Property Law Perspectives VIII

Property Law Perspectives VIII

Jill Robbie, Flore Vavourakis, Víðir Smári Petersen, Ivan Allegranti and Aleksa Radonjić (Eds.)

eleven

Published, sold and distributed by Eleven
P.O. Box 85576
2508 CG The Hague
The Netherlands
Tel.: +31 70 33 070 33
Fax: +31 70 33 070 30
e-mail: sales@elevenpub.nl
www.elevenpub.com

Sold and distributed in USA and Canada
Independent Publishers Group
814 N. Franklin Street
Chicago, IL 60610, USA
Order Placement: +1 800 888 4741
Fax: +1 312 337 5985
orders@ipgbook.com
www.ipgbook.com

Eleven is an imprint of Boom uitgevers Den Haag.

ISBN 978-90-4730-171-4
ISBN 978-94-0011-331-2 (E-book)

Table of Contents

Preface

This book contains contributions from the XIth and XIIth editions of the Young Property Lawyers' Forum (YPLF), which both took place in a virtual environment. The XIth edition of the YPLF was held between 26th May and 23rd June 2021 when there were ongoing restrictions due to the Coronavirus pandemic. As a result, there were five online panels, each hosted by a different university. These were entitled "Property and Land" hosted by the Universidad de Monterrey; "Property and Technology" hosted by Maastricht University; "Property and Sustainability" hosted by University of Glasgow, "Property and Justice" hosted by University of Groningen; and "Property Law for the Future" hosted by Universität Würzburg. Members of the YPLF Board of Advice were crucial in facilitating the conference in this way with Prof Rafael Ibarra Garza, Prof Bram Akkermans, Prof Björn Hoops and Prof Caroline Rupp all helping to organise the respective panels with assistance from Dr Laura Velázquez, Alexander Appelmans, Tiddo Bos, Dr Shona Norbash and Calum Stewart. In order to raise the spirits when the pandemic was still affecting our lives in substantive ways, there was an innovative intervention during each panel, including a musical intermezzo by Marc Weerts and a poetry reading from Sophie Cooke. The poem which Sophie read, entitled "Clockwork World", is included within this collection.

This online format was repeated in 2022 for the XIIth edition, when five online panels took place between 25th May and 22nd June. However, in this year, the majority of the organisation was carried out by early career researchers, as is the aim of the YPLF. A panel on "Contemporary Property Theory" was hosted by Víðir Smári Petersen of University of Iceland. Flore Vavourakis of KU Leuven hosted a panel on "Property and Natural Resources". A panel on "Property and Values" was hosted by Dr Aleksa Radonjić of the Union University, School of Law. Ivan Allegranti of University of Camerino hosted a panel on "Property and Society in Extraordinary Times". Finally, University of Glasgow hosted a panel on "Property Law for the Future". This organising committee with representation from five universities then went on to edit this collection of papers, which originated from these conferences.

As the XIIth edition of the YPLF came to a close, I announced that after 5 years in the post I was stepping down as Chair of the Board of Advice of the YPLF. The position was advertised and in August 2022, the three new co-Chairs of the YPLF were announced as Dr Aleksa Radonjić, Union University, School of Law; Dr Ernesto Vargas Weil, Selwyn College, University of Cambridge; and Konstanze von Schütz, McGill University. Under their joint leadership, the XIIIth edition of the YPLF was held at Universität Osnabrück in person in June 2023 and was well attended by up-and-coming property law researchers. Personally, I am so delighted to see the YPLF continuing in the hands of its new leaders.

I feel like a parent, who finally sees their child grown up and flourishing without their daily attention and input. The aim of the YPLF has always been to enhance the capacities of, and opportunities for, early career researchers, and for its leadership to be taken over by the next generation is a milestone in the history of the organisation.

I wish to thank everyone who has been involved in the YPLF during my time as Chair. I called on many people for help and advice during this time. Thank you also to the presenters at each of the conferences for their stimulating presentations, questions and discussions. The YPLF has always provided an encouraging and inspiring environment for sharing property law ideas and allowing researchers to grow. I hope it continues to do this for many years to come.

Dr Jill Robbie
University of Glasgow

Clockwork World

Sophie Cooke

This independence of depending parts,
rigged for time with pendulum and wheels
within the slap that started stars –
was flung on a slow arc, still moving,
swinging between opposites for ages –
dark and light, the anchor teeth
of death and life –
balancing.

It kept on, in silence, wind,
til acids were ribo-nucleic.

The turning wheel turned others, also slow, whose life was tiny.
The vast wee populations lay down to die in oceans (Devonian):
algae, microbes. Rock and shale grew over them.
It took a while before the wheels with bells on turned.

Life was vociferous, bursting, scaly. It steamed and crashed,
crashed and burned.
The buried small things cooked; jungles popped. The ringing stopped.
Now just the gentle tick-tock
of wheels that had been turning slowest, softest, long.
In ditches, the dinosaur gears still smoked; broken off.

Nature stripped back to its centre
swinging its orderly weight
right - left, life - death
real in its anchor teeth,
though the centre is neither – both - the same.

Turned the wheels that were in first place:
stuff of life, and smallest life,

waiting to grow a better sixth and eighth,
a three hundred and thirtieth that might be of interest.

Warm heartbeats were part of the new arrangement.
The dark and tiny dead still hid beneath Cretaceous seas,
condensed. The human gear clicked in.
Keenly we mapped out borders with dirks and rifles.
Lands were said to belong to the folk who happened to stand upon them,
and you could take other folk's if you were stronger,
said a beardie-man called Cortez.
We made a lot of noise, we competed with the dinosaurs.

As land belonged to the folk, same for what was inside it:
we opened the land right up, like a patient, a coffin, a purse,
put its riches into a clear glass jar, and said the glass jar made them,
on the label wrote the name of an economic system.
Folk in love with different systems fought to stuff their jars the fullest,
to show that theirs was best, to disbelieving farm-hands
who thought they knew – you get back what you put in,
all harvests must be seeded, calves or oats.
You put back what you get out, skimming it for need,
slipping the movement in with the wheels.

Wealth never came from nowhere.

The dark small dead in the shale and rock
fuelled torches, engines, factories, and empires.
All their life, stopped over time as wide as a desert,
flowed into our rigs, flared in a future that wouldn't stop.
We could scoop their deaths back to use. This rounded off
a little from one tooth of the pendulum's anchor,
adding more to the other.

The teeth of the anchor were huge.
Relative to their size, the shifting amounts were inconsequential,
and no-one could say the shifting had been caused by us
because the reality of the pendulum itself was doubtful (it wasn't visible:
only showed up on the underside of logic and mathematics
and in music).

We thought we'd always have enough of that stuff –
the small bodies
turned to liquid.
It was like water.
It came up from wells, and ran through pipes, it was as plentiful.
Only, we were burning it up.
Our way of living ran on the borrowed blood - a gilded Cadillac.
We were magnificent, our arts and cities shone, our medicine and jumbo jets.
We conquered outer space, and snowy wastes. Our way of living was us.
How could we give our selves up?

We grew gigantic by transfusion. Grown so tall,
the other wheels were toy ones, tools. We knew
we were cleverer than the logic of the clock that spawned us.
We knew how to use things. Perhaps we were the whole point of the clock
and, having been born, could dispense with those parts of the contraption
for which we had no use. We surveyed its unproductive reaches
and wondered why it was we found them beautiful?

Nature was - a dependence of independent parts: dependent on us.
We took care of Nature, our less capable but beautiful relation, or rather
we paid other people to do this for us (they were experts, it was safer).
And death's side of the anchor kept on getting smaller,
we were making that tooth rounder, adding more to life's tooth, adding faster.

The first wheel, confused, began to click out of gear.
Floods washed Colorado. Forest blazed. Ice melted. Our leaders said:
Pay no attention. The only bit of the clock that matters is our part:
cleverest and best. The human wheel and culture that can split time into atoms:
we are nature's full refinement. The 'pendulum' – if it exists –
is many gears away from here.

The pendulum's anchor was an irrelevance which needed not be mentioned;
it had been dealt with in a previous stanza.

Mainly, life went on as normal. The wheels still worked:
upsets were occasional, so mainly the rich folk looked right.
In the back greens of tenements,
on Morvern at sundown, on the slants of Torridon,

Nature continued to branch, and gather, and divide:
folk had barbecues in summer, ash leaves stamped the blue and fell.

The logic of chrysanthemum petals, in the vase,
mirrored the spirals of the fern, out of doors.
Nature's knowing doing lay in our genes, our bones,
as in the seeming-wild lands outside our eyes' wee windows.
Could be this kinship was why we found nature beautiful
despite her uselessness for many money-raising purposes.
Nettle and dahlia, collie and fox, stag and rat and chicken, were nature,
and our toes that stretched beneath the sheets - our hopes for happiness,
reaching for it, brushing against the world around us, this bed we dreamt inside –
were nature.
The pigeon, as the peewit;
the urge to accumulate in banks, as the wisdom of the well-run farm,
no less a part of nature than those inhuman mountains, than Quinag, Suilven.

The thing with the clock was, its escapement mechanism –
to engage the first wheel by the opposite teeth of the anchor,
in turn attached to the pendulum – had been designed
to release the wheel one tooth at a time.
With the teeth of the anchor uneven –
thanks to our undoubtedly clever interventions,
our operations on death performed as a side-effect,
at a distance
of four hundred thousand millennia –
the wheel, which at first had just skipped out of gear now and then,
looked by turns like it might
race its weight to speed to the end of the universe first
    or stop where it was, frozen still.
Our leaders said: Disregard this! It's part of Nature's habit
to have hiccups. Our wheel is strong.
The 'anchor', whatever it is,
can always be fixed by us, if we want to.

The anchor teeth grew more and more uneven.
Everyone knew – with their bodies, that chimed with the clockwork,
with the ribonucleic being of the wheel that means the most
in all their cells, in their hearts and brains and guts -

if that first wheel failed to engage, or got stuck,
the rest would all follow suit; all stop.
Even if it were free, without an answering nudge
the pendulum itself might soon not budge.

People had their suspicions
the barbecues would not have existed,
because life, with its time, would be gone.

Nature is a clock in which life blooms from time,
lives in the motion of the wheels, and we see them, while
the pendulum swings out of sight.

Part I
Property and Sustainability

1 Framing Waste as a Common Treasury to Facilitate the Circular Economy

*Katrien Steenmans**

1 Introduction

There is a global waste crisis. Huge amounts of waste are being generated yet not properly managed. The World Bank, for example, estimates that 2.01 billion tonnes of municipal solid waste are produced annually with at least a third 'not managed in an environmentally safe manner'.[1] Worryingly, this number is only expected to increase to 3.40 billion tonnes by 2050.[2] Management of these critical amounts of waste has been described as a wicked problem,[3] characterised by complexity interconnectedness, lack of clarity, ambiguity, limited understanding, and uncertainty.[4] These characteristics result from, for example, its link to resource use and consumption, tensions and trade-offs between waste prevention and the usefulness of some generated wastes to avoid other types of waste (*e.g.* packaging to reduce food waste), and varying characteristics of different types of wastes. Moreover, where waste is generated, it can be managed in different ways (*e.g.* prevention, reuse, recycling, reclamation, restoration, repair, remanufacturing, landfill, incineration, *etc.*).[5]

---

* Postdoc, Centre for Private Governance, Faculty of Law, University of Copenhagen.

1 S. Kaza *et al.*, *What a Waste 2.0. A Global Snapshot of Solid Waste Management to 2050*, Washington D.C., World Bank, 2018, p. 3.

2 *Ibid.*

3 In relation to waste management generally, see, *e.g.*: K.U. Shah *et al.*, 'Plastics Waste Metabolism in a Petro-island State: Towards Solving a "Wicked Problem" in Trinidad and Tobago', *Sustainability*, Vol. 11, No. 13, 2018, pp. 6580; G. Salvia *et al.*, 'The Wicked Problem of Waste Management: An Attention-based Analysis of Stakeholder Behaviours', *Journal of Cleaner Production*, Vol. 326, 2021, 1292200. Particular types of waste have also been described as wicked problems, see, *e.g.* radioactive waste – A. Brunningräber, 'The *Wicked* Problem of Long Term Radioactive Waste Governance', *in* A. Brunnengräber & M.R. Di Nucci (Eds.), *Conflicts, Participation and Acceptability in Nuclear Waste Governance*, Wiesbaden, Springer, 2019, pp. 335-355; B.D. Solomon, 'Solving a Wicked Problem in Deep Time: Nuclear Waste Disposal', *Science and Engineering Ethics*, Vol. 27, 2021, p. 21; food waste – Jamie Murphy *et al.*, 'Wicked Problem: Reducing Food Waste by Tourist Households', *Journal of Gastronomy and Tourism*, Vol. 3, No. 4, 2019, p. 247.

4 H.W.J. Rittel & M.M. Webber, 'Dilemmas in a General Theory of Planning', *Policy Sciences*, Vol. 4, 1973, pp. 161-167; J. Pryshlakivsky & C. Searcy, 'Sustainable Development as a Wicked Problem', *in* S.F. Kovacic & A- Sousa-Poza (Eds.), *Managing and Engineering in Complex Situations*, Dordrecht, Springer, 2013, p.110.

5 There are different ways in which to categorise waste management. Beyond landfill and incineration, there are the "3Rs" (reduce, reuse, recycle) or "5Rs" (refuse, reuse, reduce, repurpose, recycle). Potter even distinguishes between 12 Rs: refuse, reduce, reuse, repair, refill, retail, rent, redirect, recycle, resources,

Wicked problems do not have a "single, specific solution" and instead "require a range of activities directed at achieving a number of different objectives".[6] At international, national, and sub-national governance levels, a myriad of laws and policies have been introduced to tackle the waste crises, including on product design,[7] landfill tax,[8] waste recycling targets,[9] and plastic bag charges and bans.[10] A concept that has particularly gained traction over the past decade is the circular economy,[11] in which waste is prevented and, where it cannot be prevented, waste and resources are reused, recycled, or recovered for sustainable development (*i.e.* for environmental quality, economic prosperity, and social equity).[12] For example, internationally, a legally binding agreement currently being developed on plastics is to include provisions on the circular economy;[13] the European Commission adopted a new Circular Economy Action Plan in 2020 (following an initial plan in 2014, which was withdrawn and replaced by the Circular Economy Package in 2015);[14] and there are also a growing number of circular economy laws at national level – such as China's 2008 Circular Economy Promotion Law,[15] Germany's Circular Economy Act 2012,[16] France's 2020 Anti-waste and Circular Economy Law,[17] and Mexico's General

regenerate, and regulate and restructure – C. Potter, *Welcome to the Circular Economy. The Next Step in Sustainable Living*, London, Laurence King, 2021.

6 E. Mumford, 'Problems, Knowledge, Solutions: Solving Complex Problems', *Journal of Strategic Information Systems*, Vol. 7, 1998, p. 260. See also Rittel & Webber, 1973, pp.161-167.

7 *E.g.* in the EU: European Parliament and Council Directive 2009/125/EC of 21 October 2009 establishing a framework for the setting of eco-design requirements for energy-related products (Ecodesign Directive), OJ 2009 L 285/10.

8 *E.g.* in the UK: The Landfill Tax Regulations 1996.

9 *E.g.* in the EU targets for packaging and packaging waste are set out in the European Parliament and Council Directive 94/62/EC of 20 December 1994 on packaging and packaging waste (Packaging Directive), OJ 1994, L 365/10.

10 *E.g.* in Rwanda: Law No 17/2019 of 10/08/2019 relating to the prohibition of manufacturing, importation, use and sale of plastic carry bags and single-use plastic items.

11 The origin of circular economy can be traced much further back, see, *e.g.* F. Lesniewska & K. Steenmans, *Circular Economy and the Law: Bringing Justice into the Frame*, Oxon, Routledge, 2023, ch 1.

12 J. Kirchherr, D. Reike & M. Hekkert, 'Conceptualizing the Circular Economy: An Analysis of 114 Definitions', *Resources, Conservation and Recycling*, Vol. 127, 2017, p. 229.

13 UNEP/EA.5/Res.14 includes a mandate to develop an international legally binding agreement on plastics pollution by 2024. The treaty is to include provisions "[t]o promote sustainable production and consumption of plastics through, among other things, product design and environmentally sound waste management, including through resource efficiency and circular economy approaches" (Art 3(b)).

14 European Commission, *A new Circular Economy Action Plan*, 2020, COM(2020) 98 final.

15 The Circular Economy Promotion Law of the People's Republic of China, adopted at the 4th session of the Standing Committee of the 11th National People's Congress of the People's Republic of China on August 29, 2008.

16 *Gesetz zur Förderung der Kreislaufwirtschaft und Sicherung der umweltverträglichen Bewirtschaftung von Abfällen (Kreislaufwirtschaftsgesetz - KrWG)* (Circular Economy Act), 24 February 2012.

17 *Loi no. 2020-105 du 10 février 2020 relative à la lutte contre le gaspillage et à l'économie* circulaire (Anti-waste and Circular Economy Law).

Circular Economy Law 2021[18] and policies at sub-national level – such as the Amsterdam Circular Strategy 2020-2025 (the Netherlands)[19] and Circular Glasgow (UK).[20] Despite some progress, implementation of circular approaches are still limited and the 'circularity gap' – the amount of resources extracted compared to the amount of material loss due to waste generation and stock depletion – is increasing.[21] None of the laws and policies have thus yet had the desired and required transformative effect to mitigate the local and global waste crises. This chapter examines another possible avenue to promote the prevention and sustainable circular management of waste: the reconceptualisation of waste as a common treasury.

In order to assess the viability and usefulness of reconceptualising waste as a common treasury, this chapter considers four questions: (1) What is a common treasury? (Section 2) (2) Can waste be reconceptualised as a common treasury? (Section 3.1) (3) What are the benefits of reconceptualising waste as a common treasury? (Section 3.2) (4) What is the most appropriate property scheme for waste to operate as a common treasury? (Section 4) These questions are explored predominantly within the English common law system within this chapter, though many of the insights may be relevant more widely. Despite differences between the details and appearance of civil and common law property regimes, there is increased recognition that the leading principles, underlying policies, fundamental concepts, and basic rules of civil law and common law traditions are quite similar.[22]

2 THE CONCEPT OF COMMON TREASURY

The concept of common treasury used in this chapter is based on Malcolm and Clarke's development of True Leveller and Digger Gerrard Winstanley's principle that resources of

18 *Ley General de Economía Circular, OFICIO No. DGPL-1P1A.-2934, Ciudad de México, a 17 de noviembre de 2021* (General Circular Economy Law).

19 City of Amsterdam, *Amsterdam Circular 2020-2025 Strategy*, Amsterdam, Municipality of Amsterdam, 2020. Available at: www.amsterdam.nl/en/policy/sustainability/circular-economy/#:~:text=Amsterdam%20Circular%20Strategy%202020%2D2025,to%20preserve%20valuable%20raw%20materials. (accessed 25 October 2022).

20 Glasgow Chamber of Commerce 'Circular Glasgow', 2021. Available at: www.circularglasgow.com (accessed 25 October 2022).

21 J.A. Mathews & H. Tan, 'Circular Economy: Lessons from China', *Nature*, Vol. 531, 2016, p. 441; N. Gregson *et al.*, 'Interrogating the Circular Economy: The Moral Economy of Resource Recovery in the EU', *Economy and Society*, Vol. 44, No. 2, 2015, p. 218; Circle Economy, *The Circularity Gap Report 2022*, PACE 2022, p. 21. Available at: www.circularity-gap.world/2022#Download-the-report (accessed 23 October 2023).

22 For example, Mattei writes that in the property-theory literature, civil and common law have "a much more uniform language than the one used by practical lawyers" – U. Mattei, *Basic Principles of Property Law: A Comparative Legal and Economic Introduction*, Westport, Greenwood Press, 2000, p. 13. See also: S. van Erp, 'Comparative Property Law', *in* M. Reimann & R. Zimmermann (Eds.), *The Oxford Handbook of Comparative Law*, Oxford, Oxford University Press, 2006, pp. 1049-1050; S. van Erp, *European and National Property Law: Osmosis or Growing Antagonism*, Zutphen, Europa Law Publishing, 2006, p. 16.

the earth are to be used in common by all.[23] The Diggers, also known as True Levellers (to distinguish themselves from the Levellers), were a religious and political group calling for the fundamental restructuring of land ownership in the aftermath of the English Civil War and execution of Charles I, the King of England, and have been called "Europe's first communists".[24] Winstanley developed the common treasury concept in 1649 within the context of the enclosure of common land as a challenge to private property in the vision that the earth and its land should be a "common treasury for all".[25] Malcolm and Clarke embraced the common treasury concept for its normative component:

> *because* of [a resource's] physical characteristics and its importance to all, it *ought* to be available to all ("all" is to be understood here as encompassing all creatures of the earth today and into the future, and the environment as a whole).[26]

Thus, common treasury describes the physical nature of the resource and its importance to all forms of life, rather than its legal nature.[27] Beyond perfunctory mentions, subsequent literature has not yet applied or developed the concept within legal contexts since Malcolm and Clarke re-introduced it.[28]

The normative description of the resource distinguishes common treasury from other concepts, such as communal property, which is a property concept, and public goods and common pool resources, which are both types of economic goods. Table 1.1 provides an

---

23 A. Clarke & R. Malcolm, 'The Role of Property in Water Regulation: Locating Communal and Regulatory Property Rights on the Property Rights Spectrum', *in* C. Godt (Ed.), *Regulatory Property Rights: The Transforming Notion of Property in Transnational Business Regulation*, Leiden, Brill Nijhoff, 2016, pp. 121-140; R. Malcolm & A. Clarke, 'Water a Common Treasury', *in* T. Xu & A. Clarke (Ed.), *Legal Strategies for the Development and Protection of Communal Property*, Oxford, Oxford University Press, 2018, pp. 202-229. See also: G. Winstanley *et al.*, *The True Levellers Standard Advanced: or the State of Community Opened, and Presented to the Sons of Men*, 26 April 1649, reprinted Oxford, Benediction Classics, 2009.

24 G. Kennedy, 'Digger Radicalism and Agragarian Capitalism', *Historical Materialism*, Vol. 14, No. 3, 2006, p. 114. See also: A. Hughes, 'Diggers, True Levellers and the Crisis of the English Revolution', *in* P. Baker & E. Vernon (Eds.), *The Agreements of the People, the Levellers and the Constitutional Crisis of the English Revolution*, Basingstoke, Palgrave MacMillan, 2012; D. Loewenstein, 'Gerrard Winstanley and the Diggers' *in* L.L. Knoppers (Ed.), *The Oxford Handbook of Literature and the English Revolution*, Oxford, Oxford University Press, 2012, pp. 327-345.

25 For a history of Winstanley and how a common treasury was developed, including how it fit with other contextual and socio-cultural developments, see, *e.g.* Loewenstein, 2012, pp. 327-345; Clarke & Malcolm, 2016, pp. 122-123; Malcolm & Clarke, 2018, pp. 204-207.

26 Malcolm & Clarke, 2018, p. 207 (emphasis in original). See also: Clarke & Malcolm, 2016, pp. 123-5.

27 Clarke & Malcolm, 2016, pp. 123-4.

28 S. Davey, 'Plastic "Highways" to the Sea: The Problem of Litter in English Inland Waterways', *Social Sciences*, Vol. 10, No. 473, 2021, p. 4; K. Grecksch, 'Out of Sight – Out of Regulation? Underground Space Governance in the UK', *Journal of the British Academy*, Vol. 9, No. 10, 2021, p. 52; K. Steenmans & R. Malcolm, 'Transitioning towards Circular Systems: Property Rights in Waste', *Journal of Property, Planning & Environmental Law*, Vol. 12, No. 3, 2020, p. 229.

overview of the similarities and differences between the concepts. The characteristics of the three concepts (common treasury, communal property, and public goods/common pool resources) are independent and a resource can therefore be all three simultaneously – though not both a public good and common pool resource, as public goods are non-excludable and not subtractable (*e.g.* national defence, knowledge), whereas common pool resources are non-excludable but highly subtractable (*e.g.* groundwater basins, forests).[29] Goods are subtractable (also known as rivalrous) if, once a good has been exchanged, it is no longer available for others to use.[30] Exclusion "relates to the difficulty of restricting those who benefit from a good or service".[31] Inland waters, for example, are argued to be a common treasury by Clarke and Malcolm,[32] certain forms of inland waters, such as lakes and river basins, are often used as examples of common pool resources,[33] and water can (and according to Malcolm and Clarke should) be communal property.[34]

29 E. Ostrom, *Understanding Institutional Diversity*, Princeton, Princeton University Press, 2005, p. 24; E. Ostrom, 'Beyond Markets and States: Polycentric Governance of Complex Economic Systems', *American Economic Review*, Vol. 100, No. 3, 2010, pp. 642 & 644.

30 F. Berkes & M. T. Farvar, 'Introduction and Overview' *in* F. Berkes (Ed.), *Common Property Resources: Ecology and Community-based Sustainable Development*, London, Belhaven Press, 1989, p. 7.

31 Berkes & Farvar, 1987, p. 7; E. Ostrom, R. Gardner, & J. Walker, *Rules, Games, and Common-pool Resources*, Ann Arbor, The University of Michigan Press, 1994, p. 24; Ostrom, 2005, p. 23.

32 Clarke & Malcolm, 2016, pp.138-139; Malcolm & Clarke, 2018, pp. 227-228.

33 (Inland) waters are one of the most studied forms of common pool resources – A. Sarker, H. Ross & K.K. Shrestha, 'A Common-Pool Resource Approach for Water Quality Management: An Australian Case Study', *Ecological Economics*, Vol. 68, 2008, p. 461. *E.g.* lakes – P.M. Mvula & T. Haller, 'Common Pool Resource Management in Lake Chilwa, Malawi: A Wetland Under Pressure', *Development Southern Africa*, Vol. 26, No. 4, 2009, p.539; M.E. Malott & S.S. Glenn, 'Integrating Institutional and Culturo-behavioral Analyses in the Management of Common Pool Resources: Application to an Inland Lake in Michigan', *Behavioral and Social Issues*, Vo. 28, 2019, p. 248; rivers – M. Schlüter & C. Pahl-Wostl, 'Mechanisms of Resilience in Common-pool Resource Management Systems: An Agent-based Model of Water Use in a River Basin', *Ecology and Society*, Vol. 12, No. 2, 2007, p. 4; P.R. van Oel, M.S. Krol & A.Y. Hoekstra, 'A River Basin as a Common-pool Resource: A Case Study for the Jaguaribe Basin in the Semi-arid Northeast of Brazil', *International Journal of River Basin Management*, Vol. 7, No. 4, 2009, p. 345.

34 Malcolm & Clarke, 2018, pp. 227-228.

Table 1.1 Overview of the distinction between common treasury, communal property, and public goods / common pool resources

	Common treasury	Communal property	Public goods / common pool resources
Concept type	Normative	Property	Economic good
Property holdings[*]	X	✓	X
	Private, state, communal, or res nullius.	Either open access (everyone in the world is a member of the community, e.g. digital commons) or limited access (where there is closed or restricted access for a limited community)	Private, state, communal, or res nullius. These property interests can inform the excludability characteristic, which helps determine the type of economic good.[**]
Physical nature	X	X	✓
	Normative component is informed by physical nature, but not determined by it. So far literature limited to water, but arguments could be made in relation to other sources.	Examples of communal property having different physical characteristics ranging from fisheries to space.[***]	Depending on whether common pool resource or public good, defined whether it is subtractable.
Normative	✓ A resource that should be available to all.	X	X

[*] See Section 4 for understanding of property types within this chapter.

[**] E. Ostrom, L. Schroeder & S. Wynne, *Institutional Incentives and Sustainable Development: Infrastructure Policies in Perspective*, Boulder, Westview Press, 1993, p. 81.

[***] Examples depend on the particular context – for example, as in some contexts fisheries and outer space may be communal property whereas in other contexts they may be state or private property. *E.g.* fisheries as communal property – F. Berkes, 'The Common Property Resource Problem and the Fisheries of Barbados and Jamaica', *Environmental Management*, Vol. 11, No. 2, pp. 225-235; space as communal property – J. Tjandra, 'The Fragmentation of Property Rights in the Law of Outer Space', *Air & Space Law*, Vol. 46, No. 3, pp. 373-394.

Despite it seemingly being of relevance, the concept of the commons has not been included in the preceding discussion as it is "ambiguous and comprehensive".[35] A generic definition

35 M.A. McKean, 'Building Common Property Regimes to Deter Resource-Wrecking' *in* T. Murota & K. Takeshita (Eds.), *Local Commons and Democratic Environmental Governance*, Tokyo, United Nations University Press, 2013, p. 375.

is "almost impossible to formulate"[36] as a result of its many different, inconsistent understandings across different fields as well as within fields.[37] The commons has, for example, been treated as an economic good, a type of property, and a normative concept within academic literature.[38]

3 Waste as a Common Treasury

In contrast to Malcolm and Clarke's works examining water,[39] waste is both a man-made and often unwanted good. Some arguments are equally applicable to water as to waste, whereas others deviate as expected. In this section, waste and its particular physical characteristics and importance are first described to explain why waste should be reconceptualised as a common treasury to support circular economy transitions, before focusing on particular advantages of such reconceptualisation.

3.1 *Waste*

For the purposes of this chapter, waste is defined as "any substance or object which the holder discards or intends or is required to discard".[40] There are uncertainties and debates about the meaning of intention and discard, but these have already been much discussed in extant literature.[41]

---

36 J.B. Holder & T. Flessas, 'Emerging Commons', *Social & Legal Studies*, Vol. 17, No. 3, 2008, p. 300.

37 K. Steenmans, *Enabling Industrial Symbiosis through Regulations, Policies, and Property Rights*, PhD thesis, University of Surrey, 2018, pp. 99-100.

38 Commons as an economic good – *e.g.* R.J. Oakerson, 'Analyzing the Commons: A Framework' *in* D.W. Bromley (Ed.), *Making the Commons Work: Theory, Practice and Policy*, San Francisco, ICS Press, 1992, p. 41; commons as a type of property – *e.g.* U. Mattei, 'First Thoughts for a Phenomology of the Commons' *in* D. Bollier & S. Helfrich (Eds.), *The Wealth of the Commons: A World Beyond Market and State*, Amherst, Levellers Press, 2012, p. 37; and commons as a normative concept – e.g. J.L. Vivero-Pol, 'Food as Commons or Commodity? Exploring the Links between Normative Valuations and Agency in Food Transition', *Sustainability*, Vol. 9, No. 3, 2017, 442. See also Steenmans, 2018, pp. 99-100.

39 Clarke & Malcolm, 2016, pp. 121-140; Malcolm & Clarke, 2018, pp. 202-229.

40 This is the definition from art. 3(1) of Directive 2008/98/EC of 19 November 2008 on waste and repealing certain Directives (Waste Framework Directive), OJ 2008, L 312/3, as s. 75(2) of the Environmental Protection Act 1990 defines waste as 'anything that is waste within the meaning of Article 3(1) of the Waste Framework Directive'.

41 *E.g.* I. Cheyne & M. Purdue, 'Fitting Definition to Purpose: The Search for a Satisfactory Definition of Waste', *Journal of Environmental Law*, Vol. 7, No. 2, 1995, p. 149; G. Van Calster, 'The EC Definition of Waste: The Euro Tombesi Bypass and the Basel Relief Routes', *European Business Law Review*, Vol. 8, No. 5/6, 1997, p. 137; E. Scotford, 'Trash or Treasure: Policy Tensions in EC Waste Regulation', *Journal of Environmental Law*, Vol. 19, No. 3, 2007, p. 367; K. Steenmans, R. Malcolm & J. Marriott, 'Commercial Waste: Industrial Symbiosis, Legal and Theoretical Methods of Circular Economy', *Scientific Research on World Life and Values*, Vol. 2, No. 9, 2017, p. 1; M. Thürer, I. Tomasevic & M. Stevenson, 'On the Meaning of "Waste": Review and Definition', *Production Planning & Control*, Vol. 28, No. 3, 2017, p. 244; M.

The physical characteristics of waste can vary; waste can be solid (*e.g.* plastic waste), liquid (*e.g.* wastewater), or gaseous (*e.g.* greenhouse gas emissions). The generation of waste forms part of natural eco and energy systems. An often-used example is that of leaves becoming waste when falling off trees, but then providing nutrition for the soil.[42] Moreover, according to the second law of thermodynamics, processes produce waste heat, as there are no perfectly closed systems. Combined with the law of conservation of energy, which states that energy cannot be created or destroyed, only converted from one form to another, waste contributes to self-sustaining systems. Waste is thus a necessary and important part of natural processes, but the issue is with the types and amounts of waste currently produced, as well as their management.

The management of waste is in part informed by its conceptualisation as a pollutant or resource. This dichotomy has been covered elsewhere in the literature.[43] In essence: waste generation should be minimised wherever possible, as waste is a result of production and consumption processes. Simultaneously, where waste generation is unavoidable, then waste should be viewed as a resource. If it is not viewed as a resource then the conceptualisation of waste as a pollution results in the 'waste' of resources. If, however, waste is only viewed as a resource, then prevention is unlikely to sufficiently be encouraged. This is because waste as a resource results in its commodification and secondary markets.[44] Once secondary markets or other systems reliant on waste are established (*e.g.* industrial symbiosis or district heating),[45] there may be lock-ins to systems based on continued waste generation, resulting in little incentive to reduce or prevent waste generation.

The determination of waste as a common treasury is useful. Within the context of water, the concept:

Wiprächtiger *et al.*, 'Waste Not, Want Not – Ambiguities around Waste and Waste Prevention', *Resources, Conservation & Recycling*, Vol. 173, No. 105742, 2021, p. 1.

42 *E.g.* R. Davis, 'Trees and the Circular Economy', *The LEAF Charity*, 24 November 2020. Available at: www.theleafcharity.com/blog/treesandthecirculareconomy (accessed 25 October 2022).

43 *E.g.* European Environment Agency, 'Waste: A Problem or a Resource?', *European Environment Agency*, 5 November 2021. Available at: www.eea.europa.eu/publications/signals-2014/articles/waste-a-problem-or-a-resource (accessed 25 October 2022); Lesniewska & Steenmans, 2023, ch. 4.

44 M.E. Ferguson & G.C. Souza, *Closed-loop Supply Chains: New Developments to Improve the Sustainability of Business Practices*, London, CRC Press, p. 204; Steenmans & Malcolm, 2020, p. 227 & 229.

45 Industrial symbiosis "engages traditionally separate industries and other organisations in a collective exchange of waste and by-products resulting in economic, environmental, and social benefits" – Steenmans, 2018, p. 10. Available at: https://openresearch.surrey.ac.uk/esploro/outputs/doctoral/Enabling-industrial-symbiosis-through-regulations-policies/99512498802346 (accessed 25 October 2022). See also: M.R. Chertow, '"Uncovering" Industrial Symbiosis', *Journal of Industrial Ecology*, Vol 11, No. 1, p. 13. District heating uses waste fuel or heat sources to provide heating for local customers by using a heat distribution network of pipes – see *e.g.* B. Rezaie & M.A. Rosen, 'District Heating and Cooling: Review of Technology and Potential Enhancements', *Applied Energy*, Vol. 93, 2012, pp. 2-10; S. Werner, 'International Review of District Heating and Cooling', *Energy*, Vol. 137, No. 15, 2017, pp. 617-631.

> dictates that water is a right and responsibility of us all, giving us all a right to use it in common with all others and putting us all under a duty to ensure that it is used for the common good and the preservation of the environment – both anthropocentric and ecocentric aims.[46]

Similarly in the context of waste, the common treasury concept facilitates both the view that waste is unavoidable and necessary, and that some waste can be useful (arguably a 'right to waste' perspective),[47] while also encompassing the view of waste as a pollutant that society has a duty and responsibility to manage in a manner that protects the environment and human health.

3.2 *Benefits of Reconceptualisation for Circular Economy*

At its simplest, the reconceptualisation of waste as a common treasury is a relabelling to emphasise its normative dimensions. Research within other contexts has demonstrated that labels influence perception[48] and can help activate concepts through supporting dissemination of messages and understanding of particular environmental issues.[49] Within the context of waste management, evidence exists that messages may influence or change future behaviour, so that past factors and behaviour do not continue to influence intentions and future behaviour in the same way.[50] The message that the common treasury concept can help disseminate is that past behaviour of 'wasting' waste and considering

46 Malcolm & Clarke, 2018, p. 223.

47 Right to waste is beyond scope of this chapter, but others have written about it in different contexts. *E.g.* E.J. McCaffery, 'Must We Have the Right to Waste?', *in* S. Munzer (Ed.), *New Essays in the Legal and Philosophical Theory of Property*, Cambridge, Cambridge University Press, 2007; B. Chaturvedi & V. Gidwani, 'The Right to Waste: Informal Sector Recyclers and Struggles for Social Justice in Post-reform Urban India', *in* W. Ahmed, A. Kundu & R. Peet (Eds.), *India's New Economic Policy: A Critical Analysis*, Oxon, Routledge 2010, pp. 125-154; M. Liboiron, 'An Ethics of Surplus and the Right to Waste', *Society + Space*, 14 August 2015. Available at www.societyandspace.org/articles/an-ethics-of-surplus-and-the-right-to-waste (accessed 23 October 2022).

48 *E.g.* "The power of labels that describe and introduce a stimulus to influence subsequent perception of that stimulus has been documented in numerous students" in relation to the evaluation of classroom behaviour and how procedures were labelled – A.E. Woolfolk, R.L. Woolfolk & G.T. Wilson, 'A Rose by Any Other Name …: Labeling Bias and Attitudes Toward Behavior Modification', *Journal of Consulting and Clinical Psychology*, Vol. 45, No. 2, 1977, p. 184.

49 M.A. Hajer, *The Politics of Environmental Discourse: Ecological Modernization and the Policy Process*, Oxford, Oxford University Press, 1995, p. 42-72; R. Lilja, 'From Waste Prevention to Promotion of Material Efficiency: Change of Discourse in the Waste Policy of Finland', *Journal of Cleaner Production*, Vol. 17, No. 2, 2009, p. 129-136.

50 C. Knussen, 'An Analysis of Intentions to Recycle Household Waste: The Roles of Past Behaviour, Perceived Habit, and Perceived Lack of Facilities', *Journal of Environmental Psychology*, Vol. 24, 2004, p. 238; F. Corsini *et al.*, 'Exploring Waste Prevention Behaviour through Empirical Research', *Waste Management*, Vol. 79, 2018, p. 139.

waste another person's problem should be abandoned, and instead that waste prevention and management are a common responsibility with waste to be treasured (*i.e.* waste does not need to exist in abundance and, where it does exist, it should be treated as a resource).

The particular label of common treasury is also valuable for waste as it incorporates a normative component. Social norms influence consumers' intentions and behaviour,[51] and these currently are a barrier to some circular activities in particular contexts. Consumers, for example, do not want to throw away food at restaurants, but social norms prevent them from asking servers to handle their leftovers: "Personal norms, in relation with culture, education and environmental concern, encourage respondents not to waste; but at the same time, salient social norms encourage restaurant consumers to leave their leftovers".[52] Relabelling of waste may help increase, for example, the "biospheric value orientation" or "environmental concern" in relation to waste, which may help change current social norms to promote circular economy behaviour.[53]

Thus, the primary benefits of recasting waste as common treasury are the intended impacts on perception, attitude, and social norms. There is, however, a limit to the effect of relabelling on perception and attitude. Within the context of water conservation, Huddleston *et al.* observed water conservation practices at home informed research participants' decisions rather than labels or any information on signs.[54] Moreover, this chapter does not claim that the reconceptualisation of waste as a common treasury will suddenly result in immediate and effective implementation of circular economy approaches, but instead that it may influence sociocultural factors that inform such behaviour together with other regulatory and non-regulatory mechanisms that triggers more transitions towards circular economies.

---

51 F. Fornara, *et al.*, 'Distinguishing the Sources of Normative Influence on Proenvironmental Behaviors: The Role of Local Norms in Household Waste Recycling', *Group Processes & Intergroup Relations*, Vol. 14, No. 5, 2011, p. 631; L. In relation to, for example, food waste: L. Sirieix, J. Lála & K. Kocmanová, 'Understanding the Antecedents of Consumers' Attitudes towards Doggy Bags in Restaurants: Concern about Food Waste, Culture, Norms and Emotions', *Journal of Retailing and Consumer Services*, Vol. 34, 2017, p. 153; Erica van Herpen, 'Take It or Leave It: How an Opt-out Strategy for Doggy Bags Affects Consumer Food Waste Behavior and Restaurant Evaluations', *Journal of Cleaner Production*, Vol. 325, 2021, p. 8.

52 Sirieix *et al.*, 2017, p. 157.

53 These terms are used in (and refers to literature that introduced them): K.K. Mintz *et al.*, 'What Predicts Household Waste Management Behaviors? Culture and Type of Behavior as Moderators', *Resources, Conservation & Recycling*, Vol. 145, 2009, p. 12.

54 P. Huddleston *et al.*, 'Can You Read the Sign? Consumers' Utilization of Water Use Information and Price as Sign Cues', *in* M.D. Groza & C.B. Ragland (Eds.), *Marketing Challenges in a Turbulent Business Environment. Developments in Marketing Science: Proceedings of the Academy of Marketing Science*, London, Springer, 2016, p. 651. See also: M.J. Knuth *et al.*, 'Water Conserving Message Influences Purchasing Decision of Consumers', *Water*, Vol. 12, No. 12, 2020, p. 3487.

Relabelling can also help shift emphasis of problem identification, which can then be used to inform deliberate and structured interventions for environmental governance.[55] This is one of the ways in which the common treasury concept is applied in this chapter: the next section uses the concept to frame the exploration of different property interests in waste to support sustainable circular waste governance.

4 PROPERTY SCHEMES IN WASTE AS A COMMON TREASURY

To effectively regulate resources, including waste as a common treasury to support circular economy transitions, existing schemes of property interests need to be taken into account.[56] Yet, Thomas observes that implications of current property regimes "are curiously absent from the literature, even though property regimes, and the ownership structures they produce, could be a substantial block in circular economies".[57] Since Thomas's observation, there has been emerging literature exploring the effects of property rights in waste generally and in relation to circular economy specifically.[58]

Winstanley argued that common treasuries should not be the subject of private property,[59] but Malcolm and Clarke's understanding and discussions emphasise that it should not be presupposed that common treasuries should be governed by an open access regime.[60] Winstanley only considered the dichotomy of open access and private commodification, whereas Malcolm and Clarke clarify that the property rights system is more nuanced.[61] This chapter similarly considers there to be a spectrum of property interests, and specifically uses the categorisations of private, communal (also known as *res communis* or *res communes omnium*), state, and no (also known as *res nullius*) property. This categorisation is used for three reasons: (1) it is also used by Malcolm and Clarke in relation to the common treasury concept; (2) other (common law) property theorists also

55 B.C. Chaffin *et al.*, 'Transformative Environmental Governance', *Annual Review of Environment and Resources*, Vol. 41, 2016, p. 409.

56 J.B. Baron, 'Property and "No Property"', *Houston Law Review*, Vol. 42, No. 5, 2016, p. 1449.

57 S. Thomas, 'Law and the Circular Economy', *Journal of Business Law*, Vol. 1, 2019, p. 76. Thomas identified as the sole exception: G. Hieminga, *Rethinking Finance in a Circular Economy. Financial Implications of Circular Business Models*, ING 2015, p.6. Available at: https://think.ing.com/reports/rethinking-finance-in-a-circular-economy-financial-implications-of-circular-business-models/ (accessed 25 October 2022).

58 A.B. Bottomley, 'Property's Competing Values: The Public House Re-cycled as "Community Asset"', *Journal of Property, Planning & Environmental Law*, Vol 12., No. 3, 2020, p. 251; Steenmans & Malcolm, 2020; G. Danese, '*One Person's Trash is Another Person's Treasure*: In Search of an Efficient Property Regime for Waste in the Global South', *Waste Management*, Vol. 128, 2021, p. 251; K. Steenmans, 'Do Property Rights in Waste and By-products Matter for Promoting Reuse, Recycling and Recovery? Lessons Learnt from Northwestern Europe', *Current Research in Environmental Sustainability*, Vol. 3, 2021, 100030.

59 Winstanley, 1649.

60 Malcolm & Clarke, 2018, pp. 214-228.

61 *Ibid.*

use it in other contexts;[62] and (3) it builds on nascent work on property rights in waste within the circular economy context.[63] Even though this categorisation has its limitations – Heller, for example, states that the division into four schemes 'renders invisible many new forms of property'[64] and Barry and Meinzen-Dick consider these 'ideal types' to rarely exist in practice,[65] with instead boundaries of property interests fraying at the edges often having overlapping sets of rights[66] – it is nonetheless recognised as a useful analytical device.[67]

The definitions of waste (see Section 3.1), waste holder ("anyone who imports, produces, carries, keeps, treats, disposes of, or are a dealer or broker that has control of, controlled waste"),[68] and waste producer ("any person whose activities produce waste. This includes: private sector businesses ... [,] public sector services .... [, and] permitted operations or exempt facilities")[69] neither dictate nor prevent any of the property interests. Some property rights that may exist are, however, included in the definition (*e.g.* in Hohfeldian-Honoré terms: claim right to possess, privilege to possess, *etc.*).[70] Any of the four property interests may therefore apply. Similarly, nothing hinders the application of the property systems in definitions of waste broker and waste manager.[71] Figure 1.1 provides examples of the different property interests in waste as well as illustrates the fluidity that may exist between the interests. Sometimes changes in the relevant property scheme are through actual changes, whereas others as a result of perceived changes.[72] For

62 *E.g.* J. Waldron, *Right to Private Property*, Oxford, Oxford University Press, 1998; D.W. Bromley, 'Property Relations and Economic Development: The Other Land Reform', *World Development*, Vol. 17, No. 6, 1989, p. 867; A. Clarke & P. Kohler, *Property Law: Commentary and Materials*, Cambridge, Cambridge University Press, 2005.

63 Steenmans & Malcolm, 2020; Steenmans, 2021.

64 M.A. Heller, 'Three Faces of Private Property', *Oregon Law Review*, Vol. 79, 2000, p. 417.

65 D. Barry & R. Meinzen-Dick, 'The Invisible Map: Community Tenure Rights', *in* S.B. Hecht, K.D. Morrison & C. Padoch (Eds.), *The Social Lives of Forests: Past, Present, and Future of Woodland Resurgence*, Chicago, Chicago University Press, 2014, p. 298.

66 Heller, 2000, p. 417; Barry & Meinzen-Dick, 2014, p. 298.

67 Heller, 2000, p. 418.

68 S. 2.1 of the Waste Duty of Care: Cody of Practice. Available at: www.gov.uk/government/publications/waste-duty-of-care-code-of-practice/waste-duty-of-care-code-of-practice (accessed 25 October 2022). This is similar, but not identical, to the definition at EU level: Article 3(6) of the Waste Framework defines waste holder as "the waste producer or the natural or legal person who is in possession of the waste".

69 S. 2.1 of the Waste Duty of Care: Cody of Practice. This definition is again similar, but not identical, to the definition at EU level: Article 3(5) of the Waste Framework Directive defines waste producer as "anyone whose activities produce waste (original waste producer) or anyone who carries out pre-processing, mixing or other operations resulting in a change in the nature or composition of this waste".

70 See Steenmans & Malcolm, 2020, pp. 223-227 for a discussion of Hohfeldian-Honoré property rights that may exist in waste as a result of the definitions.

71 These are also defined in the Waste Duty of Care: Code of Practice (*supra* note 69).

72 For more examples and discussion on tensions between actual versus perceived property rights in waste see Steenmans, 2021, pp. 8-9. See also G. Danese, '*One Person's Trash is Another Person's Treasure:* In Search of

example, the *de jure* (formal) property rights in steam produced while showering are that steam produced often belongs to person who pays for the water. In practice, however, the physical nature of steam means that it is usually treated as there being no property in steam. This example is, however, context dependent, as in other instances, like in some industrial symbiosis and district heating systems, private property in steam is maintained with the steam captured and sold for other purposes.[73] Actual change from no property to private property may occur, for instance, as a result of Locke's labour theory, which broadly encompasses the idea that applying labour to *res nullius* or communal goods turns the goods into private property,[74] or from perceived no property (due to no identifiable private, communal, or state owner) to private property as a result of so-called "rights of finders",[75] "rule of first possession",[76] or "first in time, first in right".[77] Different types of property and their effects in waste are detailed in the following subsections.

The question is which property scheme is most appropriate for facilitating the minimisation of waste generation and maximisation of reuse, recycling, and other recovery (in that priority order) where its generation is unavoidable for the purposes of circular economy transitions? The preceding common treasury discussions frame insights and inform recommendations set out in the following sections, as the concept dictates governance mechanisms, of which property is one, through considering normative dimensions. The remainder of this section considers each regime: how it applies to waste, what the challenges are, and how framing waste as common treasury affects it within the context of circular economy transitions.

---

an Efficient Property Regime for Waste in the Global South', *Waste Management*, Vol. 128. 2021, p. 252 (refers to formal and factual property rights).

73 *Supra* note 45. For an example of where steam is sold, see the Kalundborg industrial symbiosis – T.A. Domenech Aparisi, *Social Aspects of Industrial Symbiosis Networks*, PhD thesis, University College London, 2010, pp. 170-171. Available at: https://discovery.ucl.ac.uk/id/eprint/762629/ (accessed 25 October 2022).

74 J. Locke, *Second Treatise of Government*, C.B. Macpherson (Ed.), Cambridge, Hackett Publishing Company, 1980, ch. 5, s. 25 & 26. Criticisms of Locke's labour theory exist, but are beyond the scope of this chapter. See *e.g.* J. Waldron, *Right to Private Property*, Oxford, Clarendon Press, 1979; G. Sreenivasan, *The Limits of Lockean Rights in Property*, Oxford, Oxford University Press, 1995.

75 See R.W. Aigler, 'Rights of Finders', *Michigan Law Review*, Vol. 21, 2913, p. 664.

76 See D. Lueck, 'The Rule of First Possession and the Design of Law', *The Journal of Law & Economics*, Vol. 38, No. 2, 1995, p. 393.

77 See L. Berger, 'An Analysis of the Doctrine that "First in Time is First in Rights"', *Nebraska Law Review*, Vol. 64, 1985, p. 349.

Figure 1.1 Examples of the different property interests in waste, which also illustrates the fluidity that may exist between the interests.

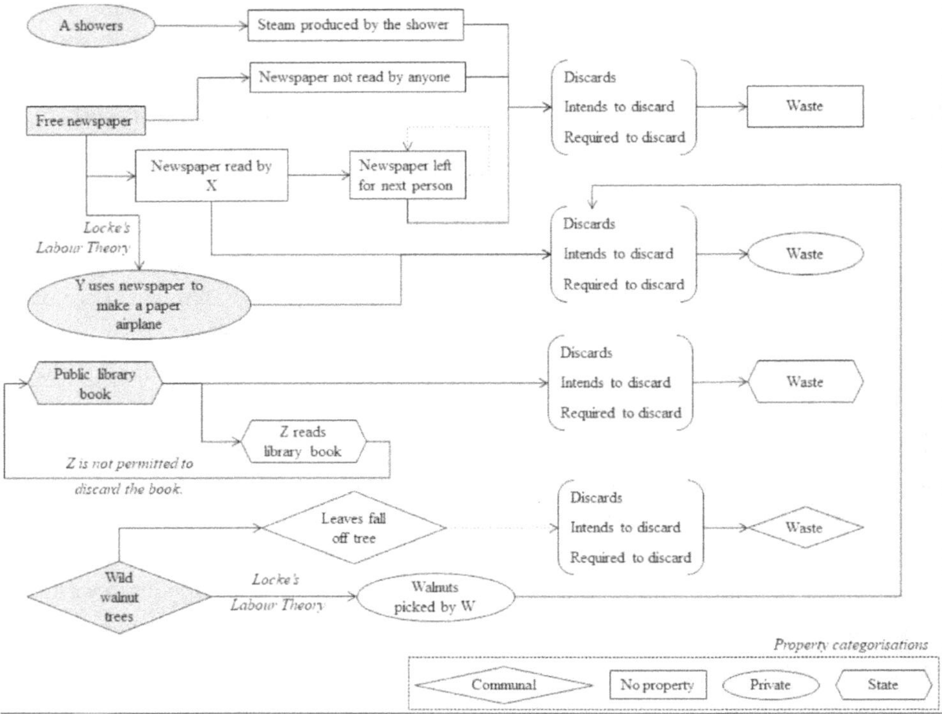

4.1 *Private Property*

The Blackstonian understanding of private property is adopted in this chapter: private property is where one person claims and exercises all rights over a thing.[78] Private property interests are currently the most dominant approach to waste and underpin waste management frameworks.[79] Household waste, for instance, is private property of the household until the household places it outside for collection and it is collected by the council (or an operator contracted by the council).[80]

Private property interests can align with the common treasury concept if the private owner makes waste available to all. There are, however, many examples where there are

78 W. Blackstone, *II Commentaries on the Laws of England*, Oxford, Clarendon Press, 1765/1769, ch. 1 & 2.

79 For a comparative analysis on approaches to waste, see: Steenmans, 2021, p.8. For a general discussion of private law approaches to waste, see: K. Steenmans, R. Malcolm & J. Marriott, 'Commodification of Waste: Legal and Theoretical Approaches to Industrial Symbiosis as Part of a Circular Economy', *University of Oslo Faculty of Law Research Paper No. 2017-26*, p. 11; Steenmans & Malcolm, 2020, p. 227.

80 Steenmans & Malcolm, 2020, pp. 225-226.

tensions between private property interests and making wastes available for all. Private property interests enable the commodification of waste and support secondary markets,[81] resulting in financial gains for those entities producing waste. The possible financial reward disincentivises making waste freely available to all. Moreover, even though secondary markets facilitate the reuse, recycling, and other recovery of waste, they simultaneously do not incentivise waste minimisation, which should be the priority of a circular economy, as waste is perceived as a valuable resource. Private property interests have also prevented waste reuse. The Crown Prosecution Service, for example, has considered prosecuting individuals for 'dumpster diving' and reclaiming food from bins outside a supermarket.[82] In such instances, Thomas argues that freegans (*i.e.* those who take goods that appear abandoned, without paying for them) should not be guilty of theft under current English criminal law,[83] though abandoned private property generally remains a grey area of law and also a barrier to circular approaches.[84]

Simultaneously, private property in waste also facilitates many of the legal mechanisms adopted to promote a circular economy. Physical extended producer responsibility, which is where the producer retains physical responsibility of a product that they have designed at the end-of-life, and leasing-based models,[85] for example, are possible because of the use of private property interests. Private property interests and such approaches have, however, not resulted in the necessary transformation to date.

Regulatory changes are needed for private property interests to be used in such a way that incentivises circular economy approaches, as they "are not self-enforcing; thus 'private' property schemes require governments".[86] Incentives are needed to move away from the status quo of transferring the ownership of waste from one private entity (*e.g.* households) to a waste management company. Both existing and innovative regulatory mechanisms, as well as legal rules that stimulate innovation in relation to private property, need to be re-examined and proposed for private property interests to cause the necessary systemic shift – for example, extended producer responsibility is observed to have limited

81 *Supra* note 44.

82 *E.g.* E. Saner, 'Skipping: Is There Anything Wrong with Taking the Food that Supermarkets Throw Away?', *The Guardian*, 29 January 2014. Available at: www.theguardian.com/lifeandstyle/shortcuts/2014/jan/29/skipping-food-waste-supermarkets-dumpster-diving (accessed 24 October 2022).

83 S. Thomas, 'Do Freegans Commit Theft?', *Legal Studies*, Vol. 30, N0. 1, 2010, p. 98.

84 Steenmans & Malcolm, 2020, p. 227.

85 For extended producer responsibility, see *e.g.* T. Lindhqvist, *Extended Producer Responsibility in Cleaner Production: Policy Principle to Promote Environmental Improvements of Product Systems*, PhD thesis, Lund University, 2000, pp. 37-40. Available at: https://lucris.lub.lu.se/ws/portalfiles/portal/4433708/1002025.pdf (accessed 25 October 2022). For leasing-based models, see *e.g.* M.G. Gnoni *et al.*., 'Supporting Circular Economy through Use-based Business Models: The Washing Machines Case', *Procedia CIRP*, Vol. 64, 2017, pp. 49-54.

86 J.B. Baron, 'Property and "No Property"', *Houston Law Review*, Vol. 42, No. 5, 2016, p. 1426.

impact in various contexts,[87] so what (innovative) amendments to the regime could make it effective and reach its touted potential in stimulating green design?[88] Reconceiving waste as a common treasury facilitates rethinking the regulatory framework needed.

4.2 State Property

State property is where the waste is owned or provided by a public body (*e.g.* the state). Such property interests may be appropriate in contexts where the perception is that state should be responsible for environmental management.[89] But, where public bodies currently are responsible for waste (*e.g.* for household waste), practices indicate that waste is often transferred to waste management companies that do not incentivise the prevention of waste as it is the reason for their revenue. Instead, the focus is on recycling or other recovery, which are lower on the priority order of the circular economy concept. The state may also manage waste in the most cost-efficient manner rather than implement the necessary laws and policies to minimise waste generation and to avoid, for example, waste incineration that is not the most environmentally effective way to manage waste and the environmental benefits of which are sometimes overstated.[90]

4.3 No Property

Within the English common law system, no property is where everyone can access the resource but no one has enforceable rights to this access against others, including the state. This is arguably what exists in waste generated by nature. For man-made waste, there should usually be an identifiable person (or other entity) with enforceable rights.[91] This

87 Limited impact in relation to the European Union, see *e.g.* K. Steenmans, 'Extended Producer Responsibility: An Assessment of Recent Amendments to the European Union Waste Framework Directive', *Law, Environment and Development Journal*, Vol. 15, No. 2, p. 112. For a discussion of its limited effectiveness in relation to electronic waste, see *e.g.* M. Compagnoni, 'Is Extended Producer Responsibility Living up to Expectations? A Systematic Literature Review Focusing on Electronic Waste', *Journal of Cleaner Production*, Vol. 367, No 133101, 2022, p. 7-8.

88 For a discussion on the rationale for extended producer responsibility policies, see *e.g.* OECD, *Extended Producer Responsibility: Updated Guidance for Efficient Waste Management*, Paris, OECD, 2016, s. 1.2.1.

89 This is, for example, considered to be the case in Greece: N. Jones *et al.*, 'Social Factors Influencing Perceptions and Willingness to Pay for a Market-based Policy Aiming on Solid Waste Management', *Resources, Conservation & Recycling*, Vol. 54, 2019, p. 538.

90 See *e.g.* I. Steenmans, *Integrated Infrastructure Systems: Strategic Planning Practice and Problem Structuring Support*, PhD thesis, University College London, 2017, pp. 92. Available at: https://discovery.ucl.ac.uk/id/eprint/1553325/ (accessed 25 October 2022); ClientEarth, 'What are the Environmental Impacts of Waste Incineration', *ClientEarth*, 9 March 2021. Available at: www.clientearth.org/latest/latest-updates/stories/the-environmental-impacts-of-waste-incineration/ (accessed 25 October 2022).

91 'Person' is used interchangeably with 'entity'.

may be the person who generates the waste, as a result of Locke's labour theory, or it could also be another person. For example, where person A trims their neighbour's (person B) tree that is overhanging person A's property, the pruned branches, which could be waste, may belong to B and A should offer them back to B.[92] Even though man-made waste will usually not exist in the no property state, there are nonetheless examples where there is perceived to be no property in man-made waste as a result of its physical properties (such as earlier steam example)[93] or because the property holder cannot be identified (for example, as a result of littering or fly-tipping).[94]

Actual or perceived no property in waste can be advantageous in certain contexts. There is, for instance, perceived to be no property in abandoned plastic waste recovered from the New Meuse River in Rotterdam, which facilitates their use in building floating islands.[95] The common treasury concept is complementary as this waste ought to be available to all, as it allows others to take action, as well as that the concept states that the waste is also the responsibility of all. But, the common treasury concept only supports a solution-based approach once the plastic has already been abandoned, as it does not address the problem that the abandoned plastic waste should not have ended up in the river in the first place. In fact, the concept may even disincentivise earlier action as the positive label of the concept may encourage littering as it could be perceived as facilitating a common treasury for all approach.

No property in waste would need to be supported by a regulatory framework to ensure that action is taken and that waste is not left without anyone taking responsibility.[96] If duties are imposed on no property, it then becomes open-access communal property instead of no property.[97] This does not mean waste needs to be subject to private, state, or communal property, though this could help support in allocating and enforcing responsibility.

4.4 *Communal Property*

Communal property is where each member of the community has the right to access property and not to be excluded from it. A community may be open to everyone (*i.e.* open access communal property) or restricted to a limited community (*i.e.* limited access communal property). In contrast to private and state property, which are both top-down

92 Lemmon v. Webb [1894] UKHL 1, [1895] 1 AC 1; Mills v. Brooker [1919] 1 KB 555.
93 See introduction to Section 4.
94 Fly-tipping is the illegal dumping of waste.
95 Steenmans, 2021, pp. 6-7.
96 Steenmans *et al.*, 2017, pp. 10-11.
97 Steenmans & Malcolm, 2020, p. 299.

regimes, communal property is bottom-up.[98] Many effective waste management examples are bottom-up – such as the informal recycling sector and industrial symbiosis as previously discussed.

In relation to common treasury:

> [t]he classification of a resource … as a common treasury … must also dictate that the governance mechanisms adopted are such as to give first priority to preserving and retaining its critical status as a common treasury, that is, that it is available to all.[99]

As previously stated, (open access) communal property is not necessary for the concept, but it patently is facilitative of it. Communal property may enable duties to be imposed (through a regulatory framework) to ensure circular management of waste by the community and generally contribute to social responsibility arrangements that drive improved waste sorting engagement, and the minimisation and elimination of pollution.[100] The shared opportunities and responsibilities of communal property and the effects on social norms from the reconceptualisation of waste as a common treasury could thus be mutually reinforcing.

The possible benefits of communal waste in waste as a common treasury may be illustrated by the informal recycling sector. The informal recycling sector is a critical contributor to circular economies with evidence suggesting that waste pickers recycle more than entire formal waste industry combined.[101] It describes individuals or other entities extracting recyclable materials from mixed municipal solid waste[102] – it is not always clear who owns the waste from which the sector extracts, but likely to be private or state property. Danese concluded that no property schemes might foster competition between different stakeholders of waste and may encourage beneficial specialisation.[103]

98 Malcolm & Clarke, 2018, 227.

99 Malcolm & Clarke, 2018, p. 214.

100 Y.T. Negash *et al.*, 'Engagement Factors for Household Waste Sorting in Ecuador: Improving Perceived Convenience and Environmental Attitudes Enhances Waste Sorting Capacity', *Resources, Conservation & Recycling*, Vol. 175, No. 105893, 2021, p. 10.

101 E. Cook & C. Velis, *Global Review on Safer End of Engineered Life*, Engineering X, 2020, p. 9. Available at: https://raeng.org.uk/media/ko0adleh/engineeringx-global-review-engineer-life.pdf (accessed 25 October 2020); C. Velis, 'Plastic Pollution Global Treaty to Cover Waste Pickers and Open Burning?', *Waste Management & Research*, Vol. 40, No. 1, 2021, p. 1; World Business Council for Sustainable Development (WBCSD), World Resources Forum (WRF) and Swiss Federal Laboratories for Materials Science and Technology (EMPA), *Informal Approaches towards a Circular Economy*, World Business Council for Sustainable Development, 2017, p. 3. Available at: www.sustainable-recycling.org/reports/informal-approaches-towards-a-circular-economy/ (accessed 25 October 2022).

102 C. Ezeah, J.A. Fazakerley & C.L. Roberts, 'Emerging Trends in Informal Sector Recycling in Developing and Transition Countries', *Waste Management*, Vol. 33, 2013, p. 2510.

103 Danese, 2021, p. 257.

Waste pickers who have readiest access to waste will pick and sort waste, whereas companies and intermediaries might focus on requalifying and commercialising the recyclables.[104] Communal property may, however, be preferable in these circumstances. No property would result in no one having responsibility for the waste, and result in unwanted waste being left to pollute the environment. Communal property would have similar benefits in that waste pickers would have access to the waste but duties can also be imposed. Within the informal recycling sector, the common treasury concept can be complementary to such an envisioned communal property approach, as the waste ought to be available to informal recycling sector to support the livelihoods within the sector.

5 Conclusion

Current waste laws and policies are not having the required or desired transformative effects to effectively deal with the waste crises. This chapter has examined a possible avenue to support transitions towards a circular economies alongside other mechanisms and initiatives. Specifically, the possible value of reconceptualising waste through the use of a label of "common treasury" was explored together with possible complementary property governance structures. These discussions have made a two-fold contribution in wider context: (1) it has extended Malcolm and Clarke's work on common treasury to a man-made resource, and (2) it has examined another way to support transitions towards a circular economy. Critically, this chapter has not argued that the common treasury reconceptualisation is sufficient on its own. It is instead one part of a larger landscape of various policies and regulatory measures that aim to minimise waste generation and sustainably manage any waste that is produced.

The main observations presented in this chapter have included that waste as a common treasury is a valuable reconceptualisation as a result of the inevitability and importance of waste generation in natural ecosystems, and the value of labels. Private, state, and communal property are compatible with the common treasury concept (no property would require duties, which would result in open access communal property), but communal property is the most fitting. Further research is needed to provide (counter) evidence for the arguments presented in this chapter. This will require inter- and multi-disciplinary research to understand the impacts of relabelling.

If evidence is found to support the preliminary arguments presented in this chapter, research is needed on how to operationalise such a reconceptualisation and shift towards widespread communal property in waste regimes. Waste is currently locked into a private property system, so how can changes be effected? Can and should it be integrated with

104 Danese, 2021, p. 257.

other regulatory approaches? For example, should part of the responsibility as part of extended producer responsibility be to treat waste as a common treasury? There are many cascading effects of reconceptualisation, which is why many proponents of the circular economy concept emphasise the need for a complete (economic) systemic rethink.[105]

105 See *e.g.* L. Viva *et al.*, 'Designing Circular Waste Management Strategies: The Case of Organic Waste in Amsterdam', *Advanced Sustainable Systems*, Vol. 4, No. 9, 2020, 2000023; Z. Kovacic, R. Strand & T. Völker, *The Circular Economy in Europe: Critical Perspectives on Policies and Imaginaries*, Oxon, Routledge, 2021; Lesniewska & Steenmans, 2023.

2 Land and Real Estate as Poisoned Chalice: a Blind Spot in Property Law?

*Marie-Laure Degroote**

1 Introduction

Land is seen as a valuable commodity. Especially now, since open spaces are becoming vulnerable and building land is scarce. Nevertheless, we notice increasing derelict industrial buildings, infrastructures and vacant properties, disfiguring the landscape on a global scale.[1] If the cost of restoring, renovating or rehabilitating these properties exceeds the objective market value, it is often difficult to find interested transferees. Those negative value properties seem far less attractive and may harm society (attracting crime and vandalism)[2] and the environment (non-sustainable use and decay).[3] Each legal system tries to combat these negative externalities in idiosyncratic ways. Remarkably, most of the tools to prevent or remediate vacancy or neglect originate from public law, whereas private law remains mostly silent on the matter: the traditional conception grants a right of non-use to the owner. Therefore, from a property law perspective, it seems vacancy is perceived as a right and not as undesirable behaviour that needs to be restrained. Also, the hypothesis of negative value of real estate seems non-existent in private law. This blind spot hampers effective action, resulting in suboptimal land use. This chapter, therefore, aims to uncover the blind spot through an investigation into private law and the emerging category of

* Aspirant of the Fund for Scientific Research Flanders, PhD student of the Institute for Property Law, University of Leuven, E-mail: marielaure.degroote@kuleuven.be.

1 **BE (Fl):** I. Renson, 'Hier blijft ruimtelijk afval gewoon staan', De Standaard, 12 January 2020, www.destandaard.be; **SOU:** S. E. Mhlongo, 'A review of problems and solutions of abandoned mines in South Africa', *Int. J. Min Reclam. Environ.* 2016, vol. 30, no. 4, pp. 279-294; **US:** M.A. Pagano and A. O'M Bowman, 'Vacant land in cities: An urban resource', *The Brookings Institution Survey Series* 2000, pp. 1-9; S.B. Richardson, 'Abandonment and adverse possession', *Houst. Law Rev.* 2015, vol. 52, no. 5, pp. 1385-1430.

2 **US:** J. Accordino and G.T. Johnson, 'Addressing the vacant and abandoned property problem', *J. Urban Aff.*, vol. 22, no. 3, p. 303; K. Hirokawa and I. Gonzalez 'Regulating Vacant Property', *Urban Lawyer* 2010, vol. 42, no. 3, p. 628; S.B. Richardson, *supra* note 1, p. 1388. See also K. Von Schütz: 'Keeping it Private: the Impossibility of Abandoning Ownership and the Horror Vacui of the Common Law of Property', *McGill Law Journal* 2021, vol. 66, no. 4, pp. 723.

3 **BE:** M. Deweirdt and B. Mammarella, *Leegstand en onbewoonbaarheid van vastgoed in het Vlaamse Gewest*, Mechelen, Wolters Kluwer, 2013, p. 3; T. Vandromme, 'Leegstand van woning bestrijden door tijdelijke verhuring of terbeschikkingstelling', *RW* 2019-20, no. 4, p.122; **NL:** Vereniging van Nederlandse Gemeenten, 'Handreiking Leegstand te lijf 2.0: Woningen en agrarisch vastgoed', 21 June 2022, pp. 8-9. https://www.volkshuisvestingnederland.nl/documenten/publicaties/2022/06/21/handreiking-leegstand.

negative value land, and to conduct research into how legal systems (could) deal with negative value land.

This chapter starts by defining the concept of vacancy, distinguishing it from neglect and the legal act of abandonment (2). The following part will address some basic assumptions of property law (the positive value and utility assumption) and how the rising awareness of negative value things puts these assumptions under pressure (3). In doing so, the third part will provide an overview of the possible ways land can accrue negative value. Finally, the last part will investigate possible ways of regulation of land vacancy in public and private law (4). This chapter has a comparative law angle and will investigate both civil and common law legal systems. Throughout the paper, comparative examples from a range of legal systems in Europe and North-America are given.

2 CONCEPTUAL FRAMEWORK

In common parlance,[4] legal doctrine[5] and legislation,[6] addressing the topic of vacancy 'abandonment, 'vacancy' and 'neglect' are used interchangeably. Unfortunately, this leads to confusion because the three notions reflect different situations in so far they relate to immovables in property law. Vacancy refers to a *factual situation* in which land or real estate is left neglected, unattended, deserted and unoccupied for a certain amount of time.[7] Contrary to abandonment, the owner still retains his title, although he is not

4 **BE:** C. Larue, 'Remettre, grâce à des initiatives locales, de la vie dans les halls sans guichets des gares', RTBF, 19 September 2022, www.rtbf.be; **SOU:** S. E. Mhlongo, *supra* note 1, 279-294.

5 **IT:** S. Moroni, A. De Franco and B.M. Belle, 'Unused private and public buildings: Re-discussing merely empty and truly abandoned situations, with particular reference to the case of Italy and the city of Milan', *J. Urban Aff.* 2020, vol. 42, no. 8, pp. 1-22; **US:** C.A. Arnold and L.H. Gunderson, 'Adaptive Law and Resilience', *ELR* 2013, vol. 43, no. 5, pp. 10432 and 10438; B.R. Huber, 'Negative-value property', *Washington Law Rev.* 2021, vol. 98, no. 5, p. 1465; Huber differentiates between a formal and a functional abandonment; D.T. Kraut, 'Hanging out the no vacancy sign: eliminating the blight of vacant buildings from urban areas', *NYU L. Rev*, 1999, vol. 74, no. 4, p. 1140; M. Steinberg and M. Housewright, 'Addressing vacant property in the wildland urban interface', *Ida. Law Rev* 2019, vol. 55, p. 63; S.B. Richardson, *supra* note 1, p. 1391: '*the reality for city officials is that abandonment – perhaps not in the legal sense, but certainly in a practical sense occurs with rising frequency*'.

6 **US:** Note that most State Codes or other legislation usually refer to 'vacant and abandoned buildings or properties'. E.g. art. 3.60.020 Code of Ordinances (Cranston Rhode Island); Art. 19-2502 Philadelphia Code. **SC:** Part 3A of the Land Reform (Scotland) Act, as amended by the Community Empowerment (Scotland Act (2015)): '*abandoned, neglected or detrimental land*'.

7 **US:** N. Kadomatsu, J.J. Kelly Jr, R. Melot and A. Pilniok, 'Chapter 2: Municipal responses to Vacant Properties in the United States' in *Legal responses to Vacant houses, an International Comparison*, Singapore, Springer, 2020, p. 19.

interested in using his property. The owner did not give up his title, but only the factual possession of the property.[8]

There are no overarching fixed conditions to speak of (a presumption of) vacancy: the concept is interpreted differently depending on the legal system and the context in which it is used (e.g. vacancy tax or temporary requisition by public authorities). For example, In Flanders, a building is considered vacant if it has not been used for its intended function for more than 12 months.[9] In Wallonia, similar conditions are required, but recently an extra possibility was introduced. A building is presumed vacant if the consumption of water or electricity tracked during a period of 12 consecutive months does not exceed a certain threshold.[10] In France, a vacancy tax is due if the building is situated in a zone of urbanisation with more than 50,000 inhabitants and the building is left unoccupied for at least one year.[11] If the unoccupied building is not located in a zone with more than 50,000 inhabitants, the community can impose a vacancy tax, but only if the building has been vacant for more than two years.[12] The Dutch Vacancy Act ('Leegstandswet') describes the situation of vacancy as '*buildings not being used by an owner nor by a personal or real right-holder or buildings used to perform an activity which is incompatible with the Vacancy Act*.'[13] The latter indicates a functional understanding: the usage of buildings for another function for which they were intended concerns improper, non-allowed use.[14]

In turn, neglect refers to the lack of action of the owner or a personal or real right-holder, failing to maintain the property, regardless whether the owner of right-holder was legally or contractually obligated to do so. Mere neglect is legally not forbidden, but it may constitute undesirable behaviour from an ethical-philosophical perspective (see *infra* 4.2.3.) and can sometimes result in liability for damage to third parties.[15] The failure to maintain the property can signify vacancy (relinquishment of possession of the owner or right-holder), but it does not necessarily have to be so. It can also occur with occupied buildings, due to incapability of the owner or right holder (a worsening financial situation

8 **SC:** K. Swinton, 'Dealing with abandoned property', *Scottish Law Gazette* 2015, vol. 83, no. 4, p. 64. See also **US:** M.J. Samsa, 'Reclaiming Abandoned Properties: Using Public Nuisance Suits and Land Banks to Pursue Economic Redevelopment', *Clev. St. L. Rev.* 2008, vol. 56, p. 194.

9 **BE (Fl):** Art. 2.9-2.14 Vlaamse Codex Wonen van 2021, *BS* 17 July 2020.

10 **BE: (Wall):** Art. 2 4° Décret de 19 novembre 1998 instaurant une taxe sur les logements abandonnés en Région wallonne, *BS* 27 November 1998; The possibility of measuring electricity and water consumption was introduced on 1 September 2022 to take more vigorous action against situations of vacancy: See D.V. OSSEL, 'Logements inoccupés, abonnements TEC, chômage : ce qui change ce 1er septembre', RTBF 1 September 2022, www.rtbf.be.

11 **FR:** Art. 232 Code Général des Impôts.

12 **FR:** Art. 1407*bis* Code Général des Impôts.

13 **NL:** Art. 1 d) Leegstandswet, *Stb.* 1981, 337.

14 **NL :** Vereniging van Nederlandse Gemeenten, *supra* note 3, p. 5.

15 **US:** O. Liivak and E. Peñalver, 'The right not to use in Property and Patent Law', *Cornell Law Rev.* 2013, vol. 98, no. 6, pp. 1459-1460.

or old age...).[16] Also, neglect (or the associated costs) may eventually prompt an owner to (legally) abandon their property.[17]

Lastly, abandonment concerns a unilateral *legal* act in which a property right-holder voluntarily gives up his right of ownership, resulting in the extinguishment and the disappearance of the right from the patrimony of its owner.[18] Consequently, the former owner has no legal control anymore. However, not all legal systems allow the possibility to abandon land. A division applies between civil law systems that generally have a permissive regime, and common law (e.g. the United States[19]) or mixed law systems (South Africa,[20] Scotland,[21] Canada[22] except for Quebec[23]) that prohibit the possibility of abandonment of land. Poland[24] and the Netherlands[25] (two civil law systems) do not allow the abandonment of land because of evolving case law and legal doctrine.

The permissive civil law regimes are subdivided into two categories according to the exact legal consequence. In legal systems of the first category such as Belgium,[26] Italy,[27]

16 **FR:** N. Mermet, 'Un bâtiment mis en peril 'par la negligence de son propriétaire' coûte cher à la commune de Bonson', Nice-matin, 20 December 2021, www.nice-matin.com; **US:** See e.g. O. Liivak and E. Peñalver, *supra* note 15, pp. 1459-1460.

17 **CAN (QUE):** Agence du revenu du Québec c. 9110-4547 Québec inc., (Cour supérieure) 29 November 2016.

18 **BE:** M.-L. Degroote, 'De gerepareerde beslissing tot afbraak en heropbouw in het appartementsrecht: de onteigening nabij?', *RW* 2020-21 pp. 498-499, nos. 36-37; S. Demeyere, *Real Obligations at the Edge of Contract and Property*, Antwerp, Intersentia, 2020, pp. 267-312; V. Sagaert, *Goederenrecht* in *Beginselen van Belgisch Privaatrecht*, Mechelen, Wolters Kluwer 2021, pp. 1213-1214, no. 1409; **FR:** H. Perinet-Marquet, 'Droit des biens' *JCP* 2004, p. 14, no. 8; **SC:** M.M Combe and M.I Rudd, 'Abandonment of Land and the Scottish Coal Case: Was It Unprecedented?', *Edinb. Law Rev.* 2018, vol. 22, p. 303; **SOU:** R. Cramer, *The abandonment of landownership: a proposed model for Regulated Exit*, doctoral thesis Cape Town, 2020, p. 18; **US:** L.J. Strahilevitz, 'The right to abandon', *U.Pa.L.Rev* 2010, vol. 158, no. 2, pp. 360-361.

19 **US:** E.M Peñalver, 'The illusory right to abandon', *Mich. L. Rev.* 2010, vol. 109, no. 2, pp. 206-207; L.J. Strahilevitz, *supra* note 18, pp. 399-402.

20 **SOU:** R. Cramer, *supra* note 18, p. 210.

21 **BE:** S. Demeyere, *supra* note 18, p. 291, no. 377; **SC:** Scottish Environment Protection Agency v. Joint Liquidators of the Scottish Coal Co Ltd (2013) CSIH 108, 2014, SC 372, 2014 SLT 259, 2014, GWD 2-48, no. 97; M. M. Combe and M.I. Rudd, *supra* note 18, pp. 303-306.

22 **CA:** K. Von Schütz, *supra* note 2, pp. 727-728.

23 **QUE:** Y. Desjardins, 'L'abandon d'immeuble', *R. du N.* 2010, vol. 112, no. 2, pp. 247-261.

24 **PL:** The original article 179 of the Polish Civil Code (1964) allowed the 'abandonment' of immovables to the municipality on the condition of the latter's agreement. A 2003 amendment removed this required approval in article 179 resulting in a possibility for an owner of immovables to unilaterally abandon the ownership to the municipality. This amended provision was later annulled by the Polish Constitutional Court because – additionally to the legal uncertainty about the legal consequences – it found that the forced attribution is not reconcilable with the municipality's autonomy as a legal subject. The provision was replaced by a regulation allowing the owner to conclude an abandonment agreement with the municipality which amounts to the original article 179 of the Civil Code. Trybunał Konstytucyjny 15 March 2005, K9/04; E. Gniewka (ed.), *System Prawa Prywatnego - Tom 3 Prawo rzeczowe, Warschau*, Beck, 2013, p. 647, no. 491.

25 **NL:** HR 11 March 1966, *NJ* 1946, 645; HR 20 June 1997, *NJ* 1999, p. 301; A.A.J. Smelt, *Goederen met negatieve waarde in het Nederlandse vermogensrecht*, Deventer, Wolters Kluwer, 2006, p. 37.

26 **BE:** Art. 3.66 Belgian Civil Code ('BCC').

27 **IT:** Art. 827 Italian Civil Code.

Portugal,[28] Luxembourg,[29] Quebec,[30] the Civil Code attributes ownerless land (because of abandonment, there is no owner left) in principle to the State (or a corresponding public body such as a municipality). It concerns a forced attribution since the public body has no right of refusal. The same goes for France,[31] although there is an intermediate step: French municipalities have a first right to appropriate. In legal systems of the second category such as Switzerland,[32] and Germany,[33] the land can remain ownerless (*res nullius; res derelicta)* after abandonment. However, in Switzerland, the cantons are allowed to deviate from federal law, on this point and create their own regime.[34] In Germany, the tax authorities also have a right to appropriate, but a refusal does not lead to automatic (forced) appropriation to the State: it leaves the land ownerless.[35]

Abandonment and vacancy have *the (factual) relinquishment of possession* in common, but they differ regarding the effects on *title*. Contrary to vacancy, abandonment entails a loss of ownership. To ensure third-party effect, the abandonment should be entered into the land register.[36] However, in practice, the distinction is not an easy one to make. Although one would suspect that consulting the land register would suffice to qualify a situation of dispossession as abandonment, it is noted that an entry of abandonment or deletion of title is often missing. Since the entry into the land register is not a validity requirement for abandonment in all legal systems (e.g. France, Belgium),[37] the qualification of abandonment is not necessarily ruled out. In case of doubt, in the absence of a reference in the land register, and unless the owner has made it unequivocally clear that he wants to get rid of his title, unoccupied properties should be assumed vacant and not abandoned. Moreover, it was already pointed out that the possibility of abandonment is not universally accepted. At the same time, vacant land is a worldwide phenomenon appearing in all legal systems.[38]

---

28 **PO:** Art. 1345 Portuguese Civil Code.

29 **LU:** Art. 713 Code Civil Luxembourg.

30 **QUE:** Art. 936 Code Civil Québec ('CCQ').

31 **FR:** Art. 713 French Civil Code ('FCC').

32 **SW:** Art. 666 Swiss Code Civil ('ZGB').

33 **GER:** §928 German Civil Code ('BGB').

34 **SW:** Art. 658 *juncto* 664, third paragraph ZGB.

35 **GER:** §928 BGB.

36 **BE:** Art. 3.30 BCC; S. Demeyere, *supra* note 18, p. 271, no. 353; **FR:** Art. 28 Décret n° 55-22 du 4 janvier 1955 portant réforme de la publicité foncière.

37 **BE and FR:** S. Demeyere, *supra* note 18, p. 271, no. 353.

38 **In general:** N. Kadomatsu, e.a. *Legal responses to Vacant houses, an International Comparison*, Singapore, Springer, 2020, p. v (introduction).

3 PARADIGM SHIFT

3.1 *From a property-rights to a property-obligations conception*

According to classical property theories, the owner of a thing[39] has a right to exclude nor has he obligations towards others.[40] Although this conception is already mitigated today (see *infra* notes 51-59 and accompanying text), property theories emphasising entitlements rather than obligations or burdens attached to ownership are still dominating the private law field.[41] The latter is reflected in the law. Today, Civil Codes are still defining ownership according to and with emphasis on its powers or rights: the right to use (*usus*), to enjoy (*fructus*) and to dispose of (*abusus*).[42] Even the possibility of abandonment is seen as a self-evident power (civil law) or a right within the bundle of ownership (common law).[43] This traditional conception relies on the underlying assumption that each property (right) has a positive value and utility.[44] Property rights are only established on things with a specific utility[45] or something that represents a benefit to the right-holder.[46] Following this reasoning, creating or preserving property rights on useless things does not make sense. Once a thing becomes useless, property law seems to imply that its property right has come to the end of its life, and the only thing left for the owner is to exercise his power of disposal (in a legitimate way). Litter concerns a textbook example. The owner of litter is

39 This chapter focuses on corporeal, tangible property. Incorporeal goods are outside the scope of this chapter.

40 **US:** G.S. Alexander, 'The social-obligation norm in American property law', *Cornell Law Faculty Publications*, vol. 94, no. 4, 2009, p. 747; **NL:** B. Akkermans, 'Sustainable obligations in (Dutch) Property Law' in V. Sagaert and S. Demeyere (eds.), *Contract and Property with an Environmental Perspective*, Antwerp, Intersentia, 2020, p. 31.

41 **US:** N. Shoked, 'The Duty to maintain', *Duke L.J.* 2014, vol. 64, no. 3, p. 456.

42 **BE:** Art. 3.50 BCC; **NL:** Art. 5:1 Dutch Civil Code ('DCC'); **SW:** Art. 641 ZGB; **QUE:** Art. 947 CCQ; **FR:** Art. 534 Avant-Projet Capitant; B. Akkermans and K. Van Melle, 'Regeneratieve eigendom – naar een hernieuwde benadering' in B. Akkermans e.a. (eds.), *Privaatrecht 2050. De weg naar ecologische duurzaamheid*, Bruges, die Keure, 2022, pp. 193-207.

43 **BE:** S. Demeyere, *supra* note 18, p. 289, no. 374; **FR:** C. Aubry, C. Rau and P. Esmein, *Cours de droit civil* français, II, Paris, Libraries techniques, 1961, p. 239, no. 142, §191; **GER:** T. Diehn, '928 BGB' in *Staudinger BGB*, ottoschmidt/de Gruyter, 2020, pp. 159-172, no. 2; **QUE:** Y. Desjardins, 'L'abandon d'immeuble', *R. du N.* 2010, vol. 112, p. 254, no 3.2; **US:** J. Dukeminier, J.E. Krier, G.S. Alexander, M.H. Schill and L.J. Strahilevitz, *Property Law (9th edition)*, New York, Wolters Kluwer, 2019, p. 223: '*Perhaps the two most controversial and certainly most extreme rights in the bundle of ownership are the rights to abandon and to destroy property. Both rights entail the unilateral relinquishment of property.*'

44 **US:** B.R. Huber, *supra* note 5, p. 1463; FR: G. Cornu, *Vocabulaire juridique*, Paris, PUF, 2016, p. 373, no. 829; D. Chilstein, 'Les biens à valeur vénale négative', *RTD civ.* 2006, p. 663, no. 2.

45 **BE:** F. Van Neste, *Zakenrecht. 1: Goederen, bezit en eigendom*, Brussels, Story-Scientia, 1990, p. 23, no. 16B; **FR:** D. Chilstein, *supra* note 44, no. 1.

46 **NL:** Art. 3:6 DCC : '(…) *rights which, either separately or together with another right, are transferable or are intended to confer a material advantage on the holder, or are acquired in exchange for a material advantage provided or promised.*'

limited in his capabilities because he cannot exercise the right to use or to enjoy. The only 'use' one can make of waste is to dispose of or to destroy it. This follows from its description: '*any substance or object which the holder discards or intends or is required to discard*'.[47]

Because of the assumption that property rights represent wealth for their owner, abandonment and vacancy are often perceived as rare phenomena that cannot be motivated by economic rationality.[48] It also explains why, traditionally, private law is not concerned with regulating vacancy, neglect or abandonment and why legal scholarship often approaches it as a trivial act. Such an idea – together with the traditional concept of ownership – also indirectly ensures that vacancy or neglect can occur since the owner's powers include the right not to use his property.[49] Or at least, theoretically speaking. In practice, the right not to use may result in negative externalities for third parties or society in general, in which circumstances (mostly public) law can and will foresee penalties (see *infra* 4.1-4.2.2.).[50]

For several reasons, both the traditional ownership conception and the underlying (positive value and utility) assumptions become questionable. First of all, small changes sneak into the property way of thinking: the 19th-century premise of exclusiveness and individualism has been nuanced towards a more 'socially oriented' ownership right. Legal doctrine increasingly recognises limitations on the absolute nature of the ownership right (such as the doctrine of abuse of rights and nuisance law).[51] In general, the exercise of property rights may not harm (the rights of) third parties. These limitations have been acknowledged as the 'socialisation' of the ownership right in different civil law systems.[52] By extension, modern property theorists are not only emphasising limitations but they are increasingly paying attention to property-obligation relations:[53] '*Owners have obligations. They have always had obligations. We can argue about those obligations, but no one can*

47 **EU:** Art. 3(1) Waste Framework Directive 2008/98/EC of the European Parliament and of the Council of 19 November 2008, *Pb L.* 312 of 22 November 2008. An import nuance here is that we are talking about non-professional owners. A specialised recycling company has of course, the resources to recycle waste.

48 **NL:** A.G. Leijten in HR 18 April 1986, no. 12653, ECLI: NL:PHR:1986:AC9310, *NJ* 1987, 480. Leijten considers that abandonment is not a normal human action: most people hold on to their rights.

49 The right to ownership is imprescriptible even if the owner decides not to exercise his right and if a third party does not claim the right via acquisitive prescription. **BE:** V. Sagaert, *supra* note 18, p. 299; **US:** O. Liivak and E. M. Peñalver, *supra* note 15, p. 1455.

50 **US:** O. Liivak and E. Peñalver, *supra* note 15, pp. 1455 and 1459-1460.

51 **US:** G.S. Alexander, *supra* note 40, p. 747.

52 **BE:** S. Demeyere, *supra* note 18, p. 650, no. 759; V. Sagaert, *supra* note 18, pp. 315-318; V. Sagaert, 'Property law, contract law and environmental law: shaking hands with the (historical) enemy', in V. Sagaert and S. Demeyere (eds.), *supra* note 40, p. 8, no. 11; **FR:** P. Catala, 'La transformation du patrimoine dans le droit civil moderne', *Rev.trim.dr.civ.* 1966, p. 199, no. 18; **NL:** J.H. Gilissen, *Eigendomsrecht en eigendomsplichten*, Tilburg, 1946, 281p.; **GER:** L. Lau, *Die Socialpflichtigkeit des Eigentums. Würzburg*, 1997, 246p.

53 **US:** G.S. Alexander, *Property and Human Flourishing*, Oxford, OUP, 2018, p. 40; J.W. SINGER, *Entitlement: the paradoxes of property*, New Haven, Yale University Press, 2000, p. 18; See also G.S. Alexander, *supra* note 40, pp. 745-820; L.A. Fennell, 'Adjusting Alienability', *Harv. Law. Rev.* 2009, vol. 122, pp. 1404-1465; T.W. Merrill and H.E. Smith, 'The Property/Contract Interface', *CLS* 2001, vol. 101, pp. 773-852.

seriously argue that they should not exist.'[54] In this way, legal scholars are exploring and shaping the social function of the ownership right.[55] The French *Cour de Cassation* has a similar view, stating that land not only represents wealth but also a source of obligations.[56] Obviously, those obligations can be of a legal or (extra-)contractual nature, but legal scholarship is also exploring the possibility of (moral) social obligations.[57] According to that view, property rights are inherently relational and owners do have obligations to society at large.[58] Owners are part of, and interdependent from a social framework enabling them to flourish. From this reasoning follows, they have a moral obligation to maintain and contribute to this framework, also known as the human flourishing theory.[59]

3.2 *From positive to negative value things*

Once the property-obligation relation theorem is accepted, it is also imaginable that obligations can negatively influence the value of property, undermining the positive value and utility assumption. On several occasions, the burden of obligations outweighs the benefits the owner gets from his property which makes it undesirable to have but also to obtain (see *infra* 3.2.2.).[60] In that case, a negative value is established, at least objectively speaking (see the nuance *infra* note 68 and accompanying text).[61] Transferring such property rights on the market is difficult because there is often no market (or no interested transferee) for them. The same goes for useless things from which the right-holder derives no benefit (anymore). From an economic perspective, the owner can then only dispose of his property. (Il)legitimate exit-ways are open for owners of movables, but the same does not necessarily apply to useless real estate. At least in most legal systems, because the owner cannot legally abandon his property, or if the latter is possible, the ownership is – with the exception of Germany and Switzerland – allocated to a public body (see *supra* notes 26-31 and accompanying text), ensuring the existence of the right of ownership in the future. Hence, the right of ownership of immovables does not necessarily end when the property has no use (anymore).

---

54 **US:** J.W. Singer, *supra* note 53, p. 18.

55 **US:** N. Shoked, *supra* note 41, p. 443.

56 **FR:** Cass. 5 November 2015, no. 14-20.845, *D.* 2015, p. 2317; W. Dross, 'Qui répond du dommage causé par un immeuble dont personne ne veut?', *RTD Civ.* 2016, pp. 150-154.

57 **UK:** See P.M. Gerhart, *Property Law and Social Morality*, Cambridge, CUP, 2013, 332p; **US:** T.W. Merrill and H.E. Smith, 'The Morality of Property', *William Mary Law Rev.* 2007, vol. 48, pp. 1849-1895.

58 **US:** G.S. Alexander, *supra* note 40, pp. 747-748.

59 **US:** G.S. Alexander, *supra* note 40, p. 807.

60 **FR:** W. Dross, 'De la revendication à la réattribution: la propriété peut-elle sauver le climat ?', *D.* 2017, p. 2553.

61 **FR:** W. Dross, *supra* note 60.

From a private law perspective, the existence of negative value things seems problematic[62] since the property law system was shaped on the positive value assumption. Property law contains rules that should facilitate the transfer of (im)movables but negative value properties turn this system upside down,[63] which is expressed by Huber: '*It is, to speak, a bug in the system, and not one that can be easily corrected.*'[64] This becomes clear when classifying legal acts with or without consideration (see *infra* 4.2.2. (symbolic sale)). The transfer of negative value property becomes unlikely,[65] and abandonment or vacancy transforms from an irrational and rather generous act into a rational, self-serving act.

The next question is then, how negative value is exactly established? Property can accrue negative value in many different ways. The valuation of property can be variable depending on the perspective. We distinguish between a *subjective* viewpoint of the owner and an *objective* (market) viewpoint.[66]

3.2.1 Subjective negative value land

Property could accrue negative value, from a personal perspective: an owner who does not have sufficient resources to maintain his property (e.g. in case of personal insolvency). Or, an owner can simply not be interested in exercising his rights which may or may not be the result of personal circumstances (e.g. gifts from an ex-partner, other interests). Both lack of capability and disinterest can create subjective negative value things.[67] In most cases, a transfer (sale, exchange, donation) to another legal subject is possible (and likely) because the right itself is positively valued from an objective perspective, reflected through its market value.

3.2.2 Objective negative value land

According to Huber, objective negative (market) value property can be described as

> "property which not only has no positive market value but which cannot practically be alienated or discarded without improving it, bundling it with other property, or making an additional side payment."[68]

62 In a gradually increasing manner, several legal scholars both in civil and common law have raised awareness for this subject. See: **BE:** V. Sagaert, *supra* note 18, no. 106; **FR:** D. Chilstein, *supra* note 44; **NL:** A.A.J. Smelt, *supra* note 25; **SC:** M.M. Combe and M.I. Rudd, *supra* note 18, pp. 301-306; **SOU:** R. Cramer, *supra* note 18; **US:** L.A. Fennell, 'Forcings', *CLS* 2014, vol. 114, no. 6, pp. 1297-1372; N. Shoked, *supra* note 41; L.-J. Strahilevitz, *supra* note 18.

63 **FR:** D. Chilstein, *supra* note 44, no. 27.

64 **US:** B.R. Huber, *supra* note 5, p. 1467.

65 **SOU:** R. Cramer, *supra* note 18, p. 191.

66 **US:** Inspired by the taxonomy of abandoned properties elaborated by Strahilevitz, *supra* note 18, p. 362.

67 **US:** L.-J. Strahilevitz, *supra* note 18, p. 362.

68 **US:** B.R. Huber, *supra* note 5, p. 1464.

Briefly: negative value property, without alteration or additional performance, cannot be transferred to someone else.

An important nuance is that the objective negative market value does not automatically imply a subjective negative value (or *vice versa*). In general, property perceived as undesirable by the market or society can influence the perception of the owner(s) or the right-holder(s). Still, it does not necessarily have to be that way. The lack of interested buyers does not imply that the property also represents a negative value from the point of view of its current owner(s) or right-holder(s). Some owners or right-holders are still willing to hold on to those kinds of properties and see them as an asset because they value the right of ownership highly and/or because of a personal or emotional attachment.[69]

Generally speaking, there are two categories of negative market value properties. Firstly, (im)movables that represent little or no value due to intrinsic characteristics, and secondly, (im)movables burdened by external obligations of which the costs exceed the economic value of the property.[70]

Social consensus exists that some properties represent little or no value at all because of their (undesirable) intrinsic characteristics. This first category mostly represents the useless things mentioned above: the lack of utility prevents the owner from exercising use rights (see *supra* 3.1.). This category is mainly associated with movables (e.g. litter; rotten food …[71]), but one could wonder if immovables would not fit either.

Despite the paradigm shift, to this day, it is still assumed that land in itself, independently of all obligations attached to it, always has a positive value. This assumption seems a little bit unsubtle: some immovables do not contain a lot of (re)development perspectives because of their geographic (intrinsic) features: they are located in hard-to-access regions or high-risk areas for natural hazards (flood, avalanche or hurricane-prone areas, mountainous regions etc.).[72] Some land can also accrue negative value because of human actions or natural phenomena (land exhausted by drought, erosion, salinisation etc). In contrast to external negative value properties, few measures (as far as current scientific knowledge is concerned) can help (in a financially feasible way) to sustain the productivity of these low-profit lands and to undo the negative value.

The social consensus on the value of things or land may change over time. Things the market values negatively now may not necessarily be so in the future. The change from a linear to a circular economy could for example, impact the valuation of waste which could

69 In this respect, we deviate from Strahilevitz's vision, who implies that certain objective negative value (im) movables such as contaminated land or damaged chattels are automatically of a subjective negative value: **US:** L.-J. Strahilevitz, *supra* note 18, p. 362.

70 Inspired by **FR:** D. Chilstein, *supra* note 44, p. 7; **US:** L.-J. Strahilevitz, *supra* note 18, p. 388.

71 **FR:** D. Chilstein, *supra* note 44, no. 16-17.

72 **US:** S.B. Richardson, *supra* note 1, p. 1388; L.-J. Strahilevitz, *supra* note 18, p. 388. See for a recent example in Switzerland: I. Foulkens, 'Swiss village of Brienz told to flee imminent monster rockslide', BBC, 9 May 2023, www.bbc.com.

mean that waste will be a treasure in the future. The same goes for land: intrinsic characteristics on land that are considered a burden might be considered an asset in the future because of scientific progress.[73]

Furthermore, the number of these intrinsic negative value lands seems to increase because of climate change. More land becomes particularly vulnerable to extreme natural phenomena (e.g. coastal erosion because of sea level rise, floods or severe drought etc.), which makes people unwilling to take the risk of using or acquiring such lands. Earlier in this chapter, we already noted that the ways of (legal) disposal of negative real estate are limited (see *supra* 3.2.). In the vast majority of the cases, the land is simply left vacant. Remote and sparsely populated areas are especially vulnerable.[74]

A second category consists of intrinsically positive value (and useful) properties. External obligations or liabilities can reduce the market value to a low or negative value.[75] External negative value property can therefore be described as the property of which the powers or rights at a particular moment do not outweigh the obligations attached.[76] Contrary to the first category, these negative value properties can regain positive market value or may become even more valuable once discharged of obligations. Intrinsically, these properties have (redevelopment) potential (because of a strategic location, the speculation on future value etc.). But the property's value is influenced externally by increasing obligations or liabilities such as environmental obligations, property taxes and other debts attached to land or obligations related to maintenance, or even to cultural heritage.

Distinguishing between the intrinsic economic value and burdens or liabilities on land does not make sense from a conceptual point of view.[77] The land and its obligations are one entity burdening one's estate. However, from a practical viewpoint, separating the obligations or liabilities from the land can be helpful as the potential economic value can increase after fulfilling certain obligations, depending on the concrete circumstances.

3.2.3 The vacancy risk of negative value land

The burden of some of the categories of external obligations or liabilities can weigh so heavily that the exercise of use rights becomes nearly impossible. This occurs sometimes with environmental obligations. They may arise out of the necessity to remediate or

73 **US:** B.R. Huber, *supra* note 5, p. 1506.

74 **EU:** An example concerns 'agricultural abandonment': around 30% of the European Union's agricultural areas carry a moderate vacancy risk. (B. Schuh et al., *Research for Agri Committee – The challenge of land abandonment after 2020 and options for mitigating measures, European Parliament, Policy Department for Structural and Cohesion Policies*, 2020, p. 13).

75 **FR:** D. Chilstein, *supra* note 44, no. 21; See also **US:** L.A. Fennell, *supra* note 62, p. 1314.

76 Inspired by **NL:** A.A.J. Smelt, *supra* note 25, p. 19.

77 **BE:** V. Sagaert, *supra* note 18, no. 106; **FR:** D. Chilstein, *supra* note 44, no. 33.

revitalise property because of pollution or degradation, which is often the case with derelict (coal) mines, power plants or oil and gas wells.[78] Until the clean-up obligation has been completed, not many uses can be envisaged on these polluted properties. The same goes for properties burdened with debts or property taxes such as *zombie properties*: a zombie property refers to a home that is left vacant by the owner who cannot pay the mortgage and chooses to leave the property, anticipating foreclosure.[79] However, as long as the lender (often a bank) did not complete the (imminent) foreclosure process, the owner still holds title and responsibility to the property. The lender has to initiate the foreclosure process, but sometimes decides neither to initiate nor to continue the process, fearing it will be more costly than what the property could yield. In the meantime, the land or real estate is left vacant. Due to the lack of maintenance, the property deteriorates.[80] These *zombie properties* were the symbol of the economic crisis in the United States but still remain in existence.[81]

The abovementioned obligations prevent the effective exercise of the right holder's power of disposal in the same way as intrinsically negative lands: transfer and abandonment seem unlikely, leaving the option of vacancy. Many individual external obligations will not directly provide negative value to property alone but rather have a market value-reducing effect. One example concerns the Flemish (statutory) positive obligation to renovate real estate if certain energy performance requirement are not met.[82] Nonetheless, property may accrue negative value through the sum of various obligations: e.g. property taxes combined with the non-fulfillment of maintenance and environmental obligations, and/ or the poor geographical location. The 1 euro houses ('*Case a 1 euro*') in Italy provide an example: local authorities in several villages are advertising vacant, often dilapidated, homes for €1 to prevent formation of desolated ghost towns.[83] To counteract the negative externalities associated with vacancy, the community sells these vacated properties[84] for

78 **US:** B.R. Huber, *supra* note 5, pp. 1473 and following pages.

79 **US:** L.E. Fisher and J. Fox, *The foreclosure echo*, Cambridge, CUP, 2019, p. 78.

80 **US:** L.E. Fisher and J. Fox, *supra* note 79, p. 92.

81 **US:** J.G. Laitos and R. Martin, "Abandoned and unfinished residential properties in America and Europe: Comparative Strategies for Removal and Prevention", *Denv. L. Rev. F.* 2014, vol. 91, p. 65.

82 **BE:** See about the Flemish positive obligation to renovate D. Gruyaert, 'The positive obligation to renovate: Towards social responsibility for owners?' in Rethinking expropriation law IV (forthcoming).

83 **IT:** See for example: Comune di Castiglione di Sicilia (Avviso Case 1 Euro): http://www.comune.castiglionedisicilia.ct.it/News/default.aspx?1*437*0*0; also in general: https://casea1euro.it/; L. Trackray, 'Italy's one euro houses: who can buy one and how does it work?', Independent, 20th January 2022, https://www.independent.co.uk/travel/news-and-advice/italy-one-euro-homes-buy-house-b1996970.html.

84 It remains to be seen whether the community has the right to sell vacated properties since the owners did not abandon their properties, they only vacated them.

only €1 tied to the obligation to submit a renovation project and to start and finish the renovation within a certain period.[85]

4 Vacancy as a shared civil-common law challenge?

4.1 *Negative externalities*

Now that the link between vacancy and the different negative value land situations is made clear, the question rises whether and why the law should or should not intervene to avoid or diminish situations of vacancy. From a theoretical private law perspective, an owner has the right not to use his property. Nevertheless, this premise only applies if the non-use does not harm the rights of others (see *supra* 3.1.). Applied to vacancy, the non-use of real estate can trigger undesirable behaviour that may endanger the public interest and health:[86] vacancy may lead to decay, dilapidation, underuse, and property degradation.[87] Besides, it can attract crime (*broken window theory*), vandalism and squatting.[88] It is also contrary to the pursuit of sustainability, the durable use of land and the scarce housing market. Based on these reasons, it can be argued that vacancy often concerns a form of suboptimal and inefficient land management use.[89]

Although vacancy is usually negatively approached considering the abovementioned negative externalities, it should be noted that vacancy of (agricultural) lands can simultaneously encourage biodiversity and habitat preservation in some situations. Yet, there is a downside as well: deserted (agricultural) land can at the same time erode and release greenhouse gases.[90]

Therefore, a limitation on property rights to counter potential negative externalities associated with vacancy seems justified. Although this is mostly justified by the public interest (non-use triggers undesirable behaviour that may endanger the public interest),[91] this intervention could be embedded in the 'socialisation' or the social function of the ownership right (see notes 51-52 and accompanying text). Or, some even argue that the

85 Selling vacant houses for dumping prices is also happening at other places. See for example the references in the article of Shoked: N. Shoked, *supra* note 41, p. 440, no. 13.

86 **BE:** M. Deweirdt and B. Mammarella, *supra* note 3, pp. 3-4.

87 **BE:** T. Vandromme, *supra* note 3, p. 122.

88 **US:** J. Accordino and G.T. Johnson, *supra* note 4, p. 303; K. Hirokawa and I. Gonzalez, *supra* note 4, p. 628; S.B. Richardson, *supra* note 1, p. 1388. See also K. Von Schütz, *supra* note 2, p. 723 and N. Kadomatsu e.a, *supra* note 7, pp. 19-21.

89 **BE:** M. Deweirdt and B. Mammarella, *supra* note 3, pp. 3-4.

90 **In general:** A. Mirzabaev, 'Chapter 3: Desertification' in *Climate Change and Land: an IPCC special report on climate change, desertification, land degradation, sustainable land management, food security and greenhouse gas fluxes in terrestrial ecosystems*, https://www.ipcc.ch/srccl/.

91 **BE:** M. Deweirdt and B. Mammarella, *supra* note 3, pp. 3-4.

owner has a (moral) social obligation towards society to prevent negative externalities associated with vacancy to happen (see *infra* 4.2.3).

4.2 *Legal (dis)incentives for vacancy*

The existing mechanisms rely primarily on the public interest argument and consist of *incentives* to occupy and use land or *disincentives* to vacate properties. Possible mechanisms to encourage land use and occupation or to discourage vacancy are manifold. This chapter does not intend to provide a comprehensive overview of all possible measures. From a comparative law perspective, we limit ourselves to a non-exhaustive list of some main instruments in civil, common and mixed-law systems. We group them according to whether or not they represent a change in ownership. Finally, social obligations are discussed.

4.2.1 No change in ownership status

In this section, the legal mechanisms to counter vacancy without transfer of ownership are displayed. Both (1) positive and negative financial triggers are explored, together with (2) minimum safety standards, (3) anti-squat agreements and the (4) forced (temporarily) retrieval of the vacant building by local authorities.

Firstly, the financial motivations which can be twofold. The owner of (imminent) vacant property can be *encouraged* to maintain, to renovate his property or to make it more sustainable by governmental funding for renovation (e.g. in the case of cultural heritage property with a public function). This happened with the Swiss *Elisabethenkirche* in Basel. The private owner of the church did not have the financial resources to perform necessary renovation and remediation works. After successful negotiation with public authorities (*kanton, Bund* und *Stiftungen*), it was decided to split the costs.[92] Also, the government can, if financially possible, step in to anticipate vacancy, when properties or land are destroyed by a natural disaster. In this regard, in Louisiana, the federal government has invested billions of dollars to help people rebuild their homes after hurricanes Katrina and Rita.[93] Support is not only limited to governmental support: private individuals can set up initiatives as well.[94]

---

92 **SW:** D. Wahl, 'Wir brauchen die Kirche nicht', *Basler Zeitung*, 5 November 2019, www.bazonline.ch; S. Erlanger, 'Die Sanierung soll 18 Jahre dauern', *Basler Zeitung*, 5 March 2019, www.bazonline.ch.

93 **US:** S.B. Richardson, *supra* note 1, p. 1390.

94 **BE:** In Belgium, the organisation 'WarmNest' renovates vacant houses with the government's support into new sustainable homes. The owner gets the necessary support (grants etc.) in paying the costs of renovation and is accompanied by a private organisation throughout the whole process. This way, a vacancy tax is avoided. The only condition is that the owner rents his new house to a social housing agency. See also: https://www.klimaatpunt.be/projecten/warmnest.

Discouraging financial triggers exist as well, for example, the vacancy tax. This tax is due if houses or buildings are vacated for at least a specific (proven) period (see examples notes 9-12 and accompanying text). After an expiry period, vacant properties are often included in a register. This inclusion can lead to a vacancy tax or the obligation to take other measures regarding the property. This should encourage the owner to use his property, or to let it be used (rented etc.) by someone else.

One last point on effectiveness: Financial motivations can be effective if small reparations or renovations are needed in which case, the costs seem more manageable. Yet, if the property is long-time vacant, the costs are often so high that the owner is neither willing nor able to afford the investment, despite governmental force.[95]

Secondly, local governments can enact building maintenance codes, requiring that properties should meet minimum safety standards (e.g. state of good repair).[96] Owners who do not comply, could face fines. The city council can also decide to provide maintenance services themselves and to reclaim the charges from the owners afterwards.[97] While this sounds promising, enforcement is difficult in practice.[98] The same objection as with the financial motivation applies: the use of maintenance codes is not highly effective when major investments are required to comply with the minimum safety standards set by law.[99]

Thirdly, the owner can take the initiative to avoid the negative externalities of vacancy through an anti-squat agreement. This possibility emerged in the Netherlands and is slowly spreading across other jurisdictions such as France[100] or the United Kingdom.[101] It concerns a tripartite relationship in which the owner of vacant property assigns his property to an anti-squat agency. The anti-squat agency will, in turn, agree with a suitable occupier (the anti-squatter) to whom a temporary right of use is granted for a limited financial compensation. In principle, the anti-squatters do not have to pay rent, only a small compensation for electricity, water and gas use.[102] The anti-squatter is a security guard for the property's use, monitoring and maintenance. He also avoids devaluation of the property. Although this legal construction looks like rent, it must be distinguished

95 **US:** N. Kadomatsu e.a, *supra* note 7, pp. 22-23.

96 **US:** M. Steinberg and M. Housewright, *supra* note 5, p. 67. N. Kadomatsu e.a, *supra* note 7, pp. 23-24

97 **US:** J. Accordino and G.T. Johnson, *supra* note 2, p. 307.

98 **US:** M. Steinberg and M. Housewright, *supra* note 5, p. 67.

99 **US :** N. Kadomatsu e.a, *supra* note 7, p. 23.

100 **FR:** Décret n°2009-1681 du 30 décembre 2009 relatif à l'occupation de locaux en vue de leur protection et préservation par des résidents temporaires en application de l'article 101 de la loi 2009-323 du 25 mars 2009 de mobilisation pour le logement et la lutte contre l'exclusion, *JO* 31 décembre 2009.

101 **UK:** D. Taylor, 'Property guardians: reigniting the lease/license battle', *LQR* 2022, vol. 73, 35-54.

102 **NL:** H. Priemus, 'Leegstand, kraken en antikraak', *Ars Aequi* 2011, p. 364. See also C.J. Huisman, 'A silent shift? The precarisation of the Dutch rental housing market', *J. Hous Built. Environ.* 2016, vol. 31, no. 1, pp. 93-106. See also: V. Sagaert and K. Swinnen, 'Squatting in the low countries' in *Festschrift Prof A.J. Van der Walt*, Cape Town, Juta, pp. 219-242.

from it: the anti-squatter has fewer safeguards and protections than a traditional tenant. The latter, together with the legal uncertainty surrounding this agreement, is the main drawback to its use.

Lastly, in Belgium and France, public authorities can temporarily claim the use of vacant buildings ('requisition') if the vacancy status lasts at least 6 months (Belgium) or 12 months (France) and open up the building for vulnerable population groups such as homeless people. To protect property rights, a right-holder must be notified in advance and has the right to a fair compensation.[103] Dutch law knows a similar mechanism in which public authorities can – after a vacancy status of minimum 12 months – propose another user to the owner and oblige him to agree with the occupation by the other user to end the vacancy status.[104] Because there is no transfer of ownership, it appears financially attractive for public authorities. However, the procedure seems not frequently used.[105]

4.2.2 Change in ownership status

Another (more far-reaching) possibility exists in the transfer of ownership of vacant real estate or land. A first (public law) option to remedy vacancy is to (1) initiate an expropriation or a similar procedure. Another mechanism such as (2) the presumption of 'abandonment' can offer an alternative. Additionally, private law mechanisms can play a role too, such as (3) (a modified form of) adverse possession or (4) a symbolic sale of vacant, polluted property. Finally, (5) the forced sale to a private or public party can be considered.

In all legal systems, the government can expropriate property for public purposes for just compensation which results in a loss of ownership for the former (identifiable) owner. Similar results can be achieved by using pre-emption rights or because of a tax foreclosure process if the owner fails to pay his property taxes for a certain period.[106] The power to expropriate includes vacant properties. Even more: governments, especially in the United States are frequently claiming the mere taking of vacant properties serves a sufficient public purpose without taking into account the future use.[107] This possibility should be approached with care, because it may violate property rights. Contrary, to what some governments argue, using expropriation for the sole purpose of acquiring vacant properties

---

103 **BE:** Art. 134*bis* Nieuwe Gemeentewet; Koninklijk besluit van 6 december 1993 betreffende het opeisingsrecht van verlaten gebouwen, bedoeld in art. 134*bis* van de Nieuwe Gemeentewet, *BS* 30 december 1993; **FR:** Art. L-642-1 Code de la construction et de l'habitation. In France, the scope of application is limited to vacant immovables on which a legal person has a property right.

104 **NL:** Art. 5-7 Leegstandswet.

105 **BE:** D. Gruyaert, *De exclusiviteit van het eigendomsrecht*, Antwerp, Intersentia, 2016, p. 312, no. 246; **FR:** N. Kadomatsu, e.a., 'Chapter 3: Expropriation of Vacant Property in France: The Case of Substandard Housing' in *supra* note 7, p. 38.

106 **US:** J. Accordino and G.T. Johnson, *supra* note 2, p. 308.

107 **US:** N. Shoked, *supra* note 41, p. 482.

seems to provide an inadequate legal basis.[108] First of all, it should be clear that only vacant and blighted[109] (negative value) properties are targeted here. This is possible in several states in the United States because of a specific legal provision that grants government the power to expropriate blighted, neglected buildings for redevelopment purposes upon just compensation.[110]

As a result of *Kelo v. City of New London*, expropriation of non-blighted, vacated properties for the sole purpose of future economic revitalization seems valid (under the US-Constitution). In the *Kelo-decision* the Supreme Court decided that the use of eminent domain to transfer land from one private party to another in order to foster economic development constitutes a valid public purpose that does not violate the Takings Clause of the Fifth Amendment.[111] However, from a property law perspective, the expropriation to transfer property to other private parties for mere (economic) development purposes, seems difficult to reconcile with the right of ownership. The *Kelo-decision* provoked a strong public reaction and prompted States to issue balancing rules to reconcile private property rights with the municipal redevelopment purposes.[112]

But even with expropriating blighted properties, it remains difficult to ascertain whether the negative externalities arising from vacancy are so harmful that expropriation really does serve the public interest. The concept 'blighted' is often referred to as vague and unclear, and governments in the United States seem to favour a broad interpretation of it, creating a thin line between use and abuse.[113]

Inspiration for a (more) balanced public purpose interpretation can be found in other legal systems. In France, for example, a special expropriation procedure was created for vacated 'blighted' properties: the Mayor has the power to declare property manifestly 'abandoned' ('*abandon manifeste*') upon the condition that the property is not well-maintained and does not have a habitual occupant.[114] The process involves two steps. Firstly, a preliminary report is drafted, describing the nature of the defects (lack of maintenance) and the necessary measures to remedy the defects. The preliminary report must be made public for three months, and the owner(s) or other right-holder(s) should

---

108 **FR:** N. Kadomatsu, e.a. *supra* note 105, p. 35.

109 'Blight' is defined as '*the state of being a slum, a breeding ground for crime, disease and unhealthful living conditions.*'; W. Lovell, 'The Kelo: Blowback', *Ohio State Law J.*, vol. 68, no. 2, 2007, p. 618; S.C Stone, 'Two Tales of One City: Eminent Domain Post-Katrina and a Response to Kelo', *Loyola Law Rev.*, vol. 53, no.1, 2007, pp. 121-122, no. 31.

110 **US:** N. Shoked, *supra* note 41, p. 482. As example Shoked refers to the Alabama Code, §24-2-2 (c), the Iowa Code, §6A.22 and the Texas Government Code §2206.001(b)(3).

111 **US:** *Kelo v. City of New London*, 545 US. 469 (2005).

112 **US:** N. Shoked, *supra* note 41, pp. 482-483; I. Somin, 'The Limits of Backlash: Assessing the Political Response to Kelo', *Minn. L. Rev.*, vol. 93, no. 6, 2012, pp. 2102-2178; S.C. Stone, *supra* note 109, p. 128.

113 **US:** M. E. Gold and L.B. Sagalyn, 'The Use and Abuse of Blight in Eminent Domain', *Fordham Urb. L. J.* 2011, vol. 38, no. 4, pp. 1119-1173.

114 **FR:** Art. L2243-1 Code général des collectivités territoriales.

be notified.[115] If the owner(s) or right-holder(s) respond, they must negotiate with the Mayor to repair the property within a fixed period. If there is no response within three months, the Mayor drafts a final report, which is submitted to the municipal council. The latter shall decide if the property is genuinely manifestly 'abandoned' and if so, whether expropriation of the vacated building is possible. In that case, the expropriation must still pursue a sustainable or social objective. The law lists three: (1) construction or rehabilitation for housing purposes, (2) renovation, restoration or development operation which is in the collective interest, or (3) 'spare land' on which one of the two previous purposes can be achieved at a later stage.[116] Admittedly, a broad interpretation of these social objectives is not excluded either, but this procedure offers two additional safeguards compared to the *Kelo*-interpretation: (1) both the negative externalities to vacancy and the future use must be considered when determining if the public purpose condition is fulfilled and, (2) the expropriation does not depend on the mere will of the public authorities: the owner(s) or right-holder(s) are allowed to eliminate the negative externalities and can preserve their rights.

The (special) expropriation procedure seems a common denominator in all legal systems but next to the doubts of harming private property rights, the procedure is often long and burdensome. It is therefore interesting to look for alternatives. Another possibility is (also) found in France but it envisages a very specific situation. When discussing the (special) expropriation procedure, we assumed the vacated property belonged to an identifiable owner or right-holder. This second possibility only plays in case the owner could not be found or identified. In that case, municipalities (or tax authorities) can then appropriate vacant properties through a kind of '*presumption of abandonment*': properties without an identifiable owner and for which the property taxes have not been paid for three years, are presumed without an owner.[117]

The presumption only plays if a procedure is followed. At first, the municipality has to investigate the property's history of ownership, by consulting the land register and meeting with neighbours. After this, a report is made public and a notification is sent to the last known owner's last residence and (if applicable) to the last known inhabitant who should have paid the property taxes.[118] If the owner or inhabitant does not respond after six months, the property is presumed ownerless and can be appropriated by the community or the tax authorities. The municipality or the tax authorities can then decide among them both within six months who will appropriate the property. In the absence of a definitive

115 FR: Art. L2243-2 *Ibid.*

116 FR: Art. L2243-3 Code général des collectivités territoriales.

117 FR: Art. L1123-1 and L1123-3 *Ibid.*

118 FR: Art. L1123-3, 1st paragraph *Ibid.*

decision, the ownership of the property is attributed to the State.[119] Note that in this case a public purpose requirement seems absent nor should just compensation be paid.

Thirdly, leaving the field of public law solutions, American legal doctrine suggests the possibility of mitigating the requirements to acquire vacant properties through adverse possession. A Pennsylvanian legislative proposal introduces the possibility of shortening the time for adverse possession from twenty to ten years, but that proposal never became law.[120] Another possibility is the alteration of the requirement of possession itself. Richardson argues that a notice of intent to possess suffices instead of actual possession if the true owner has left his property.[121] The basic idea is to provide a more legally secure position for the occupier in case of a vacant building where the true owner is not likely to return. Nonetheless, introducing greater flexibility in adverse possession still has respect for the true owner, who can (re)claim his property for a certain period.[122] Since abuse of the adverse possessor must be considered, the legislator should clearly and strictly define the circumstances in which a flexible application of the possession requirement would apply.[123] Finally, we note that some civilian authors also criticize the imprescriptible nature of the right to ownership (see *supra* note 49 and accompanying text).[124] From this, another (although highly controversial) possibility can be derived, namely to apply the rules on extinctive prescription on land ownership, resulting in the possible extinction of land ownership through non-use.[125]

A fourth possibility has grown out of Belgian practice: the current law contains no specific mechanism to transfer negative value properties, because today's mechanisms are based on the positive value assumption (see *supra* 3.1.). A property transfer is always seen as a *quid pro quo* (sale, exchange) or as a gift (donation), even if a negative value property is transferred. When transferring the latter, the owner is discharged from a burden in his patrimony so that the transferee is always a kind of donor, unless, of course, the transferee gives another negative value thing in return.

---

119 **FR:** Art. L1123-3, 3rd and 4th paragraph *Ibid.*; for certain nature reserves and forests a possibility of appropriation by nature organisations is provided for in the 4th paragraph.

120 **US:** PA. House of Representatives, Roll Call for H.B. 1808 (2014), available at https://www.legis.state.pa.us/cfdocs/billinfo/billinfo.cfm?syear=2013&sind=0&body=H&type=B&bn=1808.

121 **US:** S.B. Richardson, *supra* note 1, p. 1391.

122 **US:** *Ibid.* pp. 1426-1427.

123 **US:** *Ibid.* p. 1424.

124 **BE:** V. Sagaert, *supra* note 18, p. 299, no. 311; **FR:** P. Jourdain, *Les biens* in *Droit Civil*, Paris, Dalloz, 1995, p. 61, no. 49.

125 In current civil law the imprescriptible character of the right of ownership is however, self-evident. See **BE:** art. 3.51, 2nd paragraph BCC; **FR:** Art. 2227 FCC; **NL:** W.J. Zwalve, *Simplex et perpetuum. Beschouwingen over eigendom en tijd*, Den Haag, Boom, Juridische Uitgevers 2006, 329p; **QUE:** S. Normand, *Introduction au droit des biens*, Montréal, Wilson & Lafleur, 2014, 100, no. 4.3; See however **BE:** H. De Page, *Traité élémentaire de droit civil*, Brussels, Bruylant, 1947, p. 782, no. 893 (proponent extinction of the right of ownership through non-use).

In practice, stakeholders could choose to agree on a symbolic sale for €1 or $1.[126] In Flanders, the Public Flemish Waste Company ('OVAM') developed, in cooperation with the Flemish Bar Association, a Protocol (not law!) in which it is agreed that if certain conditions are met, the OVAM will pre-finance the costs associated with soil investigation of polluted properties. If financially feasible, the OVAM will buy the polluted negative value land, from insolvent (legal) persons through payment of a symbolic price in order to clean up the land and repurpose it afterwards.[127]

This requires that the owner is still identifiable. Richardson points out that not all recording systems are flawless, which may cause obstacles in finding and locating the true owner of the vacated property.[128] In that case, the presumption of abandonment (see *supra* 4.2.2.) can offer a solution.

The government or a private organisation could also take the initiative: they can encourage interested buyers to buy vacant houses by providing forgivable loans and renovation funds to those buyers.[129] This technique is currently popular in Italy with regard to the abovementioned '1 euro houses' (see *supra* 3.2.3.).

Lastly, the law can provide a mechanism for the forced transfer of vacant land to a private party (e.g. a community group) or to a public body (e.g. the State, the municipality etc.). Dutch law provides for an example of the latter. The owner of the right-holder of a seriously polluted plot of land can request the municipality where the plot of land is located, to buy it. The municipality is forced to take over the property (i) if the owner or right-holder is not the polluter and if (ii) the owner of right-holder does not find an interested transferee to take over the land for a reasonable price.[130] Likewise, French law allows the forced acquisition by the municipality of moor- and marshland or uncultivated low-value land if the owner request so (in order to be discharged from taxes in the future).[131]

An example of a forced transfer to a private party was recently introduced in Scots law in Part 3A of the Land Reform (Scotland) Act 2003, as amended by the Community Empowerment (Scotland) Act 2015, which came into force on 27 June 2018. Based on this

126 **US:** L.A Fennell, *supra* note 62, p. 1343.

127 **BE:** OVAM: 'Protocol betreffende de uitvoering van bodemonderzoeken, bodemsanering en afvalstoffenverwijdering in het kader van faillissementen met vastgoed gelegen in het Vlaamse Gewest', 2016, https://ovam.vlaanderen.be/protocol-curatoren; OVAM, 'Draaiboek curatoren voor faillissementen met vastgoed in het Vlaamse Gewest', 2016, https://publicaties.vlaanderen.be/view-file/19276.

128 **US:** S.B. Richardson, *supra* note 1, pp. 1385-1430.

129 **US:** L.A Fennell, *supra* note 62, p. 1343; K. Angelova, 'Detroit will PAY you to take one of these 100 abandoned homes', *Business Insider*, 16 February 2011, https://www.businessinsider.com/abandoned-houses-detroit-2011-2?international=true&r=US&IR=T.

130 **NL:** Art. 56-63 Wet Bodembescherming; See also A.A.J. Smelt, *supra* note 25, p. 36.

131 **FR:** Art. 1401 Code général des impôts.

law, Scottish community bodies[132] can purchase '*wholly or mainly abandoned or neglected*' land or land '*being used or managed in a way that results in or causes harm to the environmental wellbeing of a relevant community*'.[133]

The provisions (ss. 97B-97Z) of the Land Reform (Scotland) Act 2003 do not define what 'abandoned or neglected' is, but, as a guideline, it is necessary to take into account the (1) physical condition of the land, (2) the use or management of the land and (3) matters relating to the designation or classification of the land.[134] Land on which there is a building that serves as an individual's home (except if occupied under tenancy) is excluded from the scope of the application.[135] If a community body identifies land they believe to be 'abandoned' or 'neglected', they can initiate an application to the Scottish Ministers to exercise the right to buy the land. Before applying, the community body must try to agree with the owner (non-compulsory). In case of non-agreement, the community body can apply to the Scottish Ministers, who can approve or reject the application. If they decide all the conditions are met, the application is successful and the owner is obliged to sell the land to the community body.[136] Still, in the whole process, there are safeguards for the owner's right to property and strict conditions a community body should meet: it has to be proven that the owner is not capable of achieving sustainable development in relation to the land while the community body is.[137] Similar to an expropriation procedure, the community body must show that its proposals for the land are in the public interest.[138]

At first sight, this compulsory sale seems a promising tool to combat inefficient land use. It can urge and encourage existing owners to make effective use of their lands themselves. If not, disinterested owners or right-holders can be replaced by dedicated community bodies who can give 'abandoned and neglected' land a new life. Still, this is only possible after a stringent procedure concerning the owner's right to property and under the watchful eyes of the Scottish Ministers. However, it seems that community bodies face numerous difficulties when trying to exercise their right to buy: in particular the burden of proof to show the lack of engagement towards sustainable development from the owner's perspective. For now, this results in few applications of which there are even fewer successful.[139] Nonetheless, this law is an important step in the right direction:

---

132 **SC:** The requirements in order to qualify as a community body are listed in s. 97D of the Land Reform (Scotland) Act 2003.
133 **SC:** s. 97C (2) of the Land Reform (Scotland) Act 2003.
134 **SC:** The Community Right to Buy (Abandoned, Neglected or Detrimental Land) (Eligible Land, Regulators and Restrictions on Transfers and Dealing) (Scotland) Regulations 2018 and more in particular regs. 3,4 and 5.
135 **SC:** s. 97C (5) (a) of the Land Reform (Scotland) Act 2003.
136 **SC:** s.97Q (4) *Ibid.*
137 **SC:** ss.97H *Ibid.*
138 **SC:** s. 97G (6) (a) (i) *Ibid.*
139 **SC:** J. Robbie, 'Babes in the wood: the decision of the Scottish Ministers on the application of Helensburgh Community Woodlands Group to exercise the right to buy abandoned, neglected or detrimental land.',

it has a clear signal function and points out that the owner should exercise his rights in a sustainable way. Meanwhile, the law provides a warning of the risk of losing property when failing the sustainability goal.

4.2.3 Social obligations

Finally, we address the possibility of social obligations as a potential remedy for vacancy. Earlier, it was explained the social obligation theory entails all individuals (including owners) are part of a social framework and have obligations to others in contributing to this framework (see *supra* 3.1.). One could therefore argue that there is a moral obligation to avoid negative externalities that harm others through the use of one's property.[140] This ensures the preservation (of the value) of property, or more in general the maintenance of the environment which is in the collective interest.[141] According to Merrill and Smith, this moral obligation also serves as a justification for takings of blighted property (see *supra* 4.2.2.):

> "The owner of blighted property is morally blameworthy in a way that the owner of non-blighted property is not, namely because the owner of blighted property is imposing harm on neighboring properties. The taking of blighted property therefore, can serve as an appropriate collective response to harm-causing or immoral behaviour (…)."[142]

Applied to the situation of vacancy (or abandonment), by relinquishing possession (or ownership), the owner simply cannot avoid the responsibility of negative value property.[143] From the acquisition of property on, owners could consider a social obligation to sustainable use of their property. This could include the amelioration of the (negative value of the) property, repurposing the land and/or a thorough research for a new (co-) owner or administrator of the property. The latter search for a co-owner or administrator can be embedded in another more radical possibility to which legal scholars recently are paying attention to: regenerative ownership. This involves sharing ownership power(s). This sharing economy of property is often cited in the context of sharing positive value properties, but can also apply if the owner is not able to maintain the value or to undo the

Edin. Law Rev. 2021, vol. 25, no. 3, pp. 347-353. Robbie mentioned that at the time of writing (2021) there were only three applications. Two have been rejected (failure to fulfill administrative requirements) and one declined (on substantive grounds).

140 **US:** J.E. Penner, *The Idea of Property Law*, Oxford, OUP, 2000, p. 79.

141 **US:** *Ibid.* p. 79.

142 **US:** T.W. Merrill and H.E. Smith, *supra* note 57, p. 1883.

143 **US:** J.E. Penner, *The Idea of Property Law*, Oxford, OUP, 2000, p. 80.

negative value of property:[144] if sharing ownership powers could maximize the utility of the property, it could also prevent devaluation and dilapidation from happening. Such a progressive solution is, however, at odds with the traditional exclusivity of the ownership right.

Whether a social obligation to sustainable use provides a solution or, it is yet another obligation inflicted on the owner is difficult to say... Legal doctrine is still exploring the field of social obligations and regenerative ownership. However, at the very least, it creates a sense of urgency that the owner should use his powers in a sustainable way. We are curious to see what the future holds.

5 Conclusion

Neglect, vacancy or abandonment, what's in a name? Today, they are used interchangeably in common and legal parlance. The similar factual appearance of neglected, vacant or abandoned properties is deceiving since the internal legal situation differs in terms of title and possession. Besides the legal differences between neglect, abandonment and vacancy, their paths cross again regarding the object they relate to: negative value land.

Negative value (im)movables increasingly invade the domain of private law. Their presence raises the question whether property law is adapted to their existence. Applying the ownership powers (*usus, fructus, abusus*) to negative value (im)movables turns the traditional perception of the ownership right upside down: this ownership often provides little power and lots of burdens. The owner is limited in exercising his use and enjoy rights, but even more in his right of disposal, which often results – with regard to land or real estate – in a situation of vacancy.

From a property law perspective, vacancy is seen as an exercise of the right not to use. However, since vacancy leads to negative externalities, public law mechanisms attempt to control the owner's behaviour requiring to ascribe the land a particular use. So, although in theory non-use is allowed, in practice, the (private) right not to use seems (as far as it concerns land), severely restricted or at least discouraged. For now, the limits or sanctions are mainly established in public law, but action on private law level is not ruled out. This is already happening on a non-regulated, ad-hoc basis (e.g. symbolic sale). Yet, in light of the developing social function of the ownership right, private law can play a more significant role. In specific cases, the owner's right not to use his property may harm third parties or the environment, justifying a restriction on the right not to use. Modifications to adverse

144 **NL:** B. Akkermans and K. Van Melle, *supra* note 42, pp. 193-207. See also: R. Dyal-Chand, 'Sharing the cathedral', *Conn. L. Rev.* 2013, pp. 647-723; S. Kreiczer-Levy, *Destabilized Property*, Cambridge, CUP, 2019, 188p.

possession or even the abolishment of the imprescriptible nature of the right of ownership are considered in legal doctrine. Also, the Scottish compulsory sale, proves there is a lot of potential in a '*tango*' of public and private law. Another, yet to explore, option involves the embedding of a social obligation of sustainable use in private law.

At the same time, all those solutions are not self-evident because they are at odds with the traditional conception of the right to ownership: the debate about expropriating blighted properties for the public purpose is still vivid, regenerative ownership is difficult to reconcile with the exclusivity of ownership and the *presumption of abandonment* compromises the perpetual nature of ownership. These deadlocks are the result of the dominant classical property rights theorem together with the criticised positive value and utility assumption. This raises the question: could the recognition of negative value things, whether or not applied in the case of vacancy give rise to a modernised perception of ownership with focus on the property obligation-relations, but above all: a sustainable ownership right? *Time will tell…*

Part II
Property and Society in Extraordinary Times

3 Cultural Heritage and Social Identity in Territories Affected by Natural Catastrophes

Roberto Garetto[*]

1 Introduction

Areas affected by natural disasters are easily exposed to the loss of cultural remains that are particularly significant for the populations living in specific territories. These can be buildings and architectural structures, sites or other artistic and/or artisanal works. This risk is particularly relevant when referring to rural or peripheral areas. These vestiges constitute in themselves expression of cultural heritage for a specific community, e.g. for a group of population in a given territory. They have a particular identifying function for the populations of a rural or otherwise peripheral territory. This identifying value takes on great relevance when populations suffer the effects of natural events. Disasters can in fact lead to a quantitative but also qualitative impoverishment of the inhabitants of marginalised territories, favouring depopulation phenomena, especially with respect to younger generations. For this reason, it is advisable to become increasingly aware of the identity value of vestiges of the past even when they have scarce artistic value. Indeed, they can be an effective tool for the revitalisation of a disaster-stricken territory, reinforcing the confidence of the populations involved and guiding them to choose to remain in the area by restoring it. It thus becomes clear how useful it is to further investigate the function of specific expression of cultural heritage, which is often considered minor and to which limited protection tends to be offered in relation to its supposedly low artistic value. For this reason, it is necessary to identify forms of recognition and protection for remains of the past that are part of the cultural heritage and that have a considerable identity value for groups of the population in rural and peripheral areas. Indeed, they can become a useful tool to help overcome the negative effects of natural disasters on a specific territory, especially when it has the highlighted characteristics of a marginalised area. A crucial point is the identification of the very notion of cultural heritage. This is a relatively recent achievement, the result of an evolution that has taken place over about a century. While

* University of Camerino, Italy.

initially the artistic value of the monument was mainly taken into account, later on the connection of the community with the artistic vestige itself also began to be considered. The latest step in this evolution is the recent notion of intangible cultural heritage.

The fragility of cultural heritage requires special attention for its protection against natural disasters. The need to prevent the dispersal of cultural heritage following a disaster takes on particular significance when considering identity values for the affected community. In the perspective of reconstruction and revitalisation of disaster-stricken areas, it is necessary to identify specific interventions. In this perspective, the regulatory framework of the European Union and in particular the most recent studies by its experts on the management of natural disasters due to climate change are of particular relevance.

2 Notion of cultural heritage

Given that humankind needs tangible evidence of the past as reminders,[1] small rural communities need the preservation of reminders of the past, even if they are not particularly relevant in an historical or artistic respect. Cultural heritage provides a specific group of population with certainties, familiar surroundings which ensures assurances and reassurances.[2] It is therefore necessary to determine what is meant by cultural heritage. In addition, it should be ascertained whether the notion of cultural heritage also takes into account sites, architectural structures or artefacts of modest artistic value, but with a high identification value for groups of population in circumscribed areas of territory.

At the international level – as we shall see below – the first definition of cultural heritage is provided by the UNESCO *Convention for the Protection of the World Cultural and Natural Heritage* (1972 Paris Convention) of 1972.[3] It is therefore useful to dwell on the definition offered by this Convention, especially bearing in mind that 'its wording has proved resilient to the passage of time.'[4]

For the purposes of the 1972 Paris Convention, Article 1 lists as 'cultural heritage:'

- monuments: architectural buildings, monumental sculptures and paintings, archaeological structures, of great value from the point of view of history, art or science;

1 D.H.R. Spennemann, 'Cultural Heritage conservation during emergency management: Luxury or necessity?', *International Journal of Public Administration*, Vol. 22, No. 5, pp. 745-804.

2 *Ibid.*

3 UNESCO (1972). *Convention concerning the protection of the world cultural and Natural Heritage.* The General Conference of the United Nations Educational, Scientific and Cultural Organization meeting, seventeenth session, Paris 17 October-21 November 1972.

4 D. Rodwell, 'The Unesco World Heritage Convention, 1972-2012: Reflections and Directions', *The Historic Environment*, Vol. 3 No. 1, 2012, p. 77.

- groups of buildings: groups of separate or connected buildings which, because of their architecture, their homogeneity or their place in the landscape, are of universal value from the point of view of history, art or science;
- sites: works of man or the combined works of nature and man which are of universal value from the historical, aesthetic, ethnological or anthropological point of view.

According to Article 3 of the 1972 Paris Convention, for the purposes of the Convention, every State Party should identify and define the 'cultural heritage' situated on its territory mentioned in Article 1. Furthermore, under Article 4 of the 1972 Paris Convention, each signatory state party has the 'duty of ensuring the identification, protection, conservation, presentation and transmission to future generations of the cultural and natural heritage (…) situated on its territory,' referred to in Article 1. Article 5 commits signatory state parties 'to ensure that effective and active measures are taken for the protection, conservation and presentation of the cultural and natural heritage situated on its territory.'

It is to be noted that the 1972 Paris Convention is intended as rather selective and is not meant to encompass everything worthy of protection.[5] The importance of heritage identification is evident. In fact, if this identification mainly takes into account the artistic value, it risks neglecting the social value, especially when referring to groups of population living in marginal rural areas.

3 'Cultural property' *v.* 'Cultural heritage': terminological evolution

As highlighted above, the term 'cultural heritage' is relatively recent; it has acquired progressively more shades due to the widespread interest in it. However, it nowadays still coexists with other terms used since the beginning of the last century in multiple international treaties.[6] The earliest international documents aimed at protecting what we normally refer to as 'cultural heritage' have mainly focused on artistic significance: the evaluation parameter has been limited to the qualitative element of the artwork itself, disregarding the value it may represent for the community that is culturally identified with it. Only gradually has the connection of cultural heritage with the territory begun to be taken into account. An accurate reconstruction of this development through an analysis

5 *Ibid.*, p. 67: '[t]he 1972 Convention was conceived as highly selective and never intended to encompass everything worthy of protection.'

6 S. Ferrazzi, 'The Notion of "Cultural Heritage" in the International Field: Behind Origin and Evolution of a Concept', *International Journal for the Semiotics of Law*, Vol. 34, 2021, p. 743.

of the text of individual documents, given their large number,[7] is beyond the scope of this chapter. It is therefore sufficient to offer below a quick overview of the most significant documents.[8]

Referring to what we now term 'cultural heritage', the International documents from the early part of the last century used the expression 'monument.' This is precisely the term used in the *Athens Charter for the Restoration of Historic Monuments* approved by the participants of the First International Congress of Architects and Technicians of Historic Monuments organised by the International Museums Office in Athens in 1931.[9] The term was later replaced by the expression 'cultural property.'[10] This expression was introduced into legal language with the *Convention for the Protection of Cultural Property in the Event of Armed Conflict* (Hague Convention) in 1954.[11] In this regard the Convention not only adopts the term 'cultural property' for the first time, but also provides adequate guarantees for it – by virtue of its importance – through distinctive emblems in order to facilitate its recognition.[12]

The term 'cultural property' used in the Hague Convention has its origin precisely in the debate that took place in those decades around the definition of a univocal and inclusive category of all historical, artistic and natural elements. The reference made to the 'cultural' element is probably due to the strong impact of the heavy destruction of World War II and the sometimes unfortunate reconstruction work carried out after the war.[13] The use of the term 'property' in the above mentioned expression denotes a prevailing focus on

7 *See* N. Silberman, 'The ICOMOS-Ename Charter Initiative: Rethinking the Role of Heritage Interpretation in the 21st Century', *The George Wright Forum*, Vol. 23, No. 1, 2006, p. 28: "'[o]f making many books there is no end,' writes the biblical author of Ecclesiastes- and so it seems that of the making of many international heritage conventions, principles, and guidelines there also seems to be no end in sight."

8 *See*, to this end for further, J. Blake, 'On Defining the Cultural Heritage', *International and Comparative Law Quarterly*, Vol. 49, No. 1, 2000, pp. 61-62. For a concise reconstruction of the protection of cultural heritage up to the 19th century, cf. R. Garetto, 'The evolution of the legislation on the artistic legacy in Italy. Proposals of reform of the code of cultural heritage and landscape', *6th SWS International Scientific Conference on Arts and Humanities, Conference Proceedings, Florence, (Italy), 22/10/2019-24/10/2019*, Vol. 6, No. 2, 2019, pp. 109-111.

9 First International Congress of Architects and Technicians of Historic Monuments CIAM I (1931). *Charter for the Restoration of Historic Monuments* (Athens Charter), Athens, 21 October-30 October 1931.

10 See, on the juxtaposition of the two expressions, M. Frigo, 'Cultural property v. cultural heritage: A "battle of concepts" in international law?', *International Review of the Red Cross*, Vol. 86, No. 854, 2004, pp. 367-369.

11 UNESCO (1954). *Convention for the Protection of Cultural Property in the Event of Armed Conflict*. Director-General of the United Nations Educational, Scientific and Cultural Organization, the Hague, 14 May 1954.

12 *See* J. Hladik, 'Marking of cultural property with the distinctive emblem of the 1954 Hague Convention for the Protection of Cultural Property in the Event of Armed Conflict', *International Review of the Red Cross*, Vol. 86, No. 854, 2004, pp. 379-380.

13 M.F. Baird, 'UNESCO's World Heritage List Process', in C. Smith (Ed.) *Encyclopedia of Global Archaeology*, New York, Springer, 2014, pp. 7445-7446: '[t]he period after World War II was characterized by large-scale restorations of war-damaged cities and monuments and a concern for the protection of cultural property. These concerns were central to the Hague Convention of 1954.'

evaluation parameters limited to the qualitative element of the artwork itself. In fact, the Hague Convention, while not neglecting the value of the territorial and national rootedness of monuments, through the explicit reference to property highlights their measurability in terms of the attribution of an economic value.

In the cultural property designed by the Hague Convention there is no mention of context, of the sphere of relations between cultural property and the groups of population linked to it. It was necessary to wait until the *International Charter for the Conservation and Restoration of Monuments and Sites* (Venice Charter), adopted in Venice in 1964,[14] to perceive the attribution of a clear 'emotional' value of the historical monuments and heritage for the people connected to them. and it is these very people who are responsible for transmitting these monuments to future generations.[15]

However, this innovative element is only drafted in this document: see, significantly, Article 1 of the Venice Charter: '[t]he concept of an historic monument embraces not only the single architectural work but also the urban or rural setting in which is found the evidence of a particular civilization, a significant development or an historic event. This applies not only to great works of art but also to more modest works of the past which have acquired cultural significance with the passing of time.'[16] As a result of the Venice Charter of 1964, the International Council on Monuments and Sites (ICOMOS) was founded in 1965 in Warsaw. It offers advice to UNESCO on World Heritage Sites.[17]

The challenge of finding an inclusive category of cultural heritage that also takes into account the emotional value for the people linked to them remains unresolved even in the subsequent UNESCO *Convention on the Means of Prohibiting and Preventing the Illicit Import, Export and Transfer of Ownership of Cultural Property*, signed in Paris in 1970.[18] In fact, in an attempt to define what cultural property is, the drafters embark on an extensive list of everything that can be included in the category. The aforementioned Convention defines 'cultural property' as that which, in the religious or secular sphere, is declared by States to be of archaeological, prehistoric, historical, literary, artistic or scientific importance (Article 1). Such a partial view of the issue is however explicable in view of the

14 International Council on Monuments and Sites ICOMOS, Second International Congress of Architects and Technicians of Historic Buildings (1964). *International Charter for The Conservation and Restoration of Monuments and Sites* (Venice Charter), Venice, 25 May-31 May 1964.

15 See C. Di Biase, "La Carta de Venecia: cincuenta años después – The Venice Charter: fifty years on', *Loggia*, No 27, 2014, p. 26: '[t]he patrimony of historical monuments and heritage belonged to peoples as a whole; it was they who would have to hand it on to future generations.'

16 *See* A. Tzika Hatzopoulou, 'The Protection of the Landscape in its Various Aspects. Proposition and Challenge!', *Sustainable Development, Culture, Traditions*, Vol. 1, 2012, p. 8.

17 See S. Madole, 'International Council on Monuments and Sites (ICOMOS) (Ethics)', in C. Smith (Ed.), Encyclopedia of Global Archaeology, Cham, Springer, 2020, pp 5872-5874.

18 UNESCO (1970). *Convention on the Means of Prohibiting and Preventing the Illicit Import, Export and Transfer of Ownership of Cultural Property*. The General Conference of the United Nations Educational, Scientific and Cultural Organization meeting, sixteenth session, Paris, 12 November-14 November 1970.

Convention's intended function: to hinder the illicit trade in works of art, frequently – today as in the past – the object of theft and misappropriation.[19] The terminological approach is therefore also justified.

In the immediately following UNESCO *Convention for the Protection of the World Cultural and Natural Heritage* (above and below mentioned as: 1972 Paris Convention), signed in Paris in 1972[20] to which we have already referred above, the term 'cultural heritage' is adopted to replace the previous 'cultural property,' bringing with it ethical, moral and political values that strengthen the role of the inclusive cultural system. A few years later, during the aforementioned Congress on the European Architectural Heritage of 1975, the Committee of Ministers of the Council of Europe enacted the European Charter of Architectural Heritage (Amsterdam Charter). This document has a focus very oriented on the territorial context of the cultural heritage. It conceives the environment as the physical place of the stratification of social, economic and institutional relations. Architectural cultural heritage is not defined exclusively by 'monuments,' but includes groups of minor buildings inserted in ancient centres, respecting their natural or man-made configuration. The Amsterdam Charter also notes that too often only monuments of outstanding value have been protected and restored, without adequate consideration of the context.

The path towards a definition of cultural and architectural heritage that takes into account both historical and artistic, as well as social interest (as to say: emotional, relational, and environmental interest) is taken with the *Convention for the Protection of the European Architectural Heritage* (Granada Convention), enacted by the Council of Europe in Granada in 1985,[21] for which the term 'architectural heritage' takes on the following identifying properties within 3 topological categories (Article1):

- monuments: all buildings and structures of conspicuous historical, archaeological, artistic, scientific, social or technical interest, including their fixtures and fittings,
- groups of buildings: homogeneous groups of urban or rural buildings conspicuous for their historical, archaeological, artistic, scientific, social or technical interest which are sufficiently coherent to form topographically definable units,
- sites: the combined works of man and nature, being areas which are partially built upon and sufficiently distinctive and homogeneous to be topographically definable and are of conspicuous historical, archaeological, artistic, scientific, social or technical interest.

---

19 M. Bouchenaki, 'Return and restitution of cultural property in the wake of the 1970 Convention', *Museum International*, Vol. 61, No 1-2, 2009, p. 140.

20 *See* above.

21 Council of Europe (1985). *Convention for the Protection of the Architectural Heritage of Europe* (Granada Convention), Granada, 3 October 1985.

The interest of the sites also – among others – for their social function is noteworthy with respect to the provisions of the Granada Convention.[22]

4 Interaction between tangible and intangible cultural heritage

Greater attention to the human person and the environment, as the space surrounding the person, requires a reconsideration of the approach to the theme of protecting cultural heritage – and its recovery in the event of natural disaster – with greater awareness of its identity value. The path outlined above bears evidence of this evolution, which comes to a fundamental turning point when, at an international level, it is realised that cultural heritage in all its forms, whether tangible or intangible, must be protected.[23]

It is the new awareness of the emotional value of cultural heritage for groups of population with ties to a local area that led to the definition by UNESCO in 2003 of the intangible cultural heritage through the *Convention for the Safeguarding of the Intangible Cultural Heritage*.[24]

This Convention is in line with the 1972 Paris Convention and intrinsically complements it, coordinating tangible heritage with intangible heritage in a logical and consequential manner.[25]

Intangible cultural heritage is a practice, representation, expression, knowledge or skill considered by UNESCO to be part of a place's cultural heritage. Intangible heritage consists of nonphysical intellectual wealth, such as folklore, customs, beliefs, traditions, knowledge, and language. Intangible cultural heritage is considered by member states of UNESCO in relation to the tangible World heritage focusing on intangible aspects of culture. This new perspective leads to emphasising the centrality of the person in relation to the artistic heritage to which they are emotionally attached.[26]

---

22 Tzika Hatzopoulou, 2012, pp. 8-9.

23 *See*, for this gradual awareness since the second half of the last century, C.A. Berryman,'Toward more universal protection of intangible cultural property', *Journal of Intellectual Property Law*, Vol. 1, No. 2, 1994, p. 296.

24 UNESCO (2003). *Convention for the safeguarding of the intangible cultural heritage*. The General Conference of the United Nations Educational, Scientific and Cultural Organization meeting, thirty-second session, Paris, 29 September-17 October 2003.

25 *See* Rodwell, 2012, p. 77: "the World Heritage Convention, with its focus on immovable material objects, has been complemented by the 2003 Convention on intangible heritage."

26 R. Di Stefano, 'Conclusion', in Id. *et al.* (Eds.), *Révolutions et biens culturels. Revolutions and cultural properties. Rivoluzioni e beni culturali. 1789-1989. Proceedings of the Scientific Symposium organized by ICOMOS (Naples 20-21 November 1989)*, Naples, Arte Tipografica, 1990, pp. 118-119: '[a]nd it is precisely considering the concept of welfare that we find the need to understand whether and how the evidences of history, art and civilization of the past must be preserved and protected; to understand and recognize the importance this heritage holds for the human survival itself, to ensure, in other words, the true welfare for the man, whose only and true wealth (as Ruskin wrote) is life.'

Cultural heritage enriches the person's life, is a driving force for a widespread well-being, and plays a role in creating and enhancing a social capital.[27] In the event of natural disasters, cultural heritage must be preserved not only for its intrinsic value (in terms of 'cultural property'), but for the emotional value it implies. On the other hand, huge economic investments for the recovery of cultural heritage can also produce a surplus entry in the balance sheet in the long run. Cultural heritage indeed can be an important resource for economic recovery and subsequent growth, employment and social cohesion. It can offer the potential to revitalise urban and rural areas affected by a disaster[28] and promote sustainable tourism.

5 CULTURAL HERITAGE AND SOCIAL IDENTITY

Cultural heritage is closely linked to the social and cultural identity of the populations established in a given territory. Therefore, the proper approach to its preservation in areas affected by natural disasters cannot disregard issues related to identity-based values.[29] It should be borne in mind that 'value' in the social perspective, is defined through emotional, and moral meanings attached to specific events, places, objects, or social practices by a group of population in a territory.[30] These values help groups of population of specific territories justify their claims or current position in relation to the rest of the population.[31] They increase the self-esteem of groups of population and shape their image (internally and externally). The value of heritage is, thus, attached to a specific group of population, its identity, and its relations with the rest of the population.[32] Social identity is based on a

27 See, with regard to heritage tourism and related risks, Silberman 2006, pp. 28-29.

28 R. Genç, 'Catastrophe of Environment: The Impact of Natural Disasters on Tourism Industry', *Journal of Tourism & Adventure*, Vol. 1, No. 1, 2018, p. 93: 'natural disasters may create long-lasting impacts on the lives of people, and as an outcome of this, tourism sector may be negatively affected due to labor power decrease and damage in tourism facilities or worsening destination image with respect to bad management of crisis (..) natural disasters are threat for the whole society in a region, thus the steps to overcome the negative impacts of a disaster would require solidarity, mutual support and collective action.'

29 D.H.R. Spennemann, 'The importance of heritage preservation in natural disaster situations', *International Journal of Risk Assessment and Management*, Vol. 7, Nos. 6/7, 2007, p. 994: '[t]he values projected onto cultural heritage places by the public are assessed against predetermined criteria to determine their significance.'

30 M. de la Torre, M.G.H. MacLean, R. Mason & D. Myers, *Heritage Values in Site Management: Four Case Studies*, Los Angeles, Getty Conservation Institute, 2005, p. 5: '[v]alue has been used to mean positive characteristics attributed to heritage objects and places by legislation, governing authorities, and other stakeholders.'

31 *See*, for this specific dynamic, the case of the Silesian group of population compared to the rest of the Polish population in: K. Wódz & J. Wódz, *Dimensions of Silesian Identity*, Katowice, Wydawnictwo Uniwersytetu Śląskiego, 2006, p. 13.

32 *See* K.V. Korostelina, 'Understanding Values of Cultural Heritage within the Framework of Social Identity Conflicts', in: E. Avrami, S. MacDonald, R. Mason & David Myers (Eds.), *Values in Heritage Management:*

strong sense of membership in a specific group, emotional connection and feelings of loyalty to this group, and perceptions of difference with respect to other groups.[33] This social identity also arises in the case of groups of population living in small towns in rural areas with a strong historical tradition. A values-based planning process calls for a clear understanding of the place where the group of population lives.[34]

In the case of catastrophic natural events (e.g. earthquake), interventions to protect and preserve cultural heritage are not only related to the value of the cultural assets in themselves, but are also functional to the identity value for the group of population connected to the cultural heritage as a whole. This is particularly true in small towns in rural areas, where the identity value of historical, artistic and cultural heritage is particularly strong. After disasters, interventions to protect and restore cultural heritage must take into account the needs of the group of population linked to a specific area. These needs, although various and heterogeneous, have been concisely categorised as follows:[35]

- enhancement: intended as confirmation of identity of the group of population through a process of 'glorification' of the past[36] and the bond with the territory affected by the disaster;
- legitimisation: namely maintaining social order within the group of population hit by a catastrophic event by means of a process of mythologising its foundation;[37]
- identification of a normative value: implying empowerment of the group of population and recognition of the right to stay on their own land after a disaster through a process of reparations for 'historical injustice';[38]
- healing achievement: a memory retrieval path for the purpose of obtaining collective and individual healing[39] aimed at maintaining a balance between remembering (the time before the disaster) and forgetting (the catastrophic event itself).

Emerging Approaches and Research Directions, Los Angeles, The Getty Conservation Institute, 2019, p. 84.

33 K.V. Korostelina, *Social Identity and Conflict: Structures, Dynamics, and Implications*, New York, Palgrave MacMillan, 2007, pp. 35-58.

34 M. Demas, 'Planning for Conservation and Management of Archaeological Sites: A Values-Based Approach', in J.M. Teutonico & G. Palumbo (Eds.) *Management Planning for Archaeological Sites*, Los Angeles, The Getty Conservation Institute, 2000, pp. 27-54.

35 *See* Korostelina, 2019, pp. 85-87.

36 P. Ricoeur, *History and Truth*, Evanston, Northwestern University Press, 1965, p. 26.

37 J. Overing, 'The Role of Myth: An Anthropological Perspective, or, The Reality of the Really Made-Up', in G. Hosking & G. Schöpfli (Eds.), *Myths and Nationhood*, New York, Routledge, 1997, p. 12.

38 M. Galanter, 'Righting Old Wrongs', in M. Minnow (Ed.), *Breaking the Cycles of Hatred: Memory, Law, and Repair*, Princeton, Princeton University Press, 2002, p. 122.

39 J. Blustein, *The Moral Demands of Memory*, Cambridge, Cambridge University Press, 2008, p. 13.

6 Fragility of cultural heritage in the face disasters and possible remedies

The fragility of cultural heritage in the face of catastrophic events calls for reflection on the need to prevent its destruction and – if it is nevertheless affected by such events – to ensure its preservation as far as possible. Our cultural heritage is indeed continuously subjected to a series of 'external' attacks that threaten to destroy and make disappear in a very short time what we have been able to preserve for centuries. In light of this, it is increasingly necessary and urgent to address the problems posed by the fragility of cultural heritage. It is therefore necessary to identify specific disaster management strategies in relation to its protection.[40] In spite of the adoption of many world programs, including the most recent: the Sendai Framework for Disaster Risk Reduction,[41] unfortunately many countries are still poorly prepared with respect to the implementation of a viable strategy in this area.[42] Nonetheless, there is a widespread awareness of the need to reduce the impact of natural disasters on cultural heritage. It has as its general consciousness-raising a disaster of planetary resonance: the Arno flood in Florence in 1966,[43] which most clearly represents the impact on collective identity – on a global level – of severe damage to cultural heritage.

A proper strategy of disaster management based on the understanding of complex security and complex risk management requires the analysis of all natural and social phenomena.[44] A disaster affects the population inhabiting an area and at the same time causes damage and/or destruction to cultural heritage. Preventive actions (and eventually subsequent interventions) must be based on the awareness that these two aspects are inseparable. Significantly, the aforementioned Sendai Framework in the preamble states that: 'It is urgent and critical to anticipate, plan for and reduce disaster risk in order to more effectively protect persons, communities and countries, their livelihoods, health, cultural heritage, socioeconomic assets and ecosystems'. Such protection implies

40 *See* R. Mason & E. Avrami, 'Heritage Values and Challenges of Conservation Planning', in J.M. Teutonico & G. Palumbo (Eds.), *Management Planning for Archaeological Sites*, Los Angeles, The Getty Conservation Institute, 2000, p. 13.

41 United Nations, *Sendai Framework for Disaster Risk Reduction 2015-2030*, United Nations, Sendai, Japan, 2015.

42 L. Antronico, R. Coscarelli, F. De Pascale & F. Condino, 'Social Perception of Geo-Hydrological Risk in the Context of Urban Disaster Risk Reduction: A Comparison between Experts and Population in an Area of Southern Italy', *Sustainability*, Vol. 11, No. 2061, 2019, p. 3.

43 G. Gerola & M. Materassi (Eds.), 'Cronaca: L'Arno straripa. Il mancato allarme. La città giorno per giorno. Quanti i Morti?', *Il ponte. Firenze Perchè*, Vol. 22, No. 11-12, 1966, pp. 1334-1357.

44 Y.V. Kostyuchenko *et al.*, 'Multi-Disaster Vulnerability Analysis Using Multisource Data', in A.G. Zagorodny *et al.* (Eds.), *FEW Nexus for Sustainable Development: Integrated Modeling & Robust Management - Взаємозв'язки в системі продовольство, енергія та вода для сталого розвитку: інтегроване моделювання та надійне управління*, Kyiv, National Academy Of Sciences Of Ukraine, 2020, p. 422: '[m]odern understanding of complex security and complex risk management requires analysis of all natural and social phenomena.'

identifying in advance the link between the group of population rooted in a territory and the places, buildings or artistic works that uniquely characterise that place and which constitute an identifying element for the group itself. Such an interaction between population group, rootedness in the territory, artistic remains and cultural significance requires coordinated interventions in a holistic perspective.[45]

In order to conserve the cultural heritage threatened by risks of natural origin, it is essential to adopt a multidisciplinary approach.[46] As stated at international level in the 1975 Declaration of Amsterdam,[47] the integrated conservation of cultural heritage requires a promotion of multiple professional skills.[48] As later enshrined in the 2005 Faro Convention,[49] this implies a synergy of competencies among all the public, institutional and private actors.[50] This goal can be achieved through a co-ordinated action between public institutions and private subjects towards innovative methods of decision-making and determination of effective policies[51] to safeguard the cultural heritage and the risks to which it is exposed and to identify efficient and timely devices to deal with and overcome natural disasters.[52] Functional to the prevention of cultural heritage from disaster risks may be the following two remedies:[53]

– implementation of a synergy between institutions in charge of disaster risk management and institutions responsible for cultural heritage. This can be achieved through a

---

45 H. Stovel, 'Two current initiatives to improve risk preparedness for cultural heritage at the national and international levels', in H. Saito (Ed.), *1997 Kobe/Tokyo International Symposium Risk Preparedness for Cultural Properties: Development of Guidelines for Emergency Response*, Tokyo, Chuo-Koron Bijutsu Shuppan, 1999, p. 228: '[we] will be able to deal with catastrophe and its consequences without having to set human life against the worth of cultural heritage; we will recognise that the two are intrinsically linked, part of the one indivisible whole.'

46 *See* 'Preface', in I. Rizzo & A. Mignosa (Eds.), Handbook on the Economics of Cultural Heritage, Cheltenham, Edward Elgar, 2013, p. xxv.

47 The Declaration of Amsterdam, Congress on the European Architectural Heritage, 21-25 October 1975.

48 *See* A.R. Genovese, 'The cultural heritage for the man', in Proceedings of ICOMOS 15th General Assembly and Scientific Symposium, Vol. I. Xi'an, China, 2005, p. 79.

49 Council of Europe (2005), *Council of Europe Framework Convention on the Value of Cultural Heritage for Society*, Faro, 27 October 2005.

50 *See* in particular Article 1 of the Convention. For further details, *see*: M. Cerreta & E. Giovene di Girasole, 'Faro Convention Network Process: Proposed Indicators for Heritage Community Self-Assessment', *Memòria viva*, 2021, pp. 69-80.

51 R. Nanda, 'Group Report: Values and Society', in N.S. Baer & F. Snickars, *Rational Decision-Making in the Preservation of Cultural Property*, Berlin, Dahlem University Press, 2001, p. 76.

52 A. Badami, 'Patrimonio culturale a rischio. Una risposta dall'Europa. Il progetto Polirisk – Politiques comparées: patrimoine, aménagement et risques naturels', *Complessità e sostenibilità: il territorio e l'architettura*, No. 7, 2008, pp. 16-19.

53 *See* D.H.R. Spennemann & D.W. Look, 'From conflict to dialogue, from dialogue to cooperation, from cooperation to preservation', in D.H.R. Spennemann & D.W. Look (Eds.), *Disaster Management Programs for Historic Sites*, San Francisco and Albury, NSW, Association for Preservation Technology, Western Chapter and Johnstone Centre, Charles Sturt University, 1998, pp.175-188 and D.H.R. Spennemann, 'Risk assessments in heritage planning in Victoria and New South Wales:a survey of the status quo', *Australasian Journal of Environmental Management*, Vol. 12, No. 2, 2005, pp.89-96.

preliminary identification of priorities in the event of a disaster and the preparation of an emergency response plan; and
- planning of an integrated multi-stakeholder system aimed at empowering private institutions and individual undertakings in the disaster risk assessment. process in order to spread support and increase local ownership of risk.[54]

In addition to these main remedies, further consideration should be given to:
- private stakeholders and the optimisation of volunteer management;
- the production of organised and useful knowledge through the development of risk maps and the consistency and location of cultural heritage;
- the identification of efficient information processes for populations exposed to risks and for safer and more aware behaviour in the event of an alert.

7 THE EU FRAMEWORK ON THE PROTECTION OF CULTURAL HERITAGE FROM NATURAL DISASTERS

At the European level, not only the Council of Europe, but also the European Union (EU) aims to preserve cultural heritage. This commitment is expressly assumed as a binding principle in Article 3(3) TEU. In this point, it is worth noting that the EU does not disregard the identity-related, emotional value of cultural heritage to the human being. One of the most important features at EU level is the publication of the *European Framework for Action on Cultural Heritage* in 2018.[55] This document is a follow up to a high impact initiative, the 2018 European Year of Cultural Heritage; it establishes a set of four principles of continued action for cultural heritage:[56]
- holistic: considering tangible and intangible cultural heritage as inseparable and interconnected;
- mainstreaming/integrated: setting out an integrated approach to cultural heritage at European level;
- evidence-based policy making: measuring the impact of actions on cultural heritage;
- Multi-stakeholder: coordinating the activities of European cultural heritage networks and international organisations.

54 J. Adekola, D. Fischbacher-Smith & M. Fischbacher-Smith, 'Inherent Complexities of a Multi-stakeholder Approach to Building Community Resilience', International Journal of Disaster Risk Science, Vol. 11, No. 2, 2020, p. 32.

55 European Commission, Directorate-General for Education, Youth, Sport and Culture. *European framework for action on cultural heritage*, Luxembourg, Publications Office of the European Union, 2019.

56 *Ibid.*, pp. 8-9.

The Framework also proposes around 60 actions to continue to promote and protect Europe's cultural heritage. The actions are organised in five areas, which can be briefly summarised as follows:

- inclusiveness
- sustainability
- resilience
- innovation
- international cooperation.

Two of these areas, sustainability and resilience, are particularly relevant in the context of protecting the identitary value of cultural heritage at EU level. The combination of sustainability and resilience, already expressed in Goal 11 of the 2030 Agenda, and now identified as an EU strategic line in the protection of cultural heritage, can effectively ensure respect for the identitary value of cultural heritage exposed to the risk of a natural disaster.

The EU Open Method of Coordination (OMC) group of Member States' experts on 'Strengthening cultural heritage resilience for climate change' published a Report in 2022.[57]

The expert group shows a clear awareness of the identitary value of cultural heritage, expressly stating that: 'it forms a visible pillar of identity and community solidarity.'[58] With regard to a specific type of natural disaster, due to climate change, it identifies gaps[59] and priorities[60] consistent with those highlighted above,[61] namely:

- the lack of awareness of the extent of cultural heritage in the context of disaster risks, both at European and national level;
- the lack of knowledge of the scope and scale of damage and losses that a natural disaster can cause on cultural heritage;
- the lack of a coherent methodology to acquire relevant information, quantitative data and knowledge of the forms of decay of cultural heritage;
- the lack of financial and human resources in research and policy development to protect cultural heritage;
- the lack of quantitative data on adaptation/mitigation costs and measures;

57 J. Leissner, A. Grady, M. Maraña, F. Baeke & A. van Cutsem, *Strengthening Cultural Heritage Resilience for Climate Change. Where the European Green Deal Meets Cultural Heritage*, Luxembourg, Publications Office of the European Union, 2022.

58 *Ibid.*, p. 7.

59 *Ibid.*, p. 8.

60 *Ibid.*, p. 9.

61 *See* paragraph 6.

- the lack of a website or platform at European level to provide information on the state of the art and the progress of actions implemented;
- the lack of a centralised inventory and entry point covering damage/loss/risk to cultural heritage following disasters at national and EU level;
- the absence of a permanent task force or forum for discussion and mutual exchange.

The expert group, in light of the highlighted gaps, further presented recommendations to help strengthen the resilience of cultural heritage to from natural and climatic disasters.

In particular:

- The European Commission should develop and regularly update, together with Member States and associated countries, a European cultural heritage risk assessment map.
- The European Commission should establish a common European platform for exchange, discussion, expertise and knowledge sharing on the impact of disasters on cultural heritage.
- National/regional and local administrations should include cultural heritage in all actions and plans to mitigate disasters. Actions must be taken to fully integrate cultural heritage issues into environmental sustainability at both national/regional/local and international levels.
- National and regional authorities need to develop multidisciplinary capacities and skills to ensure the protection of cultural heritage against natural disasters, training and updating at all levels.
- National authorities must recognise the importance of research as an indispensable driver for progress in the cultural heritage sector. In addition to EU-funded programmes, governments need to initiate research programmes at national level to improve knowledge sharing and cooperation between cultural heritage and disaster experts to create data collection mechanisms, collect and analyse data and develop tools, infrastructure, best practices and strategies.
- Governments and institutions at national/regional and local level should immediately encourage investment and incentivise the protection of cultural heritage against natural disasters through monetary and fiscal policies.
- Ministries and administrations of Member States and associated countries as well as local and regional authorities must ensure cooperation at all levels of governance in relevant policy areas, in particular in planning bodies, between those responsible for disaster prevention actions and those responsible for cultural heritage.

8 Conclusion

The path taken towards the recognition of an identity value – both social and emotional – of cultural heritage makes us fully understand how it must be preserved and recovered in the event of natural disasters. A multidisciplinary approach to the issue is certainly essential. A synergy between public institutions and private actors is also fundamental. The contribution of private actors in this perspective is absolutely central, also through the enhancement of voluntary work. The broadening of awareness of the implications of environmental disaster risk with respect to the cultural heritage must take place through the use of advanced technological tools. Their use, accompanied by detailed risk mapping, can yield great results in terms of prevention and immediate post-disaster intervention. Risk mapping and the realisation of an online platform are among the priorities emerging from EU studies on sustainability and resilience in preventive and post-disaster approaches to cultural heritage damage due to climate and environmental disasters. Prompt recovery of a cultural heritage rich in identity implications is of significant support to groups of population affected by natural disasters. This awareness with respect to identity implications of cultural heritage is in line with the full appreciation of the human person and his or her needs as opposed to considerations merely focused on the intrinsic value of artistic and/or cultural property. As has been rightly pointed out, '[t]he conservation of the cultural property may therefore become an essential part of the revolution that will replace man and his environment at the centre of the society and allow him to find again the awareness of his main purpose that is to protect the tangible and intangible values inside our heritage, the spirit of place, thus satisfying the three requests (historical, aesthetic, psychological).'[62]

Overcoming the opposition between 'cultural property' and 'cultural heritage' in favour of the latter opens the way for a broadening of the notion of cultural heritage. This is consistent with the very etymology of the term, which refers to the Latin word *hērēs*, heir in the moral (rather than patrimonial) sense.[63] The enlargement of the notion places the human person and his or her needs at the centre and makes it possible to enhance the valorisation of groups of population in marginal areas affected by disasters. Interventions for the recovery of cultural heritage compromised by natural disasters must therefore take into account not only the artistic aspect of the damaged asset, but also its identity value for the populations related to it.

---

62 A.R. Genovese, 'Protecting the spirit of place in order to construct a policy for life', in *16th ICOMOS General Assembly and International Symposium: 'Finding the spirit of place – between the tangible and the intangible', 29 Sept – 4 Oct 2008, Quebec*, p. 5. Available at: https://openarchive.icomos.org/id/eprint/158/1/78-7cyb-142.pdf, (accessed 30 September 2022).

63 G. Devoto, 'I problemi del più antico vocabolario giuridico romano', *Annali della R. Scuola Normale Superiore di Pisa. Lettere, Storia e Filosofia*, Series II, Vol. 2, 1933, p. 237.

4 The Community Land Trust Implementation in Peru: A Property Right-Based Model for a Civil Law Country

Gerson Enrique Barboza De las Casas[*]

1 Introduction

The Peruvian Sustainable Urban Development Act of 2021 ("Ley de Desarrollo Urbano Sostenible", hereinafter called LDUS) has regulated, for the very first time, the community land trust - CLT ("Fideicomiso Comunitario de Tierra") in the pursuit of affordable housing generation for low-income sector. In this regard, Art. 87 LDUS states:

> To promote the creation, development, and management of housing projects; local governments may set up or support setting up a Community Land Trust, which manages the property for the project to include total or partial Social Interest Housing, thus granting a superficies over the CLT dwellings.[1]

The CLT is a collective stewardship of private property, which differs from the traditional individual private property. The CLT model generates affordable housing by granting a right of superficies, especially for the population of the less favoured or structurally segregated socio-economic sectors.[2] In this sense, the CLT is an alternative of housing generation based on a community-led land tenure model.[3]

---

* Adjunct Professor of Property Law at Faculty of Law, Pontifical Catholic University of Peru ("Pontificia Universidad Católica del Perú" - PUCP). This chapter was developed with the finance support from the Center for Research, Training and Legal Advice ("Centro de Investigación, Capacitación y Asesoría Jurídica" - CICAJ), PUCP - Lima. Please any correspondence regarding this chapter to gbarboza@pucp.edu.pe.

1 [Author's free translation].

2 *See* K.A. Gray and J. E. Miller-Cribbs, 'The Durham Community Land Trustees', *Journal of Community Practice*, Vol. 20, 2012, pp. 402-413; and K. A. Gray and M. Galande, 'Keeping "Community" in a Community Land Trust', *Social Work Research*, Vol. 35, 2011, pp. 244-245.

3 *See* International Independence Institute, *The Community Land Trust: A Guide to a New Model for Land Tenure in America*, Massachusetts, Center for Community Economic Development, 1972.

However, can the CLT model be an effective tool for affordable housing generation in Peru? In this chapter we try to answer this question through a systematic review of the literature concerning the experiences in USA, UK, and Canada, on the one hand, and Puerto Rico and Brazil, on the other. Also, we examine the main CLT model adaptation challenges in the Peruvian legal system and how this model can improve the inadequate housing conditions.

For this purpose, first we will develop an overview of the central housing problem, that is, the inadequate housing conditions of Peruvian population, as well as the causes of this problem and how it has increased and accelerated in recent years. Second, we analyse the housing policies developed in recent decades and how, despite their implementation, the problem not only persists, but has increased. These policies focus on three aspects: (i) the formalisation of informal settlements (titling programmes), (ii) government subsidies for low-income housing, and (iii) facilities for mortgage credit access.

Third, we propose an explanation for the persistence of the problem based on an analysis of the causes and the need to adopt new models of private property management that facilitate affordable housing generation. Fourth, we analyse the figure of the CLT as a model of collective management of private property and show the evidence compiled on its operation in other jurisdictions.

Fifth, we evaluate the legal framework through the current American CLT standard model and regulation. Then, sixth, we show the evidence gathered, from the specialised literature revision, on how the CLT has worked in different countries. Seventh, we analyse the relevant legal aspects of the Peruvian CLT implementation from a comparative perspective. Finally, we provide final reflections on the opportunities, challenges, and potential objections to the implementation of the CLT in Peru.

2 Central problem: Inadequate housing conditions in Peru

According to the Housing, Construction, and Sanitation Ministry ("Ministerio de Vivienda, Construcción y Saneamiento", hereinafter called MVCS), the housing deficit in Peru is around 1.5 million and it involves mainly the moderate- and low-income population.[4] This is reflected in the inadequate housing conditions. Indeed, unable to afford a new home or to improve their own, many people are forced to squatting and live in informal settlements or shanty towns, most of them without access to public services

4 MVCS, *Política Nacional de Vivienda y Urbanismo*, Lima, MVCS, 2021. Available at: https://www.gob.pe/institucion/vivienda/informes-publicaciones/2027198-resumen-de-la-politica-nacional-de-vivienda-y-urbanismo (accessed 03 March 2023).

such as water, sewage, or electricity, or to public spaces such as parks and recreation centers.[5]

The inadequate housing conditions is caused by the limited and unfair access to adequate housing. That is, on the one hand, the supply of new dwellings is quite limited compared to the high housing demand. On the other hand, because of the limited supply of housing, the limited supply is often unaffordable for most of the population. In other words, not only is there a limited amount of suitable new housing, but it is often not targeted to the low- and moderate-income population.[6]

Figure 4.1 Inadequate housing conditions

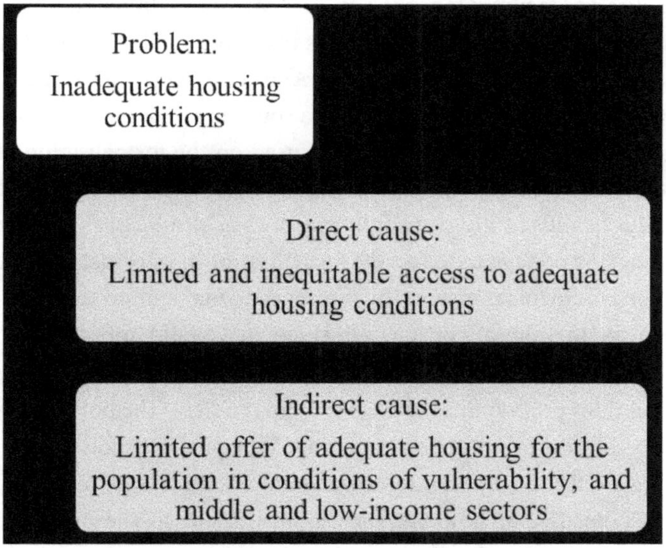

Source: Own elaboration based on the National Policy of Housing and Urbanism ("Política Nacional de Vivienda y Urbanism", hereinafter called PNVU). MVCS, Política Nacional de Vivienda y Urbanismo, Lima, MVCS, 2021. pp. 9.

However, this is proving to be an ongoing problem in fast-growing cities. Currently, almost 90% of urban growth is taking place in informal conditions, and growth is

5 *See* J. Calderón, 'El Estado y la informalidad urbana. Perú en el siglo XXI', *PLURIVERSIDAD*, Vol. 3, 2019, pp. 45-64; N. Shanee and S. Shanee, 'Land Trafficking, Migration, and Conservation in the "No-Man's Land" of Northeastern Peru, *Tropical Conservation Science*, Vol. 9, 2016; and, K. Skrabut, 'Use, Exchange, and Speculation: The Politics of Inhabitance and the Right to the City in Urban Peru, *City and Society*, Vol. 33, 2021, pp. 4-17.

6 *See* A. Espinoza and R. Fort, *Hacia una nueva política de Vivienda en el Perú: Problemas y posibilidades*, Lima, ADI, 2020. Available at: https://adiperu.pe/wp-content/uploads/Documento-Base-Hacia-una-nueva-Politica-de-Vivienda-en-el-Peru-Problemas-y-posibilidades.pdf (accessed 03 March 2023).

accelerating. As a result, if the situation is not reversed, the housing gap will tend to increase over the decades.[7] This picture reflects the need to look for alternatives to traditional housing generation that can mitigate the current shortfall.

3 Housing policies and the persistence of the problem

3.1 *Formalisation of informal ownership*

Housing policies in Peru revolve around three (3) central concepts: title programmes, government subsidies and facilities for access to mortgage loans. In relation to the first, for some decades now, the Government's priority has been to provide title deeds to families (mostly migrants from the rural areas in the Andean region) who, faced with the impossibility of accessing formal housing, opted to squatting on large tracts of land.[8]

As a result, for decades housing policy has focused on the formalisation of informal ownership, through the granting of property titles that - in principle - would provide an improvement in the quality of life of people who had a "dead asset" at their disposal. According to the housing policies based on the formalisation of informal property, families could access the formal financial system (by mortgage loans) and, in this way, be able to make improvements to their homes or start a business that would improve their quality of life. Nothing could be further from the truth.[9]

After decades of titles programmes, the work seems endless. The housing policy based on the formalisation of informal property encouraged the phenomenon of land invasions, which were no longer only of families migrating from the countryside to the city in search of a roof over their heads, but now became "sophisticated" to the point of operating through large land trafficking mafias. Organised land trafficking mafias gradually began to play a role in the provision of housing for the neediest families, giving rise to the phenomenon of "pirate subdivisions" (illegal subdivisions).[10]

---

7 A. Espinoza and R. Fort, *Mapeo y tipología de la expansión urbana en el Perú*, Lima, GRADE, 2020. Available at: https://www.grade.org.pe/wp-content/uploads/EspinozaFort_GRADEADI_expansionurbana.pdf (accessed 03 March 2023).

8 R. Lambert, 'Land Trafficking and the Fertile Spaces of Legality', *International Journal of Urban and Regional Research*, Vol. 45, 2021, pp. 21-38; J. Calderón, 'Titulación de la propiedad y mercado de tierras', *EURE*, Vol. 111, 2011, pp. 47-77; and G. Payne *et al.*, 'The limits of land titling and home ownership', *Environment and Urbanization*, Vol. 21, 2009, pp. 443-462.

9 *See* J. Calderón, 'Política de vivienda y gestión de suelo urbano. Casos de Corea, Colombia y Perú (1990-2015', Vol. 40, *Territorios*, 2019, pp. 201-226.; J. Calderón, 'The formalisation of property in Peru 2001-2002: the case of Lima', *Habitat International*, Vol. 28, 2004, pp. 289-300; and, G. Payne, 'Urban land tenure policy options: titles or rights?', *Habitat International*, Vol. 25, 2001, pp. 415-429.

10 *See* R. Lambert, 'Land Trafficking and the Fertile Spaces of Legality', *International Journal of Urban and Regional Research*, Vol. 45, 2021, pp. 21-38; and N. Shanee and S. Shanee, 'Land Trafficking, Migration, and

Large tracts of land were developed without meeting urban planification or the minimum legal requirements for access to services such as drinking water, sewage, electricity, or the necessary land contributions for the development of green areas, public spaces, hospitals, schools, etc.

Unfortunately, housing policies aimed at formalising informal property were not concerned with sustainable urban development, with urban planning or growth projections for cities and population centres. Priority was given to the titling in shanty towns and slums with populations settled in at-risk or intangible zones in accordance with environmental protection norms. In spite of this, the choice was made for unclear, immediate titling without a vision for sustainable development.

3.2 *Government subsidies*

The other central axis of housing policy is government subsidies directly granted to low-income families, after evaluation and selection. As indicated above, one of the causes of the housing deficit is that there is a limited supply of suitable housing on the real estate market, which is becoming increasingly expensive. This situation leads the state to intervene with direct subsidies.

These subsidies are granted by the public company Myhome Fund ("Fondo Mivivienda" hereinafter called FMV), through the Techo Propio programme, and allow families to buy a house for up to S/. 43,312.50 (US$ 11,458.00, approximately), build a house for up to S/. 29,700.00 (US$ 7,857.00, approximately) or improve their current house for up to S/. 11,385.00 (US$ 3,011.00, approximately).[11]

Although the FMV's subsidies are in great demand, they are insufficient to cover the large demand for housing, and it also depends directly on public funds, so it is not a sustainable measure in the long term. Though it is a palliative for the housing deficit, it is of little significance in terms of substantially reducing affordable housing gaps. In addition, the increase in the prices of land, housing and construction materials means that the subsidy granted by the state has an increasingly lower real value.

3.3 *Facilitating access to mortgage loans*

The last axis of housing policy focuses on the role of facilitator. In this case, also through the public company FMV, the state intervenes to facilitate banks granting mortgage loans

Conservation in the "No-Man's Land" of Northeastern Peru, *Tropical Conservation Science*, Vol. 9, 2016.

11 A further information of Techo Propio programme is available at: https://www.mivivienda.com.pe/portalweb/usuario-busca-viviendas/pagina.aspx?idpage=30.

to finance housing. In this case, FMV intervenes as a second-tier bank, that is, it does not grant money directly to individuals, but hands it over to commercial banks, which, in turn, grant the money to individuals. Under this scheme, the state takes the risk of non-payment of the loan.

This intervention is conducted through the Nuevo Crédito Mivivienda programme, a mortgage loan that allows a purchase, construction, or improvement of a home. The Nuevo Crédito Mivivienda finances housing between S/ 64,200.00 (approximately US$ 16,802.00) and S/ 464,200.00 (approximately US$ 121,518) with a repayment term of 5 to 25 years.[12]

The intervention of FMV as a second-tier bank means that mortgagors can make prepayments at any time and that the monthly mortgage loan instalment (and the interest rate) will always be the same. However, as it is a mortgage loan, the person applying for this programme must prove a fixed monthly income, as well as having employment and financial stability.

Under this programme, a middle-income family must allocate about 40-50% of their expenses to access a new dwelling, but it is not useful for low-income families, who cannot afford a new one under typical real estate market tools. For example, workers in informal market.[13]

In short, while this policy can be useful for the middle class, it is not an effective tool for the poor who are not in the labour and financial formalities. In this sense, it is not an effective housing policy for closing the affordable housing gap for low and extremely low socio-economic sectors.

4 Reflections on Peruvian housing policies: individual private property as the only scheme for affordable housing generation

The housing policies outlined above have been in place for decades; however, the high housing deficit figures are evidence that they are insufficient to provide a way out of the current housing crisis. It is difficult to identify a single cause for the persistence of the problem and the ineffectiveness of housing policies. However, we believe that the central problem is that the policies described above do not directly address the problem of inadequate housing conditions but, on the contrary, contribute to their exacerbation.

We pointed out above that the direct cause of the problem of inadequate housing conditions of the population is the limited and inequitable access to adequate housing

12 A further information of Nuevo Crédito Mivivienda programme is available at: https://www.mivivienda.com.pe/portalweb/usuario-busca-viviendas/pagina.aspx?idpage=20.

13 N. Libertun de Duren and R. Osorio, 'The Effect of Public Expenditure on the Housing Deficit in Peru at the Municipal Level', *Housing Policy Debate*, Vol. 30, 2020, pp. 718-740.

conditions. Likewise, this direct cause has as an indirect cause the limited supply of decent and adequate housing for the population in conditions of vulnerability, and for the middle and lower sectors.

The difficulty of housing policies is based on the premise of access to housing through the rules of the real estate market.[14] In other words, the aim is for a person or family wishing to obtain housing to be subsidised by the state in order to put themselves on an "equal footing" with other market agents. However, this generates a distortion that, in the long term, creates a fiction in the real demand for housing. This leads, on the one hand, to an increase in the value of land due to a high demand for housing subsidised or promoted by the state; and, on the other hand, to market agents such as real estate agents or people seeking to invest in real estate also entering the market.[15]

Unfortunately, government subsidies and state promotion do not keep pace with real estate development, which means that housing costs are increasingly rising without people's incomes, as well as labour formalisation and access to the formal financial system, keeping pace with them. This mismatch between the increase in the value of land (and therefore houses) and the increase in people's incomes means that the housing deficit cannot be significantly mitigated, even with state intervention.

Another relevant aspect is the housing model and the way it is managed. Much of the real estate development in the housing sector has taken place through the construction of new flats in buildings. Then, the housing policies – at least in relation to subsidy programmes and facilities for access to mortgage loans – is centred on apartment-type housing.

Inconveniently, the flats in buildings have a prohibitive cost in terms of construction, financing, and maintenance. It is a house-type that requires the intervention of various intermediaries. Consequently, it leads a quite expensive production and, as a result, low-income population are excluded from accessing them. In other words, housing policies have a serious targeting bias because the state's resources and efforts do not favour the poor. In fact, from another angle, housing policies are more beneficial for banks and real estate companies.

Finally, a fundamental aspect in our view is the implicit association between housing and individual private property. In other words, access to housing is linked to the right to exclusive property right, leaving aside other mechanisms such as rental housing, cooperative models or collective property management models. In this chapter we consider decoupling housing from individual private property. For this purpose, we

14 J. Calderón, 'El efecto Mivivienda: política de vivienda para la clase media y diferenciación social', *Ecuador Debate*, Vol. 76, 2009, pp. 107-122.

15 Z. Hawley, 'Land values, property rights, and home ownership: Implications for property taxation in Peru', *Regional Science and Urban Economics*, Vol. 69, pp. 38-47.

explore the CLT as a collective stewardship of private property mechanism that has proven to be successful in generating affordable housing, keeping it affordable even in the face of gentrification and land value increases due to speculative practices. In addition, we also analyse the challenges and potential objections in its implementation.

5 A NEW LAND TENURE MODEL: THE COMMUNITY LAND TRUST

Since its origins in American rural areas,[16] the CLT model has progressively been widespread in urban context,[17]

16 The CLT model started with the New Communities Inc. established in 1968 for African American farmers in the rural areas of Albany, Georgia, led by the African-American civil rights activists in the "Albany Movement" (1962) – described in J. E. Davis, 'Origins and Evolution of the Community Land Trust in the United States' in J. E. Davis (Ed.), *The Community Land Trust Reader*, Massachusetts, Lincoln Institute of Land Policy, 2010, pp. 11-18, and M. Cirillo *et al.*, *The Community Land Trust Handbook*, Rodale Press, 1982, pp. 39-47 – , when Martin Luther King brought Southern Christian Leadership Conference (SCLC) staff and workers to Albany "to nonviolently challenge the iron grip of legally sanctioned racial segregation in this Southern community" (International Independence Institute, *The Community Land Trust: A Guide to a New Model for Land Tenure in America*, Massachusetts, Center for Community Economic Development, 1972, p. 16).

17 As Meehan states: "Increasingly, CLTs became an urban phenomenon. Developed as a model for rural development, the CLT spread to cities and towns more rapidly than to rural areas. As mentioned, the first urban CLT had been founded in Washington, D.C., in 1976. This was followed by CLTs in Cincinnati, Ohio (1980); Minneapolis, Minnesota (1981); Trenton, New Jersey and Atlanta, Georgia (1982); Dallas, Texas (1983); Burlington, Vermont (1984); Camden, New Jersey and Boston, Massachusetts (1985); Norwich, Connecticut (1986); and New York City, New York (1988), among others" (J. Meehan, 'Reinventing Real Estate: The Community Land Trust As a Social Invention in Affordable Housing', *Journal of Applied Social Science*, Vol. 8, 2014, p. 123).

even in other jurisdictions - mainly, in England and Canada,[18] but also in Belgium,[19] Australia,[20] Kenya,[21] South Asia,[22] and Latin America[23] - proving to be a powerful tool for low-income sector housing solutions.[24]

---

18 *See* T. Archer, 'The mechanics of housing collectivism: how forms and functions affect affordability, *Housing Studies*, Vol. 37, 2022, pp. 73-102; O. Ayoade *et al.*, 'Interoperability optimization for shared equity housing model development and FTB homeownership in the UK', *Internatioonal Journal of Housing Markets and Analysis*, Vol. 12, 2019, pp. 558-580; O. Ayoade and V. Ahmed, 'An assessment of land use resources of barriers and the community-based housing model in the UK', *International Journal of Housing Markets and Analysis*, Vol. 7, 2014, pp. 539-558; L. K. Bates, 'Housing for People, Not for Profit: Models of Community-Led Housing', *Planning Theory & Practice*, pp. 1-36; S. Bunce, 'Engagement and activism in community land ownership: The emergence of community land trusts in London and Toronto' in S. Bunce *et al.* (Eds.), *Critical Dialogues of Urban Governance, Development and Activism: London and Toronto*, London, UCL Press, 2020, pp. 274-288; M. Kip and H. Oevermann, 'Neighbourhood Revitalisation and Heritage Conservation through Adaptive Reuse: Assessing Instruments for Commoning', *The Historic Environment: Policy & Practice*, 2022, pp. 1-25; E. Paterson and M. Dunn, 'Perspectives on utilizing Community Land Trusts as a vehicle for affordable housing provision', *Local Environment*, Vol. 14, 2009, pp. 749-764; and M. Thompson, 'Between Boundaries: From Commoning and Guerrilla Gardening to Community Land Trust Development in Liverpool', *Antipode*, Vol. 17, 2015, pp. 1021-1042 and 'From Co-Ops to Community Land Trusts: Tracing the Historical Evolution and Policy Mobilities of Collaborative Housing Movements', *Housing, Theory and Society*, Vol. 37, 2020, pp. 82-100.

19 *See* N. Aernouts and M. Ryckewaert, 'Beyond housing: on the role of communing in the establishment of a Community Land Trust project', *International Journal of Housing Policy*, Vol. 4, 2018, pp. 503-521.

20 *See* L. Crabtree, 'Community Land Trusts and Indigenous Housing in Australia-Exploring Difference-Based Policy and Appropriate Housing', *Housing Studies*, Vol. 29, 2014, pp. 743-759.

21 *See* E. M. Basset, 'Tinkering with tenure: The community land trust experiment in Voi, Kenya', *Habitat International*, Vol. 29, 2005, pp. 375-398, and C. Simonneau and E. M. Basset, 'Propagación de los fideicomisos comunitarios de tierras en África: lecciones de los primeros esfuerzos para establecer fideicomisos comunitarios en Kenia' in J. E. Davis *et al.* (Eds.), *En Terreno Común: Perspectivas Internacionales sobre los Fideicomisos Comunitarios de Tierras*, Wisconsin, Terra Nostra Press, 2021, pp. 267-284.

22 *See* H. Sholder and A. Hasan, 'El origen y la evolución del modelo del fideicomiso comunitario de tierras en Asia del Sur' in J. E. Davis *et al.* (Eds.), *En Terreno Común: Perspectivas Internacionales sobre los Fideicomisos Comunitarios de Tierras*, Wisconsin, Terra Nostra Press, 2021, pp. 285-303.

23 For example, L. Algoed, 'El Fideicomiso de la Tierra del Caño Martín Peña: Instrumento Notable de Regulación de Suelo en Asentamientos Informales', *Lincoln Institute of Land Policy*, WP18LA1SP, 2018, pp. i-45; O. J. Colón, 'El Fideicomiso Comunitario de Tierras: Mecanismo Municipal para Desarrollar Viviendas Asequibles', *Revista de Derecho Puertorriqueño*, Vol. 59, 2020, pp. 477-506; D. E. Davis and J. C. Fernández, 'Collective Property Rights and Social Citizenship: Recent Trends in Urban Latin America', *Social Policy and Society*, Vol. 19, 2020, pp. 319-330; T. Fidalgo-Ribeiro *et al.*, 'Los fideicomisos comunitarios de tierras en asentamientos informales: una adaptación del modelo del Fideicomiso de la Tierra del Caño Martín Peña en las favelas de Río de Janeiro, Brasil' in J. E. Davis *et al.* (Eds.), *En Terreno Común: Perspectivas Internacionales sobre los Fideicomisos Comunitarios de Tierras*, Wisconsin, Terra Nostra Press, 2021, pp. 231-257; and, M. Hernández-Torrales *et al.*, 'Propagación de los fideicomisos comunitarios de tierras en América Latina y el Caribe: orígenes, logros y el Fideicomiso de la Tierra del Caño Martín Peña como prueba de concepto' in J. E. Davis *et al.* (Eds.), *En Terreno Común: Perspectivas Internacionales sobre los Fideicomisos Comunitarios de Tierras*, Wisconsin, Terra Nostra Press, 2021, pp. 207-229.

24 *See* C. Cahen *et al.*, 'Ethical action in the age of austerity: cases of care in two community land trusts', *Housing Studies*, Vol. 37, 2022, pp. 393-413; J. F. and L. Bocarsly, 'CLTs: Growing Trend in Affordable Home Ownership', *Journal of Affordable Housing & Community Development Law*, Vol. 19, 2008, pp. 367-394; A. Decker, 'Community Land Trusts and State Legislation', *Journal of Affordable Housing & Community*

The Community Land Trust – CLT can be understood both as a legal entity "chartered to hold land in stewardship" and as a collective mechanism to manage the land "for the common good" under the traditional ownership framework.[25] In other words, a typical fee simple/full ownership property scheme is maintained, but under a collective management approach. As Meehan states:

> The CLT is an organization that holds land for what it conceives to be public interest while providing for the private use of the land through lease agreements. Through community ownership of the land, the CLT is in a position to place limits on resale prices, thus its contribution to sustained affordability. This conjunction of community ownership of land and private ownership of the economic improvements on the land – usually housing or crops – represents an innovative combination of tenure forms. In the United States, people usually think of land as either privately owned or owned by the government. The CLT is a private organization but quasi public in its aims and operations. It represents a collective ownership of land, but does not seek collective ownership of the improvements, such as housing (in contrast to public housing). It is a social invention designed to address social problems that its originators did not feel were being adequately addressed by either private or public forms of tenure.[26]

Development Law, Vol. 26, 2018, pp. 489-530; M. M. Ehlenz, 'Making Home More Affordable: Community Land Trusts Adopting Cooperative Ownership Models to Expand Affordable Housing', *Journal of Community Practice*, Vol. 26, 2018, pp. 283-307; Engelsman *et al.*, 'Community Land Trusts, affordable housing and community organising in low-income neighborhoods', *International Journal of Housing Policy*, Vol. 18, 2018, pp. 103-123; K. Gray, 'Community Land Trusts in the United States', *Journal of Community Practice*, Vol. 16, 2008, pp. 65-78; K. A. Gray and J. E. Miller-Cribbs, 'The Durham Community Land Trustees', *Journal of Community Practice*, Vol. 20, 2012, pp. 402-413; K. A. Hackett *et al.*, 'Community land trusts: releasing possible selves through stable affordable housing', *Housing Studies*, Vol. 34, 2019, pp. 24-48; R. Kruger *et al.*, 'The Production of Community in Community Land Trusts', *City and Community*, Vol. 19, 2020, pp. 683-655; J. S. Lowe and E. Thaden, 'Deepening stewardship in community land trusts', *Urban Geography*, Vol. 37, 2016, pp. 611-628; D. G. Martin *et al.*, 'Meanings of limited equity homeownership in community land trusts', *Housing Studies*, Vol. 35, 2020, pp. 395-414; K. Nelson *et al.*, 'The Commodity Effects of Decommodification: Community Land Trusts and Neighborhood Property Values', *Housing Policy Debate*, Vol. 30, 2020, pp. 823-842; K. Skobba and A. T. Carswell, 'Community land trust homeowners: Past and present housing experiences' *Family and Consumer Sciences Research Journal*, Vol. 43, 2014, pp. 4-17; Y. Sungu-Eryilmaz and R. Greenstein, 'A National Study of Community Land Trusts', *Lincoln Institute of Land Policy*, WP07YS1, 2007, pp. i-63; and, O. R. Williams, 'Community control as a relationship between a place-based population and institution: The case of a community land trust', *Local Economy*, Vol. 33, 2018, pp. 459-476.

25 International Independence Institute, *The Community Land Trust: A Guide to a New Model for Land Tenure in America*, Massachusetts, Center for Community Economic Development, 1972, pp. 1-2; and M. Cirillo *et al.*, *The Community Land Trust Handbook*, Rodale Press, 1982, p. 31.

26 J. Meehan, 'Reinventing Real Estate: The Community Land Trust as a Social Invention in Affordable Housing', *Journal of Applied Social Science*, Vol. 8, 2014, p. 116.

Also, it ought to be clarified that "land trust" expression, it should not be confused with an ordinary real estate trust. As Cirillo pointed out:

> **Real estate trusts.** A CLT is a trust in the basic sense that it holds land in trust for the entire community, but it is not a trust in the traditional legal sense. A CLT is a nonprofit corporation. A legal land trust or real estate trust, on the other hand, is a private entity with private purpose. It is a means of holding property for the good of certain specified "beneficiaries", and it is controlled by specified trustees. The legal land trust is a closed arrangement, while the CLT is open and democratic.[27]

In similar sense, the International Independence Institute's CLT Guide states:

> **The Concept of Trust.** The choice of the word "trust" is based upon our desire as authors to emphasize the notion of "trusteeship" or "stewardship". If land is limited, then its use in the face of steadily expanding human demands upon it must be regulated for the long-range welfare of all people. Our choice of the word "trust" can be explained further by our desire to emphasize Ralph Bosordi's idea of "trustery" [...] Hopefully, the community land trust will not be confused with an ordinary real estate trust which usually has individual, private beneficiaries and has as its purpose the protection of private profits.[28]

At this point, it should be noted that CLT requires a strong sense of community and a solid organisational structure. Likewise, community participation through technical assistance in dwellings construction and access to finance are key roles in this collective management model.

6 Legal framework: The CLT Standard Model

From a legal perspective, the current American CLT standard model has five key designs or core elements based in the community practice[29] as well as the federal definition in the

27 M. Cirillo *et al.*, *The Community Land Trust Handbook*, Rodale Press, 1982, p. 30. Bold emphasis in the original.

28 *Ibid.*, p. 1. Bold emphasis in the original.

29 *See* J. A. Lovett, 'Community Land Trusts: Institutionalizing the Human Flourishing Theory of Property', *Cornell Journal of Law and Public Policy*, Vol. 29, 2020, pp. 621-641; S. R. Miller, 'Community Land Trusts: Why Now is the Time to Integrate this Housing Activists' Tool into Local Government Affordable Housing Policies', *Journal of Affordable Housing & Community Development Law*, Vol. 23, 2015, pp. 349-372; and J.

Section 233 of the Cranston-Gonzales National Affordable Act (42 U.S.C. 12773) and Section 502(a) of the Housing Act of 1949 (42 U.S.C. 1472) both amended by the Housing and Community Development Act of 1992 as it follows:

> (f) DEFINITION OF COMMUNITY LAND TRUST. – For purposes of this section, the term 'community land trust' means a community housing development organization [...] – (1) that is not sponsored by a for-profit organization; (2) that is established to carry out the activities under paragraph (3);(3) that – (A) acquires parcels of land, held in perpetuity, primarily for conveyance under long-term ground leases; (B) transfers ownership of any structural improvements located on such leased parcels to the lessees; and (C) retains a preemptive option to purchase any such structural improvement at a price determined by formula that is designed to ensure that the improvement remains affordable to low- and moderate-income families in perpetuity; (4) whose corporate membership that is open to any adult resident of a particular geographic area specified in the bylaws of the organization; and (5) whose board of directors – (A) includes a majority of members who are elected by the corporate membership; and (B) is composed of equal numbers of (i) lessees pursuant to paragraph (3)(B), (ii) corporate members who are not lessees, and (iii) any other category of persons described in the bylaws of the organization.

The first core element is a non-profit entity that buys and owns the land in perpetuity, under the private property right system, and manages it on behalf of the community. Even more, this non-profit organisation provides technical assistance as "(1) homebuyer education; (2) review and approval of home purchase or refinance loans and home equity lines of credit;[30] (3) support with home repairs; and (4) financial counselling or loss mitigation counselling".[31] That is why, the CLT model should not be seen only as a mechanism to provide new dwellings, but also as a permanent community management and support for many purposes in addition to housing provision. Furthermore, professional consultancy, institutionalising voluntary work, community leaders' recruitment and training, and neighbourhood associations have always been a necessity in the early CLT's.[32]

Pierce *et al.*, 'Ownership is a habit of mind: how community land trusts expose key consensual fictions of urban property', *Urban Geography*, pp. 1-18.

30 B. Arruñada and A. Lehavi, 'Prime Property Institutions for a Subprime Era: Toward Innovative Models of Homeownership', *Berkeley Business Law Journal*, Vol. 8, 2010, p. 12.

31 J. Lowe and E. Thaden, 'Deepening stewardship in community land trusts', *Urban Geography*, Vol. 37, 2016, p. 621.

32 *See* K. A. Gray and M. Galande, 'Keeping "Community" in a Community Land Trust', *Social Work Research*, Vol. 35, 2011, pp. 244-245; K. A. Gray and J. E. Miller-Cribbs, 'The Durham Community Land Trustees', *Journal of Community Practice*, Vol. 20, 2012, p. 402; and J. Meehan, 'Reinventing Real Estate: The

The second key feature is distinguishing between the property on the ground from the property on the improvements or the building. Then, the building (dwelling) is granted to a family up to 99 years as a ground lease (superficies). The third element is the restriction on the quality of lessee-superficies owner or "entrance restrictions", for example, who can become part of the CLT model. The fourth relevant element is the limitations and controls on alienability of the leasehold interest or "exit restrictions", for instance, a pre-emptive right or "exit tax" – that reflects the land value increase. The final key feature is the CLT board that guarantees the operation of the non-profit entity that includes residents, members of the community and local authorities.[33]

The five key designs or core elements have allowed the expansion of the community-led model. In this sense, the legal framework regulating the CLT should include not only the housing rights aspects, but also the organisational structure, and the access and exit controls of the model.

7 Does the CLT model really work?

The CLT model has demonstrated to be a powerful tool to alleviate the negative impacts of gentrification in neighbourhoods, counteracting the decrease of low- and middle-class residents due to the displacement effect, mitigating the trend of lower affordability, and stabilising the excessive increase in housing prices.[34]

Also, it has been highlighted the "care" for both people and place as a defining feature of CLT, and that the success of this model depends largely on the commitment and effort of the staff and community leaders,[35] whose importance has been reflected with greater intensity in the context of the pandemic,[36] and the economic crisis.[37]

Community Land Trust as a Social Invention in Affordable Housing', *Journal of Applied Social Science*, Vol. 8, 2014, pp. 125-126.

33 J. A. Lovett, 'Community Land Trusts: Institutionalizing the Human Flourishing Theory of Property', *Cornell Journal of Law and Public Policy*, Vol. 29, 2020, pp. 626-630.

34 *See* T. Archer, 'The mechanics of housing collectivism: how forms and functions affect affordability, *Housing Studies*, Vol. 37, 2022, pp. 73-102; and M. Choi *et al.*, 'Can community land trusts slow gentrification?', *Journal of Urban Affairs*, Vol. 40, 2018, pp. 394-411.

35 *See* C. Cahen *et al.*, 'Ethical action in the age of austerity: cases of care in two community land trusts', *Housing Studies*, Vol. 37, 2022, pp. 393-413; and M. Thompson, 'From Co-Ops to Community Land Trusts: Tracing the Historical Evolution and Policy Mobilities of Collaborative Housing Movements', *Housing, Theory and Society*, Vol. 37, 2020, pp. 82-100.

36 M. Izuhara *et al.*, 'Collaborative housing communities through the COVID-19 pandemic: rethinking governance and mutuality', *Housing Studies*, 2022, pp. 1-19.

37 *See* B. Arruñada and A. Lehavi, 'Prime Property Institutions for a Subprime Era: Toward Innovative Models of Homeownership', *Berkeley Business Law Journal*, Vol. 8, 2010, pp. 3-34; and K. Nelson *et al.*, 'The

In this section we present some specific and significant experiences where CLT has proven to have positive results in improving the housing conditions of people and their environment.

7.1 The CLT consolidation: Evidence from USA, England and Canada

Some specific experiences, as the Milton Park Community in Montreal, suggest that the CLT model may be resilient in the face of political, economic, and social changes; and, at organisational level, it has shown how the internal rules and regulatory activity between the residents-owner and members causally affect the rents/prices rate.[38]

As a new phenomenon in UK, the CLT model has been applied in adaptive reuse and conservation projects with heritage buildings in London as an alternative to demolition and new construction, but it requires a professional skill and institutionalising voluntary work throughout the project.[39]

Evidence from Granby in Liverpool, England, suggests that the CLT could work as a vehicle for neighbourhood regeneration and re-appropriation of empty homes for community use, through an innovative blend of CLT and Mutual Home Ownership Society (MHOS), where instead of dwellings having individual owners, all the properties on a development are owned by a co-operative society.[40]

Other interesting case of study is the CLT community in St. Paul and Minneapolis (Twin Cities), Minnesota.[41] Herein, the impacts of CLT properties on the real estate prices of nearby homes in North Minneapolis (261 CLT units) have been studied, where the progressive growth of the CLT community reflects a positive land value increasing in the nearby homes, and it demonstrates that the price effects are strongest when affordable properties are spatially clustered.[42]

Commodity Effects of Decommodification: Community Land Trusts and Neighborhood Property Values', *Housing Policy Debate*, Vol. 30, 2020, pp. 823-842.

38 *See* T. Archer, 'The mechanics of housing collectivism: how forms and functions affect affordability', *Housing Studies*, Vol. 37, 2022, pp. 73-102.

39 *See* M. Kip and H. Oevermann, 'Neighbourhood Revitalisation and Heritage Conservation through Adaptive Reuse: Assessing Instruments for Commoning', *The Historic Environment: Policy & Practice*, 2022, pp. 1-25

40 *See* M. Thompson, 'Between Boundaries: From Commoning and Guerrilla Gardening to Community Land Trust Development in Liverpool', *Antipode*, Vol. 17, 2015, pp. 1021-1042

41 *See* J. S. Lowe and E. Thaden, 'Deepening stewardship in community land trusts', *Urban Geography*, Vol. 37, 2016, pp. 611-628; D. G. Martin *et al.*, 'Meanings of limited equity homeownership in community land trusts', *Housing Studies*, Vol. 35, 2020, pp. 395-414; and, O. R. Williams, 'Community control as a relationship between a place-based population and institution: The case of a community land trust', *Local Economy*, Vol. 33, 2018, pp. 459-476.

42 *See* K. Nelson *et al.*, 'The Commodity Effects of Decommodification: Community Land Trusts and Neighborhood Property Values', *Housing Policy Debate*, Vol. 30, 2020, pp. 823-842.

The Minnesota CLT community has shown that a lesser sense of *community* is needed when the single-family homes held by the CLT are geographically dispersed and thus CLT residency is disconnected from the neighbourhood of residence.[43] It indicates that a sense of *community* is not necessary at the beginning of the CLT constitution but can be shaped over time, as a temporal construction of the collective memory or "future-oriented" *community*.[44]

Besides, the Minnesota CLT owners are explicitly unconcerned about using their homes as an investment under the real estate market rules,[45] allowing the inclusion of the shared equity mechanism for the pursuit of affordable housing solutions for historically disadvantaged groups (i.e., single-headed, female-headed, or minority-headed households).[46]

On this last point, using the Neighborhood Change Database to explore the neighbourhood characteristics, a study carried out between 1990 and 2000 in Durham CLT in North Carolina found that a greater and significant increase in Black and Hispanic-owner-occupied rates took place in the Durham CLT tract than in Durham (comparison tract).[47] Since the beginning of the Durham CLT, there was an explicit intention to involve the black residents of the community, which is particularly important due to "Durham's long racial history".[48]

The CLT model has been a contributing factor to building a sense of safety in the community. In a study carried out at Durham CLT based on interviews with 29 homeowners, renters, board members, community members, and current and former CLT employees, "Most respondents, even the non-CLT residents, reported feeling safe in their homes and community. Several told stories of partnering with Partners Against Crime to combat crime in their neighbourhoods or simply working with working with neighbours to keep drug dealers off their streets".[49]

---

43 *See* R. Kruger *et al.*, 'The Production of Community in Community Land Trusts', *City and Community*, Vol. 19, 2020, pp. 683-655.

44 See K. A. Hackett *et al.*, 'Community land trusts: releasing possible selves through stable affordable housing', *Housing Studies*, Vol. 34, 2019, pp. 24-48; and R. Kruger *et al.* 'The Production of Community in Community Land Trusts', *City and Community*, Vol. 19, 2020, pp. 683-655.

45 See D. G. Martin *et al.* 'Meanings of limited equity homeownership in community land trusts', *Housing Studies*, Vol. 35, 2020, pp. 395-414.

46 *See* K. A. Hackett *et al.* 'Community land trusts: releasing possible selves through stable affordable housing', *Housing Studies*, Vol. 34, 2019, pp. 24-48.

47 *See* K. A. Gray and J. E. Miller-Cribbs. 'The Durham Community Land Trustees', *Journal of Community Practice*, Vol. 20, 2012, pp. 402-413.

48 *See* K. A. Gray and M. Galande. 'Keeping "Community" in a Community Land Trust', *Social Work Research*, Vol. 35, 2011, pp. 244-245.

49 *Ibid.*, p. 249.

A biographical approach examining the experiences of 20 CLT homeowners reflects a positive change in each resident's life, but the absence of a full ownership scheme, that is, the lack of land plot ownership, could mitigate the CLT residential positive experience.[50]

In other specific cases, CLT model has served for remediation of brownfield and land revitalisation. The Champlain Housing Trust in Vermont and the Dudley Neighbors, Inc. in Boston have become involved in the remediation of brownfield properties through cooperation with a community organisation.[51]

In the case of Champlain Housing Trust, the remediation also involved derelict properties and parcels in foreclosure; in Dudley's case, the CLT obtained the power of eminent domain to acquire brownfield properties for the benefit of the community; and, in both cases the Environmental Protection Agency (EPA) funded those projects by granting an amount of money.[52] In this sense, more than replicable cases in other jurisdictions, they can be taken as references of the potential of the CLT model. Therefore, it can be argued that it may be an environmental impact mitigation tool.[53]

7.2 *Dawn of the CLT in Latin America: Recent experiences in Puerto Rico and Brazil*

The growing interest of this model in Latin America must be highlighted. Particularly from the Puerto Rican and Brazilian experiences. These CLTs are the first to be implemented in Latin America in adaptation of the North American CLT, although the Brazilian CLT can be considered an adaptation of the Puerto Rican CLT.

Both experiences are particularly significant for the implementation of CLT in Peru, as they take place in contexts of informal land tenure. In this regard, the experiences in the "Global North" suggest a great potential for the generation of affordable housing and reduction of the impacts of gentrification processes; however, the experiences in Puerto Rico and Brazil reflect initial evidence that CLT can also work in the "Global South" with the problems of the "Global South".

50 *See* K. Skobba and A. T. Carswell, 'Community land trust homeowners: Past and present housing experiences' *Family and Consumer Sciences Research Journal*, Vol. 43, 2014, pp. 4-17.

51 *See* K. Wernstedt and J. Hanson, 'Community Revitalization Through Areawide Brownfield Regeneration, Community Land Trusts, and Progressive Finance', *Environmental Practice*, Vol. 11, 2009, pp. 134-143.

52 *Id.*

53 *See* S. C. Bourassa, 'The Community Land Trust as a Highway Environmental Impact Mitigation Tool', *Journal of Urban Affairs*, Vol. 28, 2006, pp. 399-418.

7.2.1 The Fideicomiso de la Tierra del Caño Martín Peña in San Juan, Puerto Rico

The Fideicomiso de la Tierra del Caño Martín Peña is a Puerto Rican CLT adaptation designed and controlled by residents of seven neighbourhoods along the Martín Peña Channel in San Juan, Puerto Rico. The Puerto Rican CLT was created with the aim to regularise land tenure and to prevent involuntary displacement and gentrification, precipitated by the government's planned dredging and clean-up of the channel.[54]

The key factors in the Puerto Rican CLT implementation were to build a community feeling among the residents and Government and to adapt it to local need, for example, the problem of land insecurity in an informal settlement. This initiative has brought together community residents and partners from the private and public sector to implement a comprehensive development plan designed to uplift a historically marginalised area, while transforming this urban area into a more habitable, just, and participatory space.[55]

The Puerto Rican CLT ensures the availability of permanently affordable housing and provides alternative housing options on its land for families who have had to relocate because of the dredging of the channel. 1,500 moderate- and low-income households are members of the CLT, which currently owns and manages more than 110 hectares of land, which previously belonged to governmental agencies.[56]

Similarly, the replicability of the Puerto Rican CLT in other countries in Latin America, the Caribbean and South Asia has been highlighted. In this sense, the communities with the greatest potential for the "Global South" CLT adaptation in these regions are those with the following characteristics:

- A significant number of residents live on lands to which they do not have a valid or legal title for lands that may be owned by the government, by private individuals, or by a corporation. Alternatively, these lands may be occupied and used under some form of communal landholdings system that has yet to be recognised and registered by the state.
- There are mechanisms available to acquire the land, including donation, adverse possession, purchase, or intervention by the state.
- A significant percentage of the population has a high sense of community cohesion and belonging.

54 M. Hernández-Torrales *et al.*, 'Sedding the CLT in Latin America and the Caribbean', *in* J. E. Davis, L. Algoed and M. Hernández-Torrales (Eds.), *Community Land Trusts and Informal Settlements in the Global South*, Wisconsin: Terra Nostra Press, 2021, p. 31.

55 *Id.*

56 *Id.*

- The informal settlement is located within an area – or proximate to one – where land values are rising or where lands are coveted by speculative investors, threatening the present population with displacement.[57]

7.2.2 The Termo Territorial Coletivo in Rio de Janerio, Brazil

The Termo Territorial Coletivo is the first Brazilian CLT adaptation project, developed by the Catalytic Communities in partnership with various public agencies, private institutions, universities and community leaders. The model provides the highest level of land tenure security possible, allowing for collective development of the territory while preserving the individual rights of residents to sell, rent or pledge their homes.[58]

This project emerged as research project between a nongovernmental organisation based in Rio de Janeiro, Catalytic Communities, and the Fideicomiso de la Tierra del Caño Martín Peña. Based on this research, recommendations were presented on essential lessons when considering the creation of a CLT in informal settlements.[59]

Rio de Janeiro has today over 1000 favela communities, ranging in size from a handful to over 200,000 residents. Over 24% of the city's population lives in favelas, which constitute the city's primary affordable housing stock. In contrast to a shanty town or a slum, Rio's favelas are well-established communities with a long history and a strong local cultural production and community investment.[60]

The Catalytic Communities concluded that, for a successful CLT adaptation in Rio de Janeiro's favelas, the following conditions need to be present:

- Consolidated communities are located on lands where residents perceive a threat of gentrification, forced eviction, or other human-induced involuntary displacement.
- A large percentage of families lack legal titles and want to address the problem of insecure land tenure.
- There is a path to acquiring title(s) to the land.
- Residents feel a strong sense of belonging and a desire to remain in their community.
- There is solid process of community organisation in place, supported by organisations that are ready to accompany the community and that can provide technical assistance.[61]

57 *Ibid.*, p. 46.

58 Further information about the Termo Territorial Coletivo is available at: https://www.termoterritorial-coletivo.org.

59 T. Fidalgo *et al.*, 'Adapting Features of Puerto Rico's Caño Martín Peña CLT to Address Land Insecurity in the Favelas of Rio de Janeiro, Barzil', *in* J. E. Davis, L. Algoed and M. Hernández-Torrales (Eds.), *Community Land Trusts and Informal Settlements in the Global South*, Wisconsin: Terra Nostra Press, 2021, p. 31.

60 *Ibid.*, pp. 56-57.

61 *Ibid.*, p. 71.

However, despite Catalytic Communities effort, the arrival of the Termo Territorial Coletivo in Brazil still faces many obstacles. These include: the difficulty of maintaining a permanent structure of mobilisation and participation, the presence of parallel power groups that can interfere with community dynamics, and the need to break with an individual private property logic.[62]

8 Implementing the CLT Model in Peru

8.1 *A property right-based model for a Civil Law country: Ground lease scheme*

The Peruvian property right system is deeply shaped by the *numerus clausus* principle. Unlike Common Law jurisdictions where this principle is defined by case law,[63] the Peruvian Civil Code clearly defines the *real rights* admitted[64] (*numerus clausus*/ Typenswang) and their content ("typicity"/Typenfixierung). Therefore, adding a new property right or appropriation scheme could be challenging. In this sense, if the lawmaker incorporates a new form of use of the properties without establishing that it is a new *real right* or that it refers to the existing ones, then it will be understood that the use will be governed by the provisions on obligations and contract, not by the property law.

Following this idea, the Peruvian CLT model uses "superficies" as equivalent for a ground lease tenancy. The superficies is regulated as *real right* or right *in rem* by the Civil Code,[65] which allows the "surface holder" to have a different ownership property right separated from the land plot, that is, an exception of the *ad coelum* doctrine.[66] This *real*

62 T. Fidalgo *et al.*, 'Experiências Internacionais de *Community Land Trusts* e Lições para a Implementação do Modelo no Brasil', *Revista Brasilera de Estudios Urbanos e Regionais*, Vol. 24, 2022, p. 19.

63 *See* H. Hansmann and R. Kraakman, 'Property, Contract, and Verification: The numerus clausus problem and the divisibility of rights', *Journal of Legal Studies*, Vol. XXXI, 2002, pp. S373-S420, and T. W. Merril and H. E. Smith, 'Optimal Standardization in the Law of Property: The Numerus Clausus Principle', *Yale Law Journal*, Vol. 110, 2000, pp. 110-170.

64 **Article 881.-** Real rights are those regulated in this Book and other legal dispositions.
[Author's free translation].

65 **Article 1030.-** The surface right can be constituted by which the surface holder enjoys the power to temporarily hold a separate property construction on or under the surface of the ground.
This right cannot last more than ninety-nine years. Upon expiration of it, the landowner acquires ownership of what was built, reimbursing its value, unless otherwise agreed.
[Author's free translation]

66 **Civil Code**
Article 938.- The owner of a property acquires by accession [*ad coelum*] what joins or materially adheres to it.
Article 954.- The ownership of the land extends to the subsoil [*ad inferos*] and the above [*ad coelum*] ground, included within the vertical of the surface perimeter and to the extent that the exercise of his right is useful to the landowner.

right may be granted up to 99 years, but it could be renewed. Upon its expiry, the landowner acquires by accession all the improvements and buildings, but compensation is due to the former surface holder. Furthermore, the superficies may be sold or mortgaged.

However, as we mentioned, this is only one aspect of the complex structure of the CLT model. The right of superficies only refers to the right over the dwelling. The legal structure of the CLT requires a comprehensive treatment of each of its elements. For this reason, we argue that the lawmaker excluded fundamental aspects of the CLT model legal scheme.

Among the fundamental aspects excluded are the "community sense" that involves "[...] organisational support, technical assistance, education, training, and continuing support [...]" (Section 233, Cranston-Gonzalez National Affordable Housing Act), the pre-emptive option to purchase any such structural improvements to ensure that the improvement remains affordable to low- and moderate-income families in perpetuity, and the board of directors' organisation.

Another relevant aspect omitted in Peruvian CLT regulation is the necessary distinction with the bank or real estate trust. Due to the Latin American tradition in the incorporation of the Common Law trust,[67] the term "fideicomiso" is directly associated with a fiduciary relationship between trustor, trustee, and beneficiary. In this regard, the Puerto Rican Integral Development of the Caño de Martín Peña District Special Planning Act 2004 ("Ley para el Desarrollo Integral del Distrito de Planificación Especial del Caño de Martín Peña") specifies the *sui generis* nature of the CLT,[68] different from the fiduciary trust.

Based on this, we argue that the CLT model should have been regulated as a new *real right* in which its whole legal structure is defined. Besides, there is not a specific statutory regulation about collective management of the land ownership in the Peruvian Civil Code. Therefore, it is necessary to assess to what extent we can overcome the Civil Code's under-regulation through a ground lease agreement between a CLT and a homeowner, and the CLT bylaw. In that sense, specific prior regulation will be required as part of the implementation of the CLT.

Subsoil ownership does not include natural resources, archaeological sites and remains, or other assets governed by special laws.
[Author's free translation]

67 *See* F. Escobar-Rozas, 'Traditions, Transplants and Inefficiencies: The Case of the "Peruvian Fideicomiso"', *Universitas*, Vol. 55, 2006, pp. 167-225, and U. Mattei and H. Hansmann, 'Trust Law in the United States. A Basic Study of Its Special Contribution', *The American Journal of Comparative Law*, Vol. 46, 1998, pp. 133-150.

68 (e) In consideration of the sui generis nature of the Land Trust, whose purpose is not envisaged in the Puerto Rico Trust Act (Act N°. 219 of August 31, 2012), this Land Trust shall be governed by this act. In case of doubt about the interpretation of its powers, faculties and functioning, the historical experience, and the doctrinal development of the "Community Land Trusts" or related figures will be used, where applicable.

8.2 The non-profit organisation as a community-based land holder

The CLT model, in its origins and its widely use current form, is based on a non-profit organisation created to hold land in perpetuity and for the benefit of a community, with a board elected by an open membership that includes residents of lease-owned land, other community residents, and public-interest representatives,[69] and this also guarantees a strong sense of community.

Although the CLT model has been run mostly under a non-profit organisation, there is evidence for running the CLT model with a for-profit organisation[70] or limited equity cooperatives.[71] In Peru, both non-profit organisations and for-profit corporations are regulated by the Civil Code and Companies General Act ("Ley General de Sociedades"), respectively, with a similar status to that of its American counterparts.

In addition, the non-profit organisation which runs the CLT has a critical role in getting land for the community purpose. Indeed, it is challenging to obtain land which will be owned through the CLT model.[72] Following this fact, the Peruvian CLT must look for mechanisms that allow obtaining unexpensive land under the rules of the real estate market. Further, specific regulation must indicate the functions of the non-profit organisation. Future regulation should also indicate the composition of the board of directors to fulfil the residents' interest and develop the tax exception system applied for this land tenure model. Likewise, participation will be relevant not only for the establishment and granting of surface rights, but also to ensure affordability during the CLT life.

8.3 Controls and limitations on alienability of the leasehold interest

As we mentioned, a relevant aspect related to this model is the entrance and exit/resale restrictions of CLT homebuyers,[73] which are not regulated in the Peruvian superficies, as

---

69 *See* J. E. Davis, 'Origins and Evolution of the Community Land Trust in the United States' in J. E. Davis (Ed.), *The Community Land Trust Reader*, Massachusetts, Lincoln Institute of Land Policy, 2010, pp. 11-18; and M. Cirillo *et al.*, *The Community Land Trust Handbook*, Rodale Press, 1982, pp. 39-47.

70 B. Arruñada and A. Lehavi, 'Prime Property Institutions for a Subprime Era: Toward Innovative Models of Homeownership', *Berkeley Business Law Journal*, Vol. 8, 2010, pp. 29-34.

71 *See* J. E. Davis, 'More Than Money: What is Shared in Shared Equity Homeownership? *Journal of Affordable Housing & Community Development Law*, Vol. 19, 2010, pp. 259-277, and M. Ehlenz, 'Making Home More Affordable: Community Land Trusts Adopting Cooperative Ownership Models to Expand Affordable Housing', *Journal of Community Practice*, Vol. 26, 2018, pp. 283-307.

72 Y. Fujii, 'Putting the pieces together: How collaboration between land banks and community land trusts can promote affordable housing in distressed neighborhoods', *Cities*, Vol. 56, 2016, pp. 1-8.

73 *See* J. J. Kelly, 'Homes Affordable for Good: Covenants and Ground Leases as Long-Term Resale-Restriction Devices', *Saint Louis University Public Law Review*, Vol. 29, 2009, pp. 9-40.

and they may infringe the general presumption in favour of alienating land[74] in the Civil Code. Indeed, the Peruvian legal system is governed by the rule of free transfer of goods. In this sense, private parties are prohibited from establishing restrictions on the free movement of goods by covenants.

However, an essential element in the CLT model is the entrance and exit/resale restrictions of CLT homebuyers to guarantee that housing is destined for low-income persons. Therefore, if the free movement of property were to be restricted by statute, this could result in a breach of the rule prohibiting such covenants.

The restrictions on the entry and exit of the CLT are essential for the proper application of this scheme, since this allows the CLT to be targeted towards the people who most need this scheme, avoiding subleasing[75] and controlling the alienation of the leasehold interest at the selling point. Additionally, it is required that these restrictions and the perpetuity of the land destination can be recorded without any obstacles in the Public Registries.[76]

8.4 *Legal structure in home financing: Shifting the individual property paradigm*

Peruvian regulation and policies are deeply based on individual property scheme.[77] The role of private property has been central in the development of housing policies, almost with the assumption that without a property title it is not feasible to have access to housing. In turn, the importance of property ownership means that the mechanisms for accessing housing finance are also geared towards it.

For this reason, a key challenge is shifting the individual property paradigm in the financing schemes for access to housing. An adequate Peruvian CLT model implementation needs a diversification of financing mechanism for the purchase of CLT dwellings. For example, banks should accept mortgages on superficies as collateral.[78]

---

74 **Article 882.**- The prohibition of alienating or collateralising cannot be contractually established, unless the law allows it.
[Author's free translation]

75 International Independence Institute, *The Community Land Trust: A Guide to a New Model for Land Tenure in America*, Massachusetts, Center for Community Economic Development, 1972, pp. 18-19.

76 According to the Peruvian legal system, the acquiring owner is not forced to register his land and get a property title. Although, to fulfil the necessary legal protection, the owner must register the land in a public registry managed by SUNARP, which aims to provide legal certainty and protection through the registration and public transparency of estates and covenants. Furthermore, land registration as an urban land implies that the land is accessible to standard utility service connections as well.

77 D. Torres and J. Ruiz-Tagle, '¿Derecho a la vivienda o la propiedad privada? De la política pública a la informalidad urbana en el Área Metropolitana de Lima (1996-2015)', *Eure*, Vol. 45, 2019, pp. 5-29.

78 *See* B. Arruñada and A. Lehavi, 'Prime Property Institutions for a Subprime Era: Toward Innovative Models of Homeownership', *Berkeley Business Law Journal*, Vol. 8, 2010, p. 34; J. F. Curtin and L. Bocarsly, 'CLTs: A Growing Trend in Affordable Home Ownership', *Journal of Affordable Housing & Community Development*

In addition, FMV subsidies and mortgage loans programmes should promote the superficies as mechanism for affordable housing.[79] Government programmes as Techo Propio or Nuevo Crédito Mivivienda should admit purchase and build to improve houses under the CLT model.

9 Conclusion

The CLT model has proven be an effective mechanism to provide new dwellings from a micro-scale intervention and it could be applied in adaptive reuse and conservation projects with heritage buildings to generate affordable dwellings, through regeneration and re-appropriation of empty homes and derelict properties for community use, in addition for brownfield's remediation and land revitalisation affected by soil pollution.

The CLT model can support to solve the Peruvian housing sector problems by both pioneering an all-new ownership tenure dynamic and promoting a collective stewardship land model. A complementary regulation is required to enhance the Peruvian CLT model functioning regarding shifting the individual property paradigm in the financing schemes for access to affordable housing. Likewise, the CLT model should be regulated as a new *real right* in which its whole legal structure and the five key elements are defined.

On the non-profit organisation, the specific regulation must indicate the functions of it. Also, a future regulation should indicate the composition of the board of directors to fulfil the residents' interest and develop the tax exception system applied for this land tenure model. Although no strong evidence has been found that CLT can be an effective tool against the growth of disorganised cities, the information gathered from Latin American experiences allows us to argue that a CLT model could be properly adapted in consolidated informal settlements.

Law, Vol. 17, 2008, pp. 743-759; M. Ehlenz, 'Making Home More Affordable: Community Land Trusts Adopting Cooperative Ownership Models to Expand Affordable Housing', *Journal of Community Practice*, Vol. 26, 2018, pp. 283-307; K. Nelson *et al.*, 'The Commodity Effects of Decommodification: Community Land Trusts and Neighborhood Property Values', *Housing Policy Debate*, Vol. 30, 2020, pp. 823-842.; and S. I. Stein, 'Wake Up Fannie, I Think Got Something to Say to You: Financing Community Land Trust Homebuyers Without Stripping Affordability Provision', *Emory Law Journal*, Vol. 60, 2010, pp. 209-249.

79 J. J. Kelly, 'Homes Affordable for Good: Covenants and Ground Leases as Long-Term Resale-Restriction Devices', *Saint Louis University Public Law Review*, Vol. 29, 2009, pp. 19-23; J. DeFilippis *et al.*, 'W(h)ither the community in community land trusts?', *Journal of Urban Affairs*, Vol. 40, 2018, pp. 755-769.

5 Dignity Restoration through Property Rights in *Thubakgale v Ekurhuleni Metropolitan Municipality*

Tanveer Rashid Jeewa and Sfiso Benard Nxumalo***

1 Introduction

Traditionally, property lawyers and scholars have fetishised the centrality of ownership and the right to exclude.[1] To these scholars, ownership and the right to exclude others are the irreducible element of property. It is simply the *sina qua non* of property.[2] For one to own property, the right to exclude is a necessary and sufficient condition.[3] Badenhorst and his co-authors note that the exclusionary focus of property demonstrates that ownership is the vertex of property. They also recognise that inherently in property, there is a hierarchy of rights with superior rights (ownership and the right to exclude) on one end

* LLB (University of Cape Town), LLM in Public Law (University of Cape Town), LLD Candidate and Constitutional Law Lecturer (South African Research Chair in Property Law, University of Stellenbosch). The South African Research Chair in Property Law is funded by the South African National Department of Science and Technology, administered by the National Research Foundation and hosted by Stellenbosch University. The views expressed in this article are those of the authors and should not be attributed to any of their affiliated institutions.

** LLB (University of Witwatersrand), BCL (University of Oxford), DPhil in Law Candidate (University of Oxford), Stipendiary Lecturer of Law at Brasenose College (University of Oxford).

1 H.E. Smith, 'The Thing about Exclusion', Vol. 3, 2014 *Brigham-Kanner Property Rights Journal*, p. 95; T.W. Merrill, 'Property and the Right to Exclude', Vol. 77, 1998 *Nebraska Review*, p. 731; J.C. Gatewood 'The Evolution of the Right to Exclude – More than a Property Right, a Privacy Right', Vol. 32, 2013 *Mississippi College Law Review*, p. 447; and D.L. Callies and J.D. Breemer 'The Right to Exclude Others from Private Property: A Fundamental Constitutional Right', Vol. 3, 2000 *Washington University Journal of Law & Policy*, p. 39. See also A.J. Van der Walt 'The modest systemic status of property rights', Vol. 1, 2015 1 *Journal of Law, Property, and Society*, p. 23.

2 Furthermore, Merrill argues "[t]here is strong evidence that, with respect to interests in land, the right to exclude is the first right to emerge in primitive property rights systems…[and that] [t]he fact that the right to exclude can be found in even the most primitive land-rights systems provides further support for the conclusion that the [right to exclude] provides the key to understanding the nature of property." *Ibid.*, Merrill 745.

3 *Ibid.*, p. 731. See L.J. Strahilevitz 'Information Asymmetries and the Rights to Exclude', Vol. 104, 2006, *Michigan Law Review*, p. 1836, who contends "American courts and commentators have deemed the 'right to exclude' foremost among the property rights, with the Supreme Court characterizing it as the 'hallmark of a protected property interest' and leading property scholars describing the right as the core, or the essential element, of ownership."

of the spectrum and weaker ones on the other.[4] Without the right to exclude, there is no property.[5] Blackstone is often enthusiastically cited to defend this position:

> There is nothing which so generally strikes the imagination, and engages the affections of mankind, as the right of property; or that sole and despotic dominion which one man claims and exercises over the external things of the world, in total exclusion of the right of any other individual in the universe.[6]

Centring the right to exclude as the fundamental facet of property has resulted in the exclusion of other values that underpin property. Values like dignity have predominantly been seen as immaterial in the property law context. Yet, there is a turn of the tide. There is a growing scholarship that recognises that property espouses other values.[7] Property, it has been argued, serves 'plural and incommensurable' values,[8] values that are even more important in the South African context.

Anyone familiar with South Africa's horrific past under apartheid and colonisation is aware of the critical role that the institution of private property played in achieving racial segregation. Pivotal to this exercise was the exclusion of communities based on their race, preventing them from enjoying property rights, diminishing their dignity, and eventually depriving them of it. Hence, it cannot be denied that under apartheid, property was used as a means to subjugate non-property owners to an inferior status in society, and inhumane treatment.[9] As Jeremy Waldron remarks, "[c]itizens of South Africa do not need me to tell them how important the idea of dignity is in our modern conceptions of human rights."[10]

4 P.J. Badenhorst et al, *Silberberg and Schoeman's The Law of Property*, 4th ed., Cape Town, LexisNexis Butterworths, 2003, p. 93.

5 *Kaiser Aetna v United States*, 444 U.S. 164, 176 (1979).

6 W. Blackstone, *Commentaries on the Laws of England, 2 vols*, New York, W. E. Dean, 1844, p. 1:425.

7 G.S. Alexander et al, 'A Statement of Progressive Property' Vol. 94, 2009, *Cornell Law Review*, p. 743; G.S. Alexander and E.M. Peñalver, *Property and Community*, Oxford, Oxford University Press, 2009; M.T. Mitchell, *Plutocratic Socialism: The Future of Private Property and the Fate of the Middle Class*, Eugene, Front Republic Books, 2022; E. Peñalver, 'Land Virtues', Vol. 94, 2009 *Cornell Law Review*, p. 821; J.W. Singer, 'Property as the law of democracy', Vol. 63, 2014, *Duke Law Journal*, p. 1287; J.W. Singer, *Entitlement: The paradoxes of property*, Connecticut, Yale University Press, 2000; and L.S. Underkuffler *The Idea of Property: Its Meaning and Power*, Oxford, Oxford University Press, 2003.

8 Alexander et al *supra* note 7 above 744.

9 Froneman J eloquently explained this in *Shoprite Checkers (Pty) Limited v Member of the Executive Council for Economic Development, Environmental Affairs and Tourism, Eastern Cape* 2015 (6) SA 125 (CC) at para 34: "[T]he pre-constitutional conception of property … entailed exclusive individual entitlement. Put simply, that is largely a history of dispossession of what indigenous people held, and its transfer to the colonisers in the form of land and other property, protected by an economic system that ensured the continued deprivation of those benefits on racial and class lines. That history of division probably explains the concerns both the previously advantaged and disadvantaged still have. The former fears that they will lose what they have; the latter that they will not receive what is justly theirs."

10 J Waldron, 'The dignity of groups', Vol. 8, 2008, *Acta Juridica*, p. 66.

It is thus not surprising that in the transition from the formal apartheid era to the 'post-apartheid' era,[11] special attention was paid to the protection that property would be given under the Constitution of the Republic of South Africa, 1996.[12] This led to an elaborately crafted property provision under section 25 of the Constitution, the so-called "property clause".[13] This clause is particularly elaborate because it is meant to be a site of historical justice and redress, as can be seen from sections 25(4) to (9) of the Constitution, which highlight South Africa's commitment to land reform.[14] In *Daniels*, Froneman J from the

---

11 There are some difficulties with the term 'post-apartheid'. The argument is that while formal (legal) apartheid came to an end, the legacy of apartheid (characterised by inequality, racism, white supremacy, and abject poverty) persists. See K van Marle, 'Jurisprudence, Friendship and the University as Heterogeneous Public Space' Vol. 127, 2010, *South African Law Journal*, p. 635 and J Modiri, 'The colour of law, power and knowledge: Introducing Critical Race Theory in (post-) apartheid South Africa', Vol. 28, 2012, *South African Journal on Human Rights*, p. 405.

12 Referred to as the Constitution from hereon.

13 There were several debates between lobbying groups that were worried about the economic fate of the white minority (mostly the National Party the ruling party at the time and responsible for apartheid), and other groups who sought restitution for the violent dispossession of other racial groups that had happened over the past decades (the African National Congress being the leading party in this case). A compromise was eventually reached after multi-party negotiations and the property clause was drawn up in such a way that it offered protection to existing property rights holders, while in the same breath facilitating a programme of restitution of land to victims who had previously been dispossessed of land under apartheid and before. For more, see M Chaskalson, 'Stumbling towards Section 28: Negotiations over the Protection of Property Rights in the Interim Constitution', Vol. 11, 1995, *South African Journal for Human Rights*, pp. 222-240.

14 The full provision of section 25 reads:

1. No one may be deprived of property except in terms of law of general application, and no law may permit arbitrary deprivation of property.
2. Property may be expropriated only in terms of law of general application
   a. For a public purpose or in the public interest; and
   b. subject to compensation, the amount of which and the time and manner of payment of which have either been agreed to by those affected or decided or approved by a court.
3. The amount of the compensation and the time and manner of payment must be just and equitable, reflecting an equitable balance between the public interest and the interests of those affected, having regard to all relevant circumstances, including
   a. the current use of the property;
   b. the history of the acquisition and use of the property;
   c. the market value of the property;
   d. the extent of direct state investment and subsidy in the acquisition and beneficial capital improvement of the property; and
   e. the purpose of the expropriation.
4. For the purposes of this section
   a. the public interest includes the nation's commitment to land reform, and to reforms to bring about equitable access to all South Africa's natural resources; and
   b. property is not limited to land.
5. The state must take reasonable legislative and other measures, within its available resources, to foster conditions which enable citizens to gain access to land on an equitable basis.
6. A person or community whose tenure of land is legally insecure as a result of past racially discriminatory laws or practices is entitled, to the extent provided by an Act of Parliament, either to tenure which is legally secure or to comparable redress.

South African Constitutional Court reasons that the Constitution, with particular reference to section 25, compels us first, to recognise and take cognisance of the past injustice; secondly, to re-appraise and think deeply about the conception of property and ownership; and thirdly, to acknowledge the changes that the Constitution inspires, rather than avoid such change and numb its force.[15] This Chapter attempts to do just that – take seriously the constitutional impact of dignity as a value that requires us to re-appraise the conception of property in South Africa in light of the historical injustices that occurred through the use of property.

It has been argued that, by including sections 25(4) to (9) directly under the constitutional protection of property against arbitrary deprivation, the property clause sought to disrupt the fetishisation of ownership and the right to exclude.[16] As a starting point, the property clause ensures that existing property rights are not inviolate. It permits an interference with existing property rights in order to restore the dignity of individuals who were stripped of their dignity and property (such as land and cattle) through land dispossession and forced removals. As explained by van der Walt and Viljoen,

> Section 25 was inherently designed to not only oversee the protection of property rights from unreasonable interference by either private parties or the State, but it was also designed in part to oversee and guide the constitutionally mandated attempt to reconstruct society through social and economic land reforms.[17]

The constitutional project, in its entirety, now demands that values like equality and dignity be considered when adjudicating constitutional rights.[18] It is argued that this is even more imperative when it comes to property disputes. While the property clause does not itself mention dignity, it foresees the use of the institution of property to restore the dignity of people who were previously dispossessed of their land. Atuahene labels this

---

7. A person or community dispossessed of property after 19 June 1913 as a result of past racially discriminatory laws or practices is entitled, to the extent provided by an Act of Parliament, either to restitution of that property or to equitable redress.
8. No provision of this section may impede the state from taking legislative and other measures to achieve land, water and related reform, in order to redress the results of past racial discrimination, provided that any departure from the provisions of this section is in accordance with the provisions of section 36(1).
9. Parliament must enact the legislation referred to in subsection (6).

15 *Daniels v Scribante and Another* 2017 (4) SA 341 (CC) at para 115.

16 A.J. van der Walt, *Constitutional Property Law*, 3rd edn., Cape Town, Juta, 2011, p. 16.

17 A.J. van der Walt and S. Viljoen 'The constitutional mandate for social welfare – Systemic differences and links between property land rights and housing rights' (2015) (18) *PER/PELJ* 4.

18 S Liebenberg, 'The Value of Human Dignity in Interpreting Socio-Economic Rights', Vol. 21, 2005, *South African Journal on Human Rights*, pp 1-31.

harm as a "dignity taking", which requires "dignity restoration".[19] Part of this dignity restoration would involve land reform. If one recognises, as mentioned earlier, that property was used to take and deprive others of their dignity, the Constitution and the property clause seek to be the means to restore said dignity. This is made clear from the Preamble of the Constitution, which states that,

> [The people of South Africa] therefore, through our freely elected representatives, *adopt this Constitution as the supreme law of the Republic so as to* heal the divisions of the past and *establish a society based on democratic values*, social justice and fundamental human rights. (Emphasis added.)

The aim of this Chapter is to argue that the Constitution requires the value of dignity to play a more significant role in the adjudication of property disputes. Principally, the Chapter posits that dignity restoration through the institution of property in South Africa should go beyond land reform, and requires courts to use the value of dignity as an interpretative *leitmotiv* when adjudicating issues related to property rights. On such a footing, dignity may be a transformative tool for achieving justice in property disputes for both property owners and non-property owners. Dignity, as a value, would cause courts to go beyond a formalistic and narrow conception of property law, which merely serves to exclude and humiliate people instead of fostering a community.

A case study of *Thubakgale* will demonstrate the role of dignity in adjudicating property disputes.[20] The argument is that if the Constitutional Court took into consideration the dignity restoration function of property in South Africa, as required by the Constitution, then the outcome would have been markedly different, bolstering the social utility of property. To advance our argument, this Chapter will be structured as follows. Part 2 explores the content of dignity, what it entails, and what it could contribute to property law adjudication. Dignity, of course, lacks a principled definition and remains notoriously hard to define.[21] In Part 3, we canvass the abominable and egregious facts of *Thubakgale*. The facts of this case, as Majiedt J writes, "are reflective of the great disparities in wealth in our society persist, manifesting in despair in almost every corner of South Africa."[22] In Part 4, we argue that the applicants in *Thubakgale* are property owners which the Court failed to recognise, frustrating the transformative ambitions of section 25. Part 5, we put

---

19 B. Atuahene, 'Dignity Takings and Dignity Restoration: Creating a New Theoretical Framework for Understanding Involuntary Property Loss and the Remedies Required', Vol. 41, 2016, *Law & Social Inquiry* 796 p. 796.

20 *Thubakgale and Others v Ekurhuleni Metropolitan Municipality and Others* 2022 (8) BCLR 985 (CC).

21 *Harksen v Lane* 1998 1 SA 300 (CC) at para 50.

22 *Ibid.*, para 6.

forward an argument about how the Constitutional Court should have used this case to restore the dignity of the applicants who are at the margins of the institution of property.

Before we move on to the substance of our argument, we lay out some key definitions. First, the Chapter focuses on immovable property – in this context, land. This is not to say that the argument is not applicable to broader types of property; however, for accuracy, we limit our argument to immovable property. Secondly, a *leitmotiv* is a recurring and dominant theme in literature. In this instance, requiring the value of dignity to be used as a *leitmotiv*, would result in dignity being a paramount concern in the jurisprudence of South African courts in relation to property matters. During the adjudication of property disputes, the value of human dignity should be actively considered in the interpretation of the affected rights of parties, so as to "ensure that conditions are created to enable [human beings] to develop their capabilities and to flourish as individual and social beings".[23]

2 Making a Case for Dignity in Property Disputes

2.1 *Understanding Dignity*

The concept of dignity has been subjected to various debates, both inside and outside of legal scholarship. For instance, Dworkin acknowledges that the concept of dignity is ambiguous and vague, but he argues that humans are conferred human rights as a result of their inherent dignity.[24] In some philosophical literature, dignity comprises two main conceptions: ideas of *worth* and *honour*.[25] Kantians assert that dignity is the invaluable worth of every human being as an end-in-itself (the 'worth' conception).[26] For Kant, no one should be treated as means to an end – in other words, individual autonomy lies in the heart of a person's dignity.[27] As Alexander puts it, "[d]ignity is indefeasible; a person cannot forfeit [their] dignity regardless of any act [they] commit."[28]

23 *Supra* note 18 p. 13.

24 R. Dworkin, *Taking Rights Seriously*, Boston, Harvard University Press, 1977, p. 198.

25 G.S. Alexander 'Property, Dignity, and Human Flourishing', Vol. 104, 2019, *Cornell Law Review*, p. 998.

26 *Supra* note 10 p. 69. Ironically, despite Kant's belief that dignity was based on inherent self-worth, he also vehemently defended his thesis of racial and sexist hierarchy. In spite of Kant's formulation of egalitarian moral principles (that he claimed were applicable to *all* human beings), he was an ardent proponent for European colonial rule and enslavement. This ought to require anyone, and not just Kantians, to question their reliance on Kant's alleged egalitarian moral principles. For more, see P. Kleingeld 'On Dealing with Kant's Sexism and Racism', Vol. 2, 2019, *SGIR Review*, p 1.

27 J. Eckert, 'Legal Roots of Human Dignity in German Law', *in* D Kretzmer and E Klein (Eds.), *The Concept of Human Dignity in Human Rights Discourse*, The Hague, Kluwer Law International, 2002, p. 46 and I. Kant, *Foundations of the Metaphysics of Morals*, Cambridge, Cambridge University Press, 1991.

28 *Supra* note 25 at 1000. Alexander makes this point when contrasting the concepts of dignity and autonomy. The argument goes that autonomy is different from dignity as it is self-authorship, involving 'self-conscious

Dignity is a concept permanently in search of a meaning. Yet, regardless of the absence of a settled meaning of dignity, it is obvious that dignity is grounded in humanity. As Weisstub asserts, "[a]lbeit ambiguous, dignity is signalling a term that goes to the heart of what constitutes the quality of humanness."[29] At a minimum, dignity comprises the inalienable, inherent and intrinsic worth or values of each individual. This much is also recognised in South African jurisprudence. Sachs J from the South African Constitutional Court remarked in *Lawrence*:

> [I]ndeed, there is a core to the individual conscience so intrinsic to the dignity of the human personality that it is difficult to imagine any factors whatsoever that could justify its being penetrated by the state.[30]

The South African Supreme Court of Appeal stated, in the *Watchenuka* judgment, that "[h]uman dignity is inherent in all people, citizens and non-citizens alike – simply because they are human."[31] The South African Constitution recognises dignity as a founding value of the Constitution,[32] as well as a right,[33] but does not provide a definition of dignity. In spite of this, South African courts have repeatedly acknowledged the importance of dignity, either as a right or value, in our constitutional framework.[34] Constitutional Court Justice O'Regan noted that "without dignity, human life is substantially diminished. Without life, there cannot be dignity."[35] In other words, to be human is to have dignity.[36]

---

choice about how one wishes to live one's life'.

29 D.N. Weisstub 'Honor, Dignity, and the framing of Multiculturalist Values', *in* D Kretzmer and E Klein (Eds.), *The Concept of Human Dignity in Human Rights Discourse*, The Hague, Kluwer Law International, 2002, p. 269.

30 *S v Lawrence* 1997 4 SA 1176 (CC) at para 168.

31 *Minister of Home Affairs v Watchenuka* 2004 4 SA 326 (SCA) at para 24.

32 Sections 1, 7, 36, and 39 identify dignity as one of the founding values of the Republic of South Africa.

33 Right to human dignity is entrenched in section 10 of the Constitution.

34 *Malan v City of Cape Town* 2014 6 SA 315 (CC) para 127; *Carmichele v Minister of Safety and Security and the Minister of Justice and Constitutional Development* 2001 4 SA 938 (CC) at para 62; *Government of the Republic of South Africa v Grootboom* 2001 1 SA 46 (CC) at para 44; *De Reuck v Director of Public Prosecutions* 2004 1 SA 406 (CC) para 63; *National Coalition for Gay and Lesbian Equality v Minister of Justice* 1999 1 SA 6 (CC) at para 28; *S v Jordan* 2002 6 SA 642 (CC); *Hoffman v South African Airways* 2001 1 SA 1 (CC) at para 43; *MEC for Education: KwaZulu-Natal v Pillay* 2008 1 SA 474 (CC) para 53; *S v Makwanyane* 1995 3 SA 391 (CC); *Prinsloo v Van der Linde* 1997 3 SA 1012 (CC) at paras 32-33; *Minister of Home Affairs v Fourie* 2006 1 SA 524 (CC) at para 50; and *Robert James Stransham-Ford v Minster of Justice and Correctional Services* (GNP) (unreported) case number 27401/15 of 4 May 2015.

35 *S v Makwanyane and Another* 1995 (3) SA 391 at para 327.

36 We interpose here to make a minor point. While western philosophers, such as Kant, have influenced how legal scholars over the world have understood dignity, the notion of dignity may be found in other systems such as Asia, Latin America and Africa. For instance, the notion of *ubuntu* is an African legal and moral concept that encompasses principles of community, solidarity, dignity and interdependence. *Everfresh Market Virginia (Pty) Ltd v Shoprite Checkers (Pty) Ltd* 2012 (1) SA 256 (CC) at para 71; Y. Mokgoro and S. Woolman, 'Where dignity ends and ubuntu begins: An amplification of, as well as an identification of a

A siloed discussion of dignity is insufficient to understand the importance of its application to property disputes in South Africa. To understand the relationship between property and dignity, it is important to understand the history of property, particularly land dispossession and forced removals, in South Africa. We want to underscore how property was used to rob Black people of their dignity. This relates to the idea of the dignity takings through property.[37] The purpose is to draw a historical nexus between property and the dignity of the dispossessed. Drawing this historical nexus nurtures the ground that dignity, as a constitutional value, ought to be an interpretative *leitmotiv* in property disputes. We turn to that now.

2.2 *The Institution of Property in Colonial, Apartheid and Democratic South Africa: Dignity Takings*

In South Africa, race-driven boundary setting and land dispossession date back to 1652, when Dutch settlers disembarked in the country.[38] Property loss was omnipresent. What started with a physical boundary through a plantation of "bitter almond hedge and all sorts of fast-growing brambles and thorn bushes" to keep the locals away from the settlers in the Cape, over time turned into legal and socio-economical boundaries.[39] An excursion of South Africa's history of land dispossession points to flagrant differences in approaches to land ownership and tenure by settlers and indigenous communities.[40]

During the first three years of settlement from 1652, Dutch settlers did not actively concern themselves with the local communities and did not have a fixed policy towards them.[41] In 1657, an agreement was concluded between the settlers and the Khoikhoi,[42] in an attempt to create "an island of Europe [within Africa], separated from the continent of

tension in Drucilla Cornell's thoughts', Vol. 25, 2010, *Southern African Public Law*, p. 406; and O. Elechil et al, 'Restoring justice (ubuntu): An African perspective', Vol. 20, 2010 *International Criminal Justice Review*, p. 75.

37 Dignity takings concern depriving subordinated and vulnerable populations of their property rights to dehumanise or infantilise that population. B Atuahene, *We Want What's Ours: Learning from South Africa's Land Restitution Program*, Cape Town, Oxford University Press, 2014, p. 2.

38 *Ibid.*

39 *Ibid.*; A Sparks, *The Mind of South Africa: The Rise and Fall of Apartheid*, South Africa, Ballantine Books, 2007, p. xv; RH Du Pre *Separate but Unequal* (1994) p. 13; and C.H. Feinstein, *Economic History of South Africa*, Cambridge, Cambridge University Press, 2005, p. 24.

40 *Ibid.*

41 At the time, the majority of Southern Africa was occupied by two main groups of people: the Khoisan (which included San hunter-gatherers and Khoikhoi nomadic herders) and Black inhabitants (pastoralists and cultivators). For more J.M. Pienaar, *Land Reform*, Cape Town, Juta, 2014, pp. 54-55 and D. van der Merwe, 'Land Tenure in South Africa: A Brief History and Some Reform Proposals', 1989, *TSAR*, p. 665.

42 The Khoikhoi are one of the indigenous people of South Africa. For more information on the different indigenous people of South Africa, and debates around the use of the word "indigenous", see P.T. Mellet, *The Lie of 1652: A Decolonised History of Land*, Cape Town, Tafelberg, 2020.

Africa".[43] However, as the number of settlers increased, so did the demand for land. Consequently, the settlers explored the inland, and frontier communities were established.[44] As the settlers pursued their exploration, they considered vacant land as *terra nullius* and claimed ownership over them, despite the fact that most local communities had, in some capacity, previously occupied the land through their migratory existence, and did not recognise an individual land tenure system.[45] Evidently, the non-recognition of this long-lasting migratory existence under the settlers' "laws" does not negate the possibility that communal land system was generally a recognisable legal system. The non-recognition instead only points to the settlers' disregard towards the locals' way of life and traditions.

Over time, the Dutch settlers had taken over a significant amount of land. Before the arrival of the settlers, there was no need for paid employment for Black people, as their subsistence depended on their communities, which in turn depended on the land. In the absence of long-held territories and communal care-taking, many Black people were forced into employment, which could only be in service to the settlers.[46] In exchange for these services, Black people were allowed to occupy land – and in certain cases, they had the right to keep some cattle.[47] Thus began the attempts of settlers to control the Black population through both labour and land.[48] Highlighting the relationship between control and land, Van der Merwe wrote:

> The important consequence of European settlement in the interior, a process which had consolidated itself by the 1860s was that the [Dutch] not only acquired dominium over the lands of the Africans, but used their control over the land to achieve sovereignty over them. In fact, evidence seems to indicate that the early settlers not only used their control over land to facilitate sovereignty over Africans, but actually saw their dominium over the land as justification for exercising imperium or, conversely, regarded their subjugation of an African tribe as justification enough to gain control over their land.[49]

---

43 J.M. Pienaar *supra* note 41 p. 55; A Sparks *supra* note 39 p. 35; CH Feinstein *supra* note 39 p. 22. This agreement led to the creation of the Cape Peninsula Boundary with settlers and locals on either side.

44 *Ibid.*

45 T.W. Bennett, *Customary Law in South Africa*, Cape Town, Juta, 2004, p. 372 and T.W. Bennett, 'African Land – A History of Dispossession' *in* R. Zimmerman and D. Visser (Eds.) *Southern Cross: Civil Law and Common Law in South Africa*, Oxford, Oxford University Press, 1996, p. 66.

46 J.M. Pienaar *supra* note 41 p. 74.

47 *Ibid.*, p. 63.

48 To control areas where people of colour were allowed to stay while employed, the Black (Urban Areas) Consolidation Act 25 of 1945 was enacted and controlled the influx of people of colour within urban areas. For more see S. Mahomedy, *Investigating the Role of Participation in the Upgrading of Informal Settlements: Identifying Challenges and Opportunities*, 2022, LLD Thesis, *Stellenbosch University*, p. 32.

49 D. van der Merwe *supra* note 41 p. 673.

This quote depicts the dehumanisation that land dispossession under colonisation entailed. Much of Black people's way of living prior to the settlers' arrival related to their migratory existence, as well as their roles as pastoralists and cultivators.[50] To be able to give effect to any of these traditions, one would undoubtedly need access to land, and what the settlers did was to effectively curtail Black people's access to land. This was done mostly through conquest and forceful possession by the Dutch settlers. However, this haphazard tenure system was not deemed adequate to the British who landed permanently in South Africa in 1795. Consequently, the British settlers moved to introduce a more formal system of land tenure which relied on the law to dispossess people of their land.

The British formally introduced the concept of individual land tenure in South Africa by recognising and implementing Roman-Dutch concepts of ownership.[51] Since traditional communal land tenure did not fit into this system of property relations, it was not recognised by the British.[52] The Glen Grey Act 25 of 1894 did away with communal land tenure and abrogated the occupational and residential rights of Black people.[53] Thus, Black people's patterns of lives were permanently disrupted through dehumanising property relations. Other people of colour were also affected by decisions taken by settlers in relation to property. For instance, Indians were not allowed to vote in Natal unless they were landowners.[54] This was implemented in an effort by the British to maintain control over the colony by controlling who had the right to vote.[55] Evidently, even prior to formal apartheid, settlers relied heavily on land and the institution of property to maintain control over the colony, and subjugate Black, Indian, and Coloured people. This, in tandem with the mounting land dispossession, caused significant harm to these individuals' dignity.

While land dispossession started from the 17th century,[56] it was cemented during apartheid through several pieces of legislation that were promulgated one after the other in a short period of time. In 1951, the apartheid government put into place the Bantu

50 *Supra* note 45.

51 *Ibid.*

52 D.L. Carey-Miller and A. Pope, *Land Title*, Cape Town, Juta, 2000, p. 16.

53 The Glen Grey Act was in actuality the blueprint which would later inform the other pieces of legislation which dispossessed people of colour of their land under apartheid. *Supra* note 10 at 69 and *ibid.*, at p. 16.

54 J. Evans and D. Philips, 'When There's No Safety in Numbers: Fear and Franchise in South Africa – The Case of Natal', *in* D. Kirby and C. Coleborne (Eds.) *Law, History, Colonialism: The Reach of the Empire*, Manchester, Manchester University Press, 2001, p. 99.

55 *Ibid.*, at p. 97.

56 The Native Land Act 27 of 1913 included a 'Schedule of Native Areas' which set aside only 8% of South African land to people of colour. Non-compliance with the Act led to criminalisation. For more see T Ngcukaitobi *Land Matters: South Africa's Failed Land Reforms and the Road Ahead*, Cape Town, Penguin Books, 2021, p. 22 and *supra* note 52 at 27. This evidences that law was once again used as a tool to legitimize land dispossession. As Dawood put it, "The Natives Land Act thus turned into law the process of dispossessing Africans of their land that had been going on for the past 200 years. Law, not war, was the final means of conquest." Z. Dawood, 'Race and Space: Dispossession through the Group Areas Act', 1994, *Surplus People Project*, p. 85.

Authorities Act 68 of 1951, which created ten independent "homelands" where Black people would be confined. Black people's movement into "white areas" were controlled by the Natives (Abolition of Passes and Co-ordination of Documents) Act 67 of 1952.[57] However, the Acts that did the most ground work to legally establish racial segregation through land relations were the Group Areas Act 41 of 1950 and the Prevention of Illegal Squatting Act 52 of 1951.[58] Together, these Acts culminated in massive forced removals; with more than three million Black people being forcibly removed.[59]

These forced removals were at the heart of the concept of dignity takings. Vast communities were dehumanised through the actions of the apartheid government. While these communities were promised job opportunities, land, and compensation in the newly allocated areas, those were false promises.[60] Instead, government threatened the communities with imprisonment and destroyed their homes with bulldozers.[61] The displacement of so many communities led to many individuals being homeless and further marginalised.[62]

It is evident that the physical boundary setting that could be seen pre-1948 turned into socio-economical and legal boundary setting during apartheid. The legislated moves towards racial segregation through the control of jobs but most importantly, movement, occupation and property relations, were aggressive. The common denominator among all of these different Acts and activities is that they all involved active dignity takings.

> [Black people] were categorised as "superfluous" and "unproductive". They were not wanted in white cities, towns and farming areas. Declared aliens in the land of their birth, they were dumped in the homelands, which were often remote rural slums, areas for which the government took no responsibility.[63]

As explained before, dignity takings concern depriving subordinated and vulnerable populations of their property rights to dehumanise or infantilise that population.[64] It

57 Commonly known as the "Pass law", this Act made it compulsory for all people of colour above the age of 16 to carry a passbook with permits that allowed them to be in white areas. For more see *supra* note 52 at p. 34.

58 Daniel F. Malan, the Prime Minister of South Africa at the time when apartheid was implemented referred to the Group Areas Act as the 'heart of apartheid'. For more see S. Rugege, 'Land Reform in South Africa: An Overview', Vol. 32, 2004, 32 *Int'l J. Legal Info*, p. 285.

59 T Ngcukaitobi *supra* note 56 p. 23.

60 *Supra* note 56 at p. 36.

61 M. Abel, 'Long-run effects of forced removal under apartheid on social capital', 2015, *Harvard Economic History Seminar*, p. 7 and G. Muller, 'The legal-historical context of urban forced evictions in South Africa', Vol. 19, 2013, *Fundamina*, p. 372.

62 *Supra* note 56 p. 38.

63 *Supra* note 52 p. 24.

64 *Supra* note 37 p. 2.

involves displacement, dispossession, and other forms of deprivation. Dehumanisation refers to the failure to recognise an individual's or group's humanity. On the other hand, infantilisation refers to the negation of independence and results in treating adults as if they were children, thus, subjecting them to the authority of another person – the effect of this, denying them of their autonomy. By involuntarily losing their property, Black people were made economically dependent on the government and the white population. Black people were rendered landless, and their property rights were radically restricted through discriminatory legislation. Crucially, they could not independently determine their relationship with property rights and their land. They were treated as inferior, sub-humans, and petulant children who could not govern their own property rights. The effect of which is reflected in this impassioned quote in *Daniels*:

> The land, our purpose is the land; that is what we must achieve. The land is our whole lives: we plough it for food; we build our houses from the soil; we live on it; and we are buried in it. When the whites took our land away from us, we lost the dignity of our lives: we could no longer feed our children; we were forced to become servants; we were treated like animals. Our people have many problems; we are beaten and killed by the farmers; the wages we earn are too little to buy even a bag of mielie-meal. We must unite together to help each other and face the Boers. But in everything we do, we must remember that there is only one aim and one solution and that is the land, the soil, our world.[65]

As Atuahene and Sibanda recognise, land dispossession under colonisation and apartheid is the archetypal example of dignity takings.[66] The institution of property showed itself to be a powerful instrument to control the lives of people of colour and harm their dignity.[67] By destroying many communities' homes, the communities themselves, and then later forbidding them access to 92% of South African land, the apartheid government proved itself to be the most cruel enemy to Black people's dignity.[68] The historical narrative above demonstrates that Black people were subject to dignity takings given that dehumanisation and infantilisation were intertwined with the dispossession of their land.

---

65 *Supra* note 15.

66 B. Atuahene and S. Sibanda, 'From Reparations to dignity restoration: The story of the Popela community', Vol. 18, 2018, *African Human Rights Law Journal*, p. 658.

67 This will come to no surprise to anyone who is familiar with the link between capitalism, power, and property. See K Pistor, *The Code of Capital: How the Law Creates Wealth and Inequality*, Princeton, Princeton University Press, 2019.

68 J.G. Gilbert, 'Land Rights as Human Rights: The Case for a Specific Right to Land', Vol. 18, 2013, *International Journal on Human* Rights, p. 114.

As a result of the instrumentality of property in dignity taking, property should be a site of redress and dignity restoration.[69] In the next section, we argue that in furtherance of the project of dignity restoration, dignity should be employed in the interpretation of the property disputes, beyond matters that concern land reform. To this end, we argue that had the Constitutional Court seriously considered the dignity of the applicants in *Thubakgale* as vulnerable individuals who have been granted property rights, the outcome would have been vastly different.

3 SETTING THE SCENE: UNDERSTANDING *THUBAKGALE*

The facts of *Thubakgale* are convoluted, representing the struggles of indigent and vulnerable people who live in precarious conditions. The case demonstrates the deplorable conditions and dire situation that a vast number of poor people find themselves in throughout the country, despite their constitutionally gauranteed rights such as the rights to housing,[70] and sufficient water and food.[71]

The applicants live in the Winnie Mandela informal settlement in Tembisa (a township found in Johannesburg, South Africa). This settlement is within the jurisdiction of the Ekurhuleni Metropolitan Municipality, which is the first respondent ('the Municipality'). The Municipality constitutes the local government, which exercises authority over this jurisdiction as envisaged in Chapter 7 of the Constitution. The applicants live in squalor and in circumstances that can only be described as absymal.[72] The applicants were effectively homeless and generally displaced.[73] They live in "squalid hovels with up to ten people each, and have to share modest structures that they have built for themselves out of wood, plastic and iron."[74]

All the applicants in this case had successfully applied for a state housing subsidy,[75] which was granted as per the Upgrading of Informal Settlements Programme (UISP).[76] Some of these applications had been submitted as far back as 1998. Following their successful applications, the residents were each allocated a *particular* stand developed

69 B. Atuahene, 'Paying for the Past: Redressing the Legacy of Land Dispossession in South Africa', Vol. 45, 2011, *Law & Society Review*, p. 955.
70 Section 26 of the Constitution.
71 Section 27 of the Constitution.
72 *Thubakhale* at paras and 12.
73 *Mathale v Linda* [2015] ZACC 38; 2016 (2) SA 461 (CC) at para 54.
74 *Thubakgale* at para 17.
75 To be specific, the first and third to 134th applicants were residents. The second applicant was a voluntary organisation by the name of Ekurhuleni Concerned Residents Association (ECRA). For ease of reference, they will all be referred to as applicants.
76 The UISP is contained in the National Housing Code 2009.

with said subsidy in Tembisa.[77] Had all things gone accordingly, the residents ought to have been given possession of the house built on the stand, and the land itself, and the property would have been registered to their names. Regrettably, this did not take place. Instead, the residents waited for their houses for over 23 years.

Aggrieved by the lacklustre attitude of the Municipality, the applicants requested it to provide reasons for its failure to provide them with housing. This bore no fruit. During this time, some of the applicants began recieiving utility bills for the houses they were allocated but had not been given access to.[78] It turns out that the subsidised houses that were intended for the residents had been unlawfully occupied by other individuals. It was established by the Special Investigations Unit (SIU) that the Municipality was engaged in a scheme that concerned allocating identical plots of land to more than one beneficiary, despite being aware that the land could only be occupied by one beneficiary.[79] Consequently, the Municipality was responsible for the unlawful occupation of plots of land through fraud and corruption. In turn, the applicants approached the High Court to compel the Municipality to provide them with the housing they had successfully been awarded. In the court of first instance, the Municipality was ordered to provide the applicants with houses at Tembisa and register them as the titleholders of their respective plot.[80]

In spite of their already dismal behaviour, the Municipality and its officials refused to comply with their constitutional duties to remedy their own mismanagement and corruption and in fact, asked for an extension literally 48 hours before the deadline was set to expire.[81] The applicants opposed the extension application and provided a counter-application for constitutional damages.[82] In this regard, the applicants contended that each applicant should receive R5 000 (approximately £250) for every month after the deadline until the Municipality provides them with housing. They argued that these constitutional damages were not for patrimonial loss, and was instead the reasonable cost for them to

77 Huchzermeyer has defined informal settlements as settlements which are unauthorised and unplanned in areas which have not been earmarked for residential purposes. M. Huchzermeyer *Cities with 'Slums': From Informal Settlement Eradication to a Right to the City in Africa*, South Africa, UCT Press, 2011, pp. 5-9. As the Constitutional Court pointed out at paragraph 12, this location is known for its dismal local level governance and maladministration. *Thubakgale* at para 12.

78 *Thubakgale* at para 14.

79 *Ibid.*, at paras 14-15.

80 *Thubakgale v Ekurhuleni Metropolitan Municipality* 2018 (6) SA 584 (GP). This decision was appealed to amend the dates on which the order had to be completed; see *Ekurhuleni Metropolitan Municipality v Thubakgale* 2018 JDR 0770 (SCA).

81 *Thubakgale* at para 22.

82 *Ibid.*, at para 23.

rent suitable accommodation per month.[83] Both the main application and the counter-application were rejected.[84]

The counter-application for constitutional damages was the subject of the appeal at the Constitutional Court. The Court handed down three judgments. The majority judgment penned by Jafta J held that the applicants had asked for the wrong remedy and that they should have explored other remedies before asking for constitutional damages. Jafta J reasoned, quite worryingly, that infringements of socio-economic rights can never attract constitutional damages.[85] According to him, constitutional damages are only available to civil and political rights, and not socio-economic rights.[86] The minority judgment, per Majiedt J, argued that the applicants were entitled to constitutional damages.[87] Majiedt J compellingly argued that section 38 of the Constitution is written in a permissive form in that it states that a court may grant appropriate relief.[88] According to the minority, 'appropriate relief' has to be granted in light of the available facts and prevailing circumstances of the case. In other words, the remedy must fit the injury.[89] Ergo, the minority held that the residents were entitled to a symbolic, once-off, sum of R10 000 (approximately £500) for constitutional damages.[90] This was because their right to access to adequate housing was infringed and the state's conduct was so egregious that constitutional damages were the most appropriate remedy. The last and third judgment partially agreed with the majority decision in so far as it held that the applicants should have exhausted all other remedies first. However, it disagreed with the majority's insistence that constitutional damages are, as a principle, not available to socio-economic rights violations. The judgments could be subjected to various criticisms; however, this Chapter

83 *Ibid.*

84 *Ibid.*, at paras 24-25. The decision of the lower court is *Ekurhuleni Metropolitan Municipality v Thubakgale*, unreported judgment of the High Court of South Africa, Gauteng Division, Pretoria, Case No 39602/2015 (13 July 2020).

85 *Thubakgale* at para 121.

86 *Ibid.*

87 *Thubakgale* at paras 84-99.

88 Section 38 of the Constitution states that:
Anyone listed in this section has the right to approach a competent court, alleging that a right in the Bill of Rights has been infringed or threatened, and the court may grant appropriate relief, including a declaration of rights. The persons who may approach a court are—
a. anyone acting in their own interest;
b. anyone acting on behalf of another person who cannot act in their own name;
c. anyone acting as a member of, or in the interest of, a group or class of persons;
d. anyone acting in the public interest; and
e. an association acting in the interest of its members.

89 This wording emerges from *Steenkamp N.O. v Provincial Tender Board of the Eastern Cape* 2007 (3) SA 121 (CC) at para 29.

90 The separate concurring judgment differed with the majority only on the issue of whether constitutional damages are competent for enforcing socio-economic rights.

focuses on the lack of property arguments in the matter and the failure by the court to use dignity as an interpretive *leitmotiv*.

4 The Missing Property Argument

All three judgments fail to consider the property rights of the applicants. This is surprising because the applicants had applied for housing and their applications were successful. They were entitled to the immovable property and each of them were given particular and specific portions of land, wherein their houses would be built. This is why some of the applicants even received utility bills relating to their allocated property. They merely did not enjoy possession of their property but this was due the administrative hodgepodge and malfeasance of the Municipality. Once the applicants had successfully applied for the housing and allocated a particular stand (with a unique identification number), the applicants should be considered property rights holders. The applicants were entitled to all the standard incidents that flow from being a property holder. Honoré argues that there are eleven incidents that flow from ownership including, the right to possess, the right to use, the right to manage, the right to appropriate income from the property, the right to derive capital from the use of the property as collateral, the right to security and transmissibility, as well as the obligation to prevent harm.[91] In our view, the applicants were deprived of all of their incidents of ownership. There is not a single entitlement that they enjoyed flowing from their ownership.

For purposes of this chapter, the constitutionalisation of property has had two denouements.[92] The first denouement was articulated by the Constitutional Court in *FNB*, where it decidedly rejected a rigid definition of property and preferred a capacious conception.[93] The justification for this rejection is that the Constitution endorses a broader notion of property rather than a limited (narrow) understanding of property. This is because section 25 recognises the need for redress for historical dispossession. If property was to be narrowly defined, it might be that certain existing rights, enjoyed by predominantly white people, might fall outside of the scope of property and therefore, remain untouched, entrenched and not subject to reform. In the converse, this means that the property rights of Black people would remain precarious and weaker. A broad

91 A.M. Honoré, 'Ownership', *in* A. Guest (Ed.), *Oxford Essays in Jurisprudence*, Oxford, Oxford University Press, 1961, p. 370.

92 By the constitutionalisation of property, we are referring to the use of constitutions as a means of "regulating state actions that have a direct or indirect impact on property rights" and property rights themselves. See A.J. van der Walt and R. Walsh, 'Comparative Constitutional Property Law', *in* M. Graziadei and L. Smith, *Comparative Property Law: Global Perspectives*, United Kingdom, Edward Elgar Publishers, 2017, p. 193.

93 *First National Bank of SA Limited t/a Wesbank v Commissioner for the South African Revenue Services and Another; First National Bank of SA Limited t/a Wesbank v Minister of Finance* 2002 (4) SA 768 at para 51.

definition of property would result in a greater class of property being available for reform where necessary.[94] This means that our conception of property and property holders, under the new constitutional dispensation, must be broadly and generously construed to ensure that the purport and spirit of the Constitution permeates thoroughly.

The second denouement is that the Constitution has underscored a social understanding of property rather than a traditional individualistic notion of property. To this end, the Constitutional Court in *Agri South Africa* instructively held that section 25, and by extension property, must be interpreted in light of the gross inequality of land distribution and wealth.[95] Notwithstanding the ambitious reform objectives of the Constitution, it does not reject the existence of property rights arising from common law, provided that such rights are in accordance with the spirit and purport of the Constitution. The Constitution constrains property rights, and thus, they cannot exist outside of its purview.[96]

Accepting the broader conception of property and the social understanding of property means that when adjudicating property disputes, courts must not rigidly apply notions of private law. Courts ought to offer protection to interests and assets, which would conventionally not be protected. That is an undeniable constitutional injunction. Concerning the interpretation of section 25(1) of the Constitution, the Constitutional Court remarked:

> [T]o determine what kind of property deserves protection under the property clause cannot be restricted to private law notions of property. To do so would exclude other potential constitutional entitlements that may deserve protection from the ambit of protection under the property clause. It could also inadvertently lead to a failure to subject private law notions of property to constitutional scrutiny in order to ensure that they accord with constitutional norms.[97]

From this footing, the argument is clearer – recognising successful applicants of housing subsidies as property owners would be constitutionally appropriate. Those applicants are entitled to protection under section 25(1), which provides that "no one may be deprived of property except in terms of law of general application, and no law may permit arbitrary deprivation of property." Those who have applied for housing and have successfully been allocated a stand should be the afforded the constitutional protections and entitlements that flow from section 25(1) of the Constitution. A failure to recognise this would

94 A.J. van der Walt, *Property and Constitution*, Pretoria, PULP, 2012, p. 123.

95 *Agri South Africa v Minister for Minerals and Energy* 2013 (4) SA 1 (CC) at para 61.

96 A.J. van der Walt, *Constitutional property clauses: A comparative analysis*, Cape Town, Juta, 1999.

97 *Shoprite Checkers (Pty) Limited v Member of the Executive Council for Economic Development, Environmental Affairs and Tourism, Eastern Cape* 2015 (6) SA 125 (CC) at para 46.

inadvertently result in narrow conception of property, which would fall squarely within the private law notions of property. It would unduly narrow the import and object of the Constitution. Furthermore, it would be a regressive step. It would thrust South Africa to a hierarchical arrangement of property rights and property interests that the Constitution has eschewed. As Sachs J in *Port Elizabeth Municipality* elucidated:

> In sum, the Constitution imposes new obligations on the courts concerning rights relating to property not previously recognised by the common law. … The expectations that ordinarily go with title could clash headon with the genuine despair of people in dire need of accommodation. The judicial function in these circumstances is not to establish a hierarchical arrangement between the different interests involved, privileging in an abstract and mechanical way the rights of ownership over the right not to be dispossessed of a home or vice versa. Rather it is to balance out and reconcile the opposed claims in as just a manner as possible taking account of all the interests involved and the specific factors relevant in each particular case.[98]

It is perspicuous that the applicants are for all intents and purposes property owners. This is bolstered by the fact the some of the applicants were receiving utilities accounts in their name, and others had been registered as title holders (despite not having possession of the properties). Furthermore, this would restore the dignity of the *Thubakgale* applicants who have been displaced as a result of the legacy of colonisation and apartheid, which is now exacerbated by the corruption of the Municipality.

The applicants did not have physical possession of the property, but they are property owners (holders). Possession should not be confused for ownership.[99] While possession and ownership may overlap, they are conceptually and analytically distinct. Possession broadly refers to a person having actual or physical control over a thing and having the requisite intention to exercise control over the thing to the exclusion of others.[100] In contrast, ownership does not require any actual or physical control. You can own something without actually being in control of it.[101] Thus, X can be an owner without being in possession and Y can be in possession without being the owner. Traditionally, the

98 *Port Elizabeth Municipality v Various Occupiers* 2005 (1) SA 217 (CC) para 23. As AJ van der Walt *supra* note 94 put it, property under the constitutional purview reflects a: "… move away from a static, typically private-law conceptualist view of the constitution as a guarantee of the status quo to a dynamic, typically public-law view of the constitution as an instrument for social change and transformation under the auspices [and I would add 'and control'] of entrenched constitutional values."

99 T.W. Merrill, 'Ownership and possession' *in* Yun-chien Chang (Ed.), *Law and Economics of Possession*, Cambridge, Cambridge University Press, 2015.

100 *Ibid.*, at 11.

101 *Ibid.*, at 17.

primary remedy for X (owner) to protect her ownership is the *rei vindicatio* (vindicatory action);[102] whereas, the primary remedy for Y (possessor) to protect her possession is *mandament van spolie* (spoliation).[103] The law regards ownership and possession differently and protects owners and possessors differently. What the *Thubakgale* applicants lack is possession – not ownership.

Furthermore, the fact that some *Thubakgale* applicants were not registered as title holders does not detract from their ownership. While personal rights are not registrable,[104] real rights must be registered in terms of section 3 of the Deeds Registries Act. However, South Africa has a negative system of registration, which means that the accuracy of the Deeds Registry is not promised or guaranteed.[105] Registration is not conclusive evidence of ownership – it is merely *prima facie* evidence. It cannot be overstated that the *Thubakgale* applicants successfully applied for housing and were respectively allocated a plot of land, accompanied by a particular stand number. Recognising said successful applications, Teffo J in the High Court (as the court of first instance) ordered the Municipality to register the residents as titleholders of those houses by 31 December 2019, and later by 30 June 2020.[106] This was an attempt to ensure that their property is registered against their names. This order may be interpreted as buttressing the applicants' proprietary entitlements – that is, the right to possess in this particular instance – by compelling the state to provide them with a house by a certain time. The Teffo J decision can be understood in two ways: (a) either it buttresses the fact that the applicants were property holders of the particular plots they were allocated; or (b) the court order establishes or concretises their property rights.

The hindrance to the registration of the property is due to the unwillingness of the Municipality to comply with two court orders. Every other step in the process to secure ownership had been completed and recognised and had been endorsed by different courts. The ongoing corrupt actions of the Municipality were the only reasons why the registration failed. For all intents and purposes, the different courts recognised that the applicants met all the requirements to be considered the due owners of the plots, and hence, ordered for their registration as titleholders.

---

102 *Chetty v Naidoo* 1974 3 SA 13(A). See also Z. Boggenpoel, '(Re)defining the contours of ownership: Moving beyond white picket fences', 2019, *Stellenbosch Law Review*, p. 234.

103 *Telkom SA Limited v Xsinet (Pty) Ltd* 2003 (5) SA 309 (SCA). See also Z. Boggenpoel, 'Questioning the use of the Mandament van Spolie in *Ngqukumba v Minister of Safety and Security* 2014 5 SA 112 (CC)', Vol. 18, 2015, *Potchefstroom Electronic Law Journal*, p. 735.

104 *Hollins v Registrar of Deeds* 1904 TS 603 at 605, 606. See also section 63 of Deeds Registries Act 47 of 1937 ("Deeds Registries Act").

105 P. J. Badenhorst, 'The Distinction Between Real Rights and Personal Rights in the Deeds Registration System of South Africa -Part One: Statutory and Theoretical Distinction between Real Rights and Personal Rights', Vol. 29, 2021, *African Journal of International and Comparative Law*, pp. 452-456.

106 *Thubakgale* at paras 20 and 21.

Beyond the fact that many of the South Africans eligible for the national housing programme had been subject to the dehumanising apartheid policies, their dignity was further trampled by the state's actions in this regard. The dignified approach to this dispute would have in part required the acknowledgment that all the applicants were in fact *bona fide* title holders, regardless of the arbitrary registration of a few of the applicants, and non-registration of numerous others.

The moment it is established that the residents are the owners of the stands and houses, then their inability to access and possess the land becomes a potential infringement of their right to not be arbitrarily deprived of their property under section 25(1). This potential infringement could be interpreted to be caused by the unlawful occupiers, or alternatively, by the Municipality that wrongfully gave the latter access to the houses.[107] However, before one comes to this conclusion, one should first consider whether the residents' rights under section 25(1) was in fact infringed.

In *FNB*, the Court held that "*any* interference with the use, enjoyment and exploitation of private property involves some deprivation in respect of that person".[108] This decision rendered the test for deprivation very wide and was quickly narrowed by the Constitutional Court only a few years later in *Mkontwana*.[109] The Court in that decision held that "at the very least, substantial interference or limitation that goes beyond the normal restrictions on property use or enjoyment found in an open and democratic society would amount to deprivation."[110] Following this approach, the interference with the property use or enjoyment would need to be significant enough to have a "legally relevant impact" on some of the entitlements of ownership.[111]

In the case of *Thubakgale*, the interference with the use and enjoyment of the residents' properties has been caused by the unlawful occupation as a result of the Municipality's corruption and mismanagement. The unlawful occupation of these properties has meant

---

107 Section 26 states that: "(1) Everyone has the right to have access to adequate housing.
(2) The state must take reasonable legislative and other measures, within its available resources, to achieve the progressive realisation of this right.
(3) No one may be evicted from their home, or have their home demolished, without an order of court made after considering all the relevant circumstances. No legislation may permit arbitrary evictions."

108 *Supra* note 93 at 57 (emphasis added).

109 *Mkontwana v Nelson Mandela Metropolitan Municipality; Bisset v Buffalo City Municipality; Transfer Rights Action Campaign v Member of the Executive Council for Local Government and Housing, Gauteng* 2005 (1) SA 530 (CC).

110 *Ibid.*, at para 32.

111 B.V. Slade, 'Constitutional Property Law', *in* G. Muller et al (Eds.), *General Principles of South African Property Law*, Cape Town, Lexis Nexis, p. 63. These two conceptions of how significant the interference needs to be to constitute deprivation has caused many debates amongst property law scholars in South Africa, but unfortunately falls outside of the scope of this Chapter. For more see A.J. van der Walt, 'Retreating from the *FNB* arbitrariness test already? *Mkontwana v Nelson Mandela Metropolitan Municipality; Bissett v Buffalo Cit Municipality; Transfer rights Action Campaign v MEC for Local Government & Housing, Gauteng*', Vol. 122, 2005, *South African Law Journal*, pp. 79-80.

that the residents have not been able to even access the properties, let alone exercise possession over their own houses, for over 23 years. It is clear that the interference at play in this case is of the most serious and consequential kind. Such an interference with the residents' entitlement to use, enjoy and exploit the properties is significant enough to meet the higher threshold held by *Mkontwana* and consequently, would also meet the requirement of *FNB*. Thus, it is clear that unlawful occupation that prevents the actual owners of the properties to enjoy its use, constitutes deprivation.[112]

Viewing the case from the lens of property ownership would have enriched the Court's jurisprudence concerning section 25(1) and broaden the scope of property and its constitutionally protected entitlements. Pivotally, a transformative approach would categorise the applicants' interests as property, worthy of protection and push back against the notion that property rights are only for the preserve of corporations or wealthy individuals. Such an interpretation would empower those who were traditionally at the margins of property and were deprived of property rights.[113] The next section explores the ways in which the Constitution mandates that property be used as an institution for dignity restoration.

5 Taking Property Rights and Dignity Seriously: Reconsidering *Thubakgale* to Restore Dignity

Dignity restoration is the "material compensation to dispossessed populations through processes that affirm their humanity and reinforce their agency".[114] As opposed to reparations, which most programmes put into place to remedy land dispossession focus on, dignity restoration is not focused only on the outcome, in this case, reimbursement for the property taken.[115] Instead, dignity restoration aims at "[rehabilitating] the dispossessed and [reintegrating] them into the fabric of society through an emphasis on process".[116]

112 This has been the case in *President of the Republic of South Africa and Another v Modderklip Boerdery (Pty) Ltd* 2005 (5) SA 3 (CC). However, in *Modderklip*, the scale of unlawful occupation was vastly different. There were more than 40,000 unlawful occupiers on Modderklip's property, and the state was unable to evict and displace said occupiers. This distinction relates to whether the property could be unoccupied, which in the case of *Thubakgale* was a possibility, as the majority judgment points out. Yet, this is a concern that will be raised in this Chapter's discussion of alternative remedies and dignity restoration in choosing said remedies.

113 This notion of 'property in the margins' comes from A.J. van der Walt, *Property in the Margins*, Oxford, Hart Publishing, 2009.

114 *Ibid.*

115 C.J. Ogletree, 'The Current Reparations Debate', Vol. 36, 2003, *UC Davis Law Review*, p. 1055 and *supra* note 37 at p. 4.

116 *Supra* note 37 p. 4. Dignity restoration is based on principles of restorative justice.

While the South African land reform programme relies heavily on reparations through either the restitution of property or the payment of compensation,[117] it is also the quintessential illustration of a programme, which is aimed at facilitating dignity restorations. This was highlighted by the former Minister of Agriculture and Land Affairs, Thoko Didiza, when she stated that "the struggle for *dignity*, equality and a sense of belonging has been the driving force behind our work as the Land Claims Commission".[118]

What should one then make of the acknowledgment that land dispossession was an act of dignity taking, and that dignity restoration is more than just reparations? Looking at the state's response, it would appear that the institution of property has not been taken into consideration when it comes to dignity restoration. South Africa has heavily relied on non-property related measures such as progressive socio-economic rights and affirmative action programs to assist in dignity restoration.[119] However, when it comes to the institution of property, dignity restoration is understood to be limited to the formal land reform programmes and reparations, as opposed to the adjudication of property disputes.

It is crucial to start viewing all property disputes, and not just those that relate directly to land reform, through the lens of dignity restoration. This can be achieved by using dignity as an interpretative *leitmotiv*. The starting point is recognising that property rights were distorted under apartheid and colonisation. To redress much of the damage that has been done would require a broader approach to property beyond just land reform. Given that the institution of property itself was used as a weapon for dignity takings, the whole institution ought to be targeted for dignity restoration. The Constitution itself recognises this through section 25. To fully realise the transformative potential of the Constitution, we need to rethink the core of property and the role property plays in society.

The Constitution is a normative break from abstract, hierarchical property rights arrangements. Such a break must be understood in the context of 'transformative constitutionalism'. Klare described transformative constitutionalism as "a long-term project of constitutional enactment, interpretation and enforcement committed … to transforming a country's political and social institutions and power relationships in a democratic, participatory, and egalitarian direction."[120] South Africa's Constitution has been described as transformative. To this end, the Constitution constitutes a bridge, between a past characterised by injustice and inequality to a society founded on justice

117 Reparations has been defined as 'the right to have restored to them property of which they were deprived in the course of the conflict and to be compensated appropriately for any such property that cannot be restored to them.' *Supra* note 37.

118 *Land Affairs Department: Annual Report, 2001-2002*, 2002, p. 7.

119 H. Klug, *The Constitution of South Africa: A Contextual Analysis*, Oxford, Hart Publishing, 2010.

120 K. Klare, 'Legal culture and transformative constitutionalism', Vol. 14, 1998, *South African Journal on Human Rights*, p. 150.

and equality.[121] This transformative nature of the Constitution means that there must be political, social and legal reform, with an awareness of the historical injustices that must be redressed.[122] With the adoption of the Constitution, our understanding of property has been significantly altered.[123]

The Constitution established one system of law, informed and shaped by the Constitution as the country's supreme law. All other forms of law, including the common law, derive their force from the Constitution. Plainly put, there is no enclave of law that operates outside of constitutional control.[124] Accordingly, the doctrinal aspect of the common law is now infused with constitutional values. The Bill of Rights, as enshrined in the Constitution, regulates and governs the common law and, by extension, property law. Common law property rights still exist within the constitutional dispensation, provided that they are not at odds with the Constitution. Of import, the reach of the Constitution is not merely limited to matters that concern the State but also extends to private relations, where there is no direct State involvement.[125] In 'post-apartheid' South Africa, property is constrained by the Constitution, which demands a redress of the historical injustices upon which South Africa is built.

Constitutional values inform *all* constitutional rights, and this is fundamental because the right to dignity is not always involved in matters in front of the court. Chaskalson P of the Constitutional Court writing extra-curially, stated that constitutional values provide a normative value system in accordance to which courts should interpret the Constitution and adjudicate matters.[126] What Chaskalson P terms a normative value system, others have termed 'backdrop of the values of South African society',[127] and 'holistic, value-based' framework.[128] What one can get from these different terms is not only the importance of constitutional values but also the need to consistently invoke them. This would explain why, although the right to dignity is not always infringed or relied on when another

121 Mhantla J in *Speaker of the National Assembly v Land Access Movement of South Africa* 2019 (5) BCLR 619 (CC) stated:"It aims to right historical wrongs, resolve unjust dispossession and heal the 'trauma of deep, dislocating loss of land' that has taken root in our country. It entails the practical disruption of racialised privilege in respect of land ownership. But it also incorporates a symbolic function of recognising histories and legacies of injustice that influence the lives of individuals, families and communities."

122 A.J. van der Walt, 'Transformative Constitutionalism and the Development of South African Property Law I', 2005, *TSAR*, p. 658.

123 Z. Boggenpoel *supra* note 102 p. 238.

124 *Ex Parte President of the Republic of South Africa: In re Pharmaceutical Manufacturers Association of South Africa* 2000 2 SA 674 (CC) at para 44.

125 See section 8(2) of the Constitution, which provides: "A provision of the Bill of Rights binds a natural or a juristic person if, and to the extent that, it is applicable, taking into account the nature of the right and the nature of any duty imposed by the right."

126 A. Chaskalson, 'Dignity as a Constitutional Value: A South African Perspective', Vol. 26, 2011, *American University International Law Review*, p. 1385.

127 *S v Williams* 1995 (3) SA 632 (CC) at para 22.

128 *Coetzee v Government of the Republic of South Africa* 1995 (10) BCLR 1382 (CC) at para 46.

primary constitutional right breach is at play, the value of dignity is still relied on to inform the shape of the right that has been breached. Consequently, dignity's paramount importance in achieving the South African democracy, requires courts to always consider constitutional values, especially that of dignity, in the adjudication of breaches of constitutional rights.

In light of this, Van der Walt contends that property should play a modest systemic role in society. He contends that the notion that property rights are sacred and should be protected by all means has been overinflated since time immemorial.[129] Property has been perceived as "the guardian of every other right."[130] To van der Walt, a systemically significant right such as life, dignity or equality (non-property rights) may, depending on the circumstances of each case, trump property rights. Accordingly, a modest systematic status of property would require us to look beyond the existing doctrinal frameworks in search of solutions.[131] Property forms part of a larger system and accordingly we should continuously challenge our conceptions of property and the value we attach to property rights.[132]

Taking heed from van der Walt, we go further. We argue that not only should dignity and other non-property rights be taken into account when adjudicating property disputes, but we argue that property should be used to restore the dignity of those who have been historically deprived of property and its enjoyment. Thus, property must be used for dignity restoration, rather than dignity taking, purposes. In *Thubakgale*, the Court failed to use property and property rights to enhance the dignity of the applicants. It failed to recognise them as property owners and further failed to adjudicate the matter in a manner that would restore the dignity of the applicants. The *Thubakgale* applicants' dignity was historically infringed and that infringement was further exacerbated by the corruption of the Municipality.

It is our contention that if the Constitutional Court took seriously the notion of dignity and dignity restoration in *Thubakgale*, then it would have awarded constitutional damages to the applicants. Beyond this, the Municipality and the Constitutional Court, by failing to *mero motu* recognise the property arguments,[133] worsened the infringement of the applicants' dignity. Awarding constitutional damages would have vindicated their rights (both property and to an extent housing rights) and restored their dignity. The applicants have been dehumanised and infantised by apartheid and colonisation, and further

129 A.J. van der Walt, *supra* note 1 pp. 26-27.

130 *Ibid.*

131 A.J. van der Walt, *supra* note 113 p. 247.

132 *Ibid.*, at 29. See also E. van der Sijde, 'Reconsidering the Relationship between Property and Regulation: A Systemic Constitutional Approach', 2015, LLD Thesis, *Stellenbosch University*, pp. 271-3.

133 Although none of the applicants made any arguments relating to their property rights, the Constitutional Court is able to raise arguments of its own accord. See *Fischer v Ramahlele* 2014 (4) SA 614 (SCA) at paras 13-5.

dehumanised and infantised by the actions of the Municipality – and the Court has not done anything to address this.

6 Concluding Remarks: *Thubakgale* – a Missed Opportunity

The Constitutional Court in *Thubakgale* did not consider the property rights of the applicants at all. This could be partly attributed to the fact that the lawyers who brought the case did not advance any property rights argument in the apex Court. This is particularly curious because the applicants are property owners (as we have argued above), and the actions of the Municipality (its corruption and fraud) led to the unlawful occupation of their property. This unlawful occupation is the direct result of the actions of the Municipality. The unlawful occupiers are similarly victims of the mismanagement and corruption of the Municipality.

Recognising the applicants' property rights restores and preserves their dignity. It would contribute to the capacity of the applicants to support themselves, and in turn their capacity to protect their human dignity. In the words of Machan, acknowledging the property rights of the applicants is a 'precondition for… [individuals'] flourishing'.[134] These property rights (or the recognition thereof) enable the restoration of dignity and humanity for those previously dispossessed and allows for societal healing, social sustainability and for democracy to flourish.

This case illustrates the dismal failure of the South African government to treat its constituencies with dignity. The treatment that the residents were subjected to, having to live in dismal conditions for more than twenty years in spite of being legitimate owners of a house, makes the promises in the Constitution sound hollow. Being mindful of the constant need for dignity restoration, warrants a different approach to such type of cases, one that involves the careful consideration of the value of dignity and how it impacts the adjudication process. A dignity-based approach to this case would have considered the impact that being denied access to their property does to a Black property owner. It would have considered the property argument at length.

Property law is dynamic, it changes with the times. So should the way one adjudicates property matters. This Chapter sought to make the contribution that the value of dignity should inform the interpretation of property rights in 'post-apartheid' South Africa. This is based on the knowledge that property as an institution was used as a weapon of mass oppression through colonial times as well as during apartheid. The dignity of people of colour in South Africa was intentionally taken away, through dignity takings. This dignity should be just as intentionally given back, through dignity restoration. This Chapter

134 T. Machan, 'Reflections on the Right to Private Property', Vol. 10, 2000, *Journale des Economistes*, p. 8.

illustrates that dignity restoration should not only be limited to formal land reform programmes, but that it should span across the adjudication of property law matters. This can best be achieved by relying on dignity as an interpretative *leitmotiv* to the property rights under the Constitution.

Part III
Property Law for the Future

6 Living on Water: on the Legal Design of Floating Real Estate Projects

*Kato De Schepper**

1 Introduction: Living on Water, a Mere (Legal) Fantasy?

1.1 *Water Juritecture*

Climate change, with rising sea levels, makes it not inconceivable that in the coming decades the development of floating housing will become extremely necessary. In addition, as a result population growth, building space is becoming scarce. Apart from this, more than 50,000 building plots lie in potential flood area in Flanders.[1] Consequently the search for alternative housing forms that occupy less land area is crucial. Floating homes, apartment blocks and even floating cities could become a new way of sustainable project development, adapted to the needs and concerns of the 21st century. However, the question arises how such floating real estate projects can be introduced in the current legal framework. This contribution attempts to explore the legal design, also called 'juritecture'[2] of such floating structures, and more specifically 'waterhouses', under current Belgian property law.[3]

Waterhouses are constructions that are built on a floating platform, consisting of concrete and polystyrene foam.[4] This platform, which is normally accessible via some kind of pier, is anchored in the underlying soil by means of brackets and poles. The floating

* PhD student at the Research Institute for Property Law of the University of Leuven (KU Leuven).

1 www.tijd.be/netto/analyse/vastgoed/als-uw-bouwgrond-in-overstromingsgevoelig-gebied-ligt/10325888.html.

2 Concept borrowed from Hendrik Ploeger: D.A. Groetelaers & H.D. Ploeger, 'Juritecture of the built environment: a different view on legal design for multiple use of land', *Structural survey* 2007, vol. 25, p. 295; H.D. Ploeger, 'Modern vastgoed: De vastgoedjurist in de eenentwintigste eeuw', *WPNR* 2009, vol. 6781, p. 14-17. See also www.juritecture.net; V. Sagaert, *De zakenrechtelijke structuur van vastgoedprojecten*, Antwerpen, Intersentia 2019, p. 2.

3 Generally, we only discuss the reformed Belgian property law as in force from the 1st of September 2021. See Act of 4 February 2020 on Book 3 "Goods" of the Civil Code, *Belgian Official Gazette* 17 March 2020, 15.753. However, where relevant, we will also refer to the former Belgian property law and to Dutch law, as a comparative legal system.

4 An important distinction exists between waterhouses and so-called 'houseboats'. The latter - although many variants exist - have in common that they are usually located within a mooring along the quay, whereas floating houses are usually placed in a specific area or as part of a harbour. See on this distinction also J.J.A.

houses are mostly disconnected from the mainland and are equipped with all the comforts of a modern home such as connection to the gas, electricity and water network. Mainly in the Netherlands, there are already some inspiring projects based on this new form of 'water architecture'. Examples include 'Woonwijk Schoonschip' near Amsterdam[5] and the floating pavilion[6] and harbour lofts[7] in Rotterdam. Architects are even already planning to create entire floating cities, consisting of several floating platforms, houses, apartment complexes, commercial and industrial zones, possibly connected by floating roads.[8]

1.2 Property Law Issues

The success rate of floating real estate projects depends – in addition to financial, political and urban planning issues – on whether and how floating homes can be legally structured. As will be explained throughout this chapter, it is necessary to create a horizontal property split between the floating superstructure or volume, being the waterhouse and the floating platform, on the one hand, and the water mass and the underlying soil on the other hand, to make waterhouses legally operational. For such a horizontal property split, some fundamental property law concepts are at stake, namely immovable property by incorporation, immovable accession, component formation and public domain. Respectively, the question arises whether floating homes – given their ability to move up and down with the water level – may or may not qualify as immovable property, whether these structures are subject to immovable accession and whether the underlying soil is

---

De Groot, 'Kan een schip onroerend zijn?', *WPNR* 2003, vol. 6517, p. 86. This chapter, however, focuses only on the legal design of waterhouses. Houseboats are in principle not discussed.

5 https://schoonschipamsterdam.org.

6 www.drijvendpaviljoen.nl.

7 www.rotterdam.nl/wonen-leven/getijdenoever-nassauhaven/.

8 A very inspiring project, supported by the United Nations, is 'Oceanix' (https://oceanix.org), where one floating platform can house up to 300 people. The European Union also has an ongoing project on floating modular islands, called 'Space@Sea' (https://spaceatsea-project.eu/about-space-at-sea). A chain of floating platforms could form a real 'floating city'. See C. Ferdinandus, 'De drijvende stad', *in* M. Hebly, H.N. Schelhaas & K. Swinnen, *Schaalvergroting in het privaatrecht*, Den Haag, Boom Juridische uitgevers, 2019, p. 120; M.B. Flikkema *et al.*, 'Legal issues for artificial floating islands', *Frontiers in Marine Science* 2021, vol. 8, article 619462. See also the inspiring designs of Waterstudio (https://waterstudio.nl) or DeltaSync (https://deltasync.co.uk). See also A.J. Mes, H.D. Ploeger & B.A.M. Janssen, 'Eigendom van onroerende zaken, met name natrekking (titels 1 en 3). Flexibele eigendomsverhoudingen in het vastgoedrecht', *in* L.C.A. Verstappen (ed.), *Boek 5 BW van de toekomst. Over vernieuwingen in het zakenrecht. KBN Preadviezen*, Den Haag, SDU, 2016, p. 186.
This contribution does not discuss floating cities any further. Also floating business premises, greenhouses, wind turbines or solar panels are excluded. See on floating solar panels in Dutch law: J.W.A. Biemans & J. Veenhof, 'Duurzaam goederenrecht: moeten drijvende zonneparken te boek worden gesteld?', *WPNR* 2021, vol. 7319, pp. 279-288; J. Veenhof & S.C. Roozenboom, 'Drijvende zonneparken– juridische verankering', *Tijdschrift voor Zakenrecht* 2020, vol. 1; D.W. Wumkes & R.A. Warning, 'Aandachtspunten bij het vestigen van zakelijke rechten ten behoeve van zonne-installaties', *Tijdschrift voor Zakenrecht* 2020, vol. 2-3.

part of the public domain. An analysis of these questions is important for the horizontal property split via a superficies right, apartment co-ownership or some form of volume ownership.[9] This contribution examines whether and how current Belgian property law does or does not facilitate the sustainable development of floating real estate.

2 MOVABLE IMMOVABLE GOODS AND INHERENT COMPONENTS

2.1 *Immovable Goods by Incorporation*

The first question is whether waterhouses can qualify as immovable goods under Belgian law. After all, all property is movable or immovable, with movable property being the residual category.[10] Four subcategories of immovable goods exist, namely immovables by their nature, by incorporation and by destination (Article 3.47 B CC) and immovables by their object (Article 3.49 CC). Floating homes potentially qualify as immovable by incorporation. Under Article 3.47, 2nd paragraph CC, immovables by incorporation are: "all buildings and plantings which, because they are incorporated in immovables by their nature, are an inherent component thereof".[11] From this wording, it follows that under the new property law, incorporation is both a necessary and sufficient condition to fall within the category of immovable property by incorporation.[12] Although there is no definition of the term 'incorporation' in the Civil Code, the Explanatory Memorandum does mention that the legislator wishes to align with the expanded incorporation criterion as interpreted in recent case law of the Belgian Court of Cassation.[13]

---

9 Given the limited scope of this chapter, we will only discuss the horizontal property split by a building right. For the legal design via apartment co-ownership and volume property in general, see K. De Schepper, 'Beweegbare onroerende eigendom: over de juritectuur van drijvende woningen', *TPR* 2022, vol. 1-2, pp. 348-354.

10 Article 3.46 Belgian Civil Code (hereafter: 'CC'); A. Apers, 'Onderscheid tussen roerende en onroerende goederen', *in* J. Baeck *et al.* (eds.), *Het nieuwe goederenrecht*, Antwerpen, Intersentia, 2021, pp. 65-66, n°. 38; C. Roussieau, 'Classifications des biens', *in* P. Lecocq *et al.* (eds.), *Le nouveau droit des biens*, Brussel, Larcier, 2020, pp. 78-79, n°. 17-18; V. Sagaert, *Goederenrecht in Beginselen van Belgisch privaatrecht*, Mechelen, Kluwer, 2021, pp. 199 & 201, n°. 202 & 204.
This was also the case under old Belgian property law. See article 516 old Belgian CC; V. Sagaert, *Goederenrecht in Beginselen van Belgisch privaatrecht*, Mechelen, Kluwer, 2014, p. 83, n°. 91.

11 For the translation *see* V. Sagaert, A. Appelmans, S. Baeyens, G. Degeest, M.-L. Degroote, B. Maeschaelck and B. Verheye, 'Act of 4 February 2020 containing Book 3 "Property" of the Civil Code Belgian Official Gazette 17 March 2020', *EPLJ* 2021, vol. 10, pp. 108-176.

12 Sagaert, 2021, pp. 208-209, n°. 212.

13 See references in the following paragraph.

The incorporation standard has developed from a traditional physical objective standard towards a larger and more functional subjective standard.[14] According to the traditional incorporation criterion, a good must be connected to the ground in such a way that it could not be removed without breaking or damage.[15] For example, a structure is incorporated if it has foundations in the ground.[16] In general, buildings, including houses and flats, but also cellars, lifts and so on, that show a material connection with land, meet this traditional incorporation criterion.[17] Gradually, case law has shifted towards a broader, more functional and subjective incorporation criterion.[18] Goods that remain permanently in a particular place and are connected durably to the ground, qualify as 'immovable by incorporation', even if they are easily movable or show limited functional mobility.[19] Under this less strict incorporation standard, building parts, such as utility lines,[20] and building equipment, such as a built-in kitchen or bathroom and air-conditioning systems,[21] can be considered immovable by incorporation.[22]

---

14 J. Kokelenberg, 'Onroerend uit zijn aard: de beperkingen van de notie beperkt', *TBBR* 2009, vol. 7, pp. 337-347; V. Sagaert, 'Onroerendmaking door incorporatie: over het verschil tussen beweegbaarheid en verplaatsbaarheid' (note under Belgian Court of Cassation 14 februari 2008), *RW* 2008-09, vol. 11, pp. 456-459.

15 Bergen 27 May 1988, *Bull. Bel.* 1989, III, p. 2127; Brussel 24 December 1898, *Pas* 1989, II, p. 138; Gent 17 May 1966, *Rec.gén.enr.not.* 1967, p. 403; H. De Page & R. Dekkers, *Traité élémentaire de droit civil belge*, V, *Des biens et des différentes modifications de la propriété*, Brussel, Bruylant, 1975, n°. 637-643; R. Dekkers & E. Dirix, *Handboek Burgerlijk recht, Zakenrecht, zekerheden en verjaring*, Antwerpen, Intersentia, 2005, p. 14, n°. 30; A. Kluyskens, *Zakenrecht* in *Beginselen van Burgerlijk recht*, V, Antwerpen, Standaard, 1953, p. 14, n°. 7.

16 Gent 28 juli 1904, *Pas.* 1905, II, p. 301; Luik 21 januari 1932, *Pas.* 1932, II, p. 212; A. Apers, *Wilsautonomie bij de kwalificatie van goederen*, Antwerpen, Intersentia, 2017, p. 78, n°. 74; B. Tilleman, 'De notie roerend en onroerend goed', *in* P. Lecocq, B. Tilleman & A. Verbeke (eds.), *Zakenrecht*, Brugge, die Keure, 2005, p. 5, n°.8.

17 Apers, 2017, p. 75, n°. 69; De Page & Dekkers, 1975, p. 603, n°. 637; R. Derine, F. Van Neste & H. Vandenberghe, *Zakenrecht* in *Beginselen van het Belgisch privaatrecht*, I, A, Antwerpen, Standaard, 1974, p. 703, n°. 41; J. Kokelenberg, 'Onroerend van nature, een begrip in beweging?' (note under Belgian Court of Cassation 15 September 1988), 1990 *TBBR*, p. 215; Sagaert, 2021, p. 207, n°. 211; Sagaert, 2014, pp. 87-88, n°. 99.

18 Belgian Court of Cassation 15 September 1988, 1988-1989 *Arr.Cass.*, p. 60; Belgian Court of Cassation 14 February 2008, *Courr. Fisc.* 2008, vol. 8, p. 456; Belgian Court of Cassation 15 March 2012, 2012 *Arr. Cass.*, p. 678; Hermand & Philippe, 2004, pp. 293-324.

19 See recently Belgian Court of Cassation 14 May 2020, 2020 *FJF*, p. 362; N. Carette & S. Dewinter, 'Actuele ontwikkelingen goederenrecht 2020', *in* R. Barbaix & N. Carette (eds.), *Tendensen vermogensrecht 2021*, Antwerpen, Intersentia, 2022, pp. 28-29.

20 Belgian Court of Cassation 8 May 1866, 1886 *Pas.*, I, p. 193; V. Sagaert, 'Het zakenrechtelijk statuut van nutsleidingen', 2004 *TPR*, pp. 1358-1359.

21 Belgian Court of Cassation 25 February 2019, 2019 *JLMB*, p. 1792; Gent 12 March 1991, 1991 *T. Vred.*, p. 212, note E. Stassijns; V. Sagaert, 'Onroerend door incorporatie: over airco's en tunnelvisies', 2020 *RW*, pp. 853-856.

22 Sagaert, 2014, pp. 211-212, n°. 216. Note that certain legal scholars require an additional physical connection for building equipment (Sagaert, 2021, p. 212, n°. 216). Other case law does not impose any additional incorporation (for example Gent 12 March 1991, 1991 *T.Vred.*, p. 212). Irrespective of this doctrinal

2.2 *Floating Homes as Incorporated Goods*

Floating houses meet this extended and more subjective incorporation criterion. Because the waterhouse is attached to the ground with piles, a sufficiently solid connection exists between the floating platform and the underlying soil. The limited functional movability of the house – moving up and down depending on the water level – does not impair the immovable qualification.[23] In addition, the connection to utilities (water, gas, electricity, telephone, etc.) indicates the immovable character of the floating object.[24] Given the similar function of waterhouses and 'normal' houses, this immovable qualification is favourable, so that both floating and normal houses are treated equally in law. Additionally, qualifying floating homes as movable goods would lead to fundamental problems: under current law it is not possible to create building rights or apartment co-ownership structures in relation to movable goods. Although this is not an issue for 'simple' single-household waterhouses (because no property split is needed if the waterhouse were movable and, consequently, immovable accession to the underlying soil would not apply), this does cause problems in case of larger floating real estate projects, such as floating apartment blocks or floating cities. In those circumstances, it will be necessary to create different rights in rem for the various actors on a floating platform. Nonetheless, there is currently no consensus about the application of building rights and appartment rights in relation to movable goods. For this, a more far-reaching redrawing of property law would be necessary, which requires a much wider debate.

In Dutch legal doctrine, however, the immovable qualification of floating real estate projects is debated.[25] Although the Dutch incorporation criterion is similar to the Belgian

---

discussion, if no additional incorporation is present, building equipment may still qualify as 'immovable by destination' (Article 3.47 last paragraph Belgian CC).

23 Bouly, 2015, p. 292, n°. 241; R. Timmermans, 'Duurzaam bouwen van flatgebouwen op waterpercelen', *T.App.* 2011, vol. 2, p. 7. However, article 531 old Belgian CC indicated otherwise, waterhouses would also qualify as immovable goods under the old property law.

24 Timmermans, 2011, p. 7.

25 See De Groot, 2003, pp. 83-86; H.D. Ploeger, 'De onroerende woonboot', *JBN* 2010, vol. 2, p. 5; I.A.F. Hendriksen, 'Drijvende woningen in het algemeen een roerende zaak' (note under Dutch Supreme court 9 March 2012), *MvV* 2012, vol. 12, p. 335 *et seq.*; H.D. Ploeger, 'Drijvend wonen. De flexibiliteit van een schip, zo vast als een huis', *WPNR* 2004, vol. 6590, pp. 717-720; P.J. Van der Plank, 'Een eerste stap naar drijvend wonen op grotere schaal', 2016 *MvV*, p. 190 *et seq.*; A.R.G. Van Dijk-Barkmeijer *et al.*, 'Waterwoningen in IJburg, tussen wal en schip? Enkele privaatrechtelijke, fiscale en ruimtelijk bestuursrechtelijke aspecten van wonen op het water', *BR* 2007, vol. 28, p. 111 *et seq.*; A.A. Van Velten, *Privaatrechtelijke aspecten van onroerend goed*, Amsterdam, Stichting tot bevordering der notariële wetenschap, 2018, pp. 87-88; A.H.H. Wouters, 'De toekomst van drijvend wonen: hoe te voorkomen dat de wal het schip keert?', *WPNR* 2017, vol. 7170, pp. 898-904.

criterion,[26] floating houses were considered movable property in recent case law.[27] As a counterreaction to this case law, some legal scholars launched a proposal to modify Dutch property law in order to qualify waterhouses as immovable property.[28]

2.3 *Immovables by Incorporation, Inherent Components and the Unity Principle under Reformed Property Law*

The new property law Act in Belgium adds a new dimension to the interpretation of immovables by incorporation. It introduces the concept of 'component formation'. Goods, directly or indirectly connected to land, are immovable by incorporation only if they are an 'inherent component' of an immovable good by its nature.[29] The reformed property law connects the category of immovables by incorporation with the theory of component formation and, by extension, the unity principle in property law.[30] According to this principle, if a movable good becomes an inherent component of an immovable good by its nature, it loses its independent existence and assimilates with the immovable qualification of the main object.[31] In order to decide whether floating homes could still qualify as immovables, we should hence consider whether they could fall under the scope of article 3.8, §2 CC.

Article 3.8, §2, 1st paragraph CC defines 'inherent components' as follows:

---

26 For the Dutch incorporation criterion the leading case is the so-called 'Portacabin case': Dutch Supreme Court 31 October 1997, ECLI:NL:HR:1997:ZC2478.. See in legal doctrine.: S.E. Bartels & A.I.M. Van Mierlo, *Mr. C. Assers Handleiding tot de beoefening van het Nederlands Burgerlijk Recht. 3. Vermogensrecht algemeen. Deel IV. Algemeen goederenrecht*, Deventer, Kluwer, 2021, n°. 91; H.J. Snijders & E.B. Rank-Berenschot, *Goederenrecht*, Deventer, Kluwer, 2022, pp. 37-40, n°. 45.

27 Dutch Supreme Court 9 March 2012, ECLI:NL:HR:2012:BV8198; Dutch Supreme Court 15 January 2010, ECLI:NL:HR:2010:BK9136.

28 Mes, Ploeger & Janssen, 2016, pp. 183-193; H.D. Ploeger & P.J. Van der Plank, 'Wetsvoorstel Drijvende opstallen: een juridisch fundament voor bouwen op water. Deel II: Boek 5 voor 'Registergoederen'', *WPNR* 2022, vol. 7356, pp. 61-68; H.D. Ploeger & P.J. Van der Plank, 'Wetsvoorstel Drijvende opstallen: een juridisch fundament voor bouwen op water. Deel I: Onroerende Drijvende opstallen', *WPNR* 2021, vol. 7319, pp. 270-277; P.J. Van der Plank, 'De introductie van drijvende percelen', *WPNR* 2015, vol. 7071, pp. 662-666.

29 See *supra* 2.1 for the definition of immovable goods by incorporation (Article 3.47, 2nd & 3d paragraph) that explicitly mentions the notion 'inherent components'.

30 Explanatory memorandum, p. 118-119; Amendment n° 13, *Parl.St.* Kamer 2019-20, n°. 55-0173/002, 18 (www.lachambre.be/FLWB/PDF/55/0173/55K0173002.pdf); Apers, 2021, pp. 67-68, n°. 44-45; Sagaert, 2021, p. 207, n°. 211; V. Sagaert, 'De hervorming van het goederenrecht', 2020 *TPR*, p. 492, n°. 137.
See before the reform already about this connection: Apers, 2017, p. 171, n°. 142; K. Swinnen, *Accessoriteit in het vermogensrecht*, Antwerpen, Intersentia, 2014, pp. 392-415, n°. 385-404; B. Verheye, 'Toekomst van de circulaire vastgoedeconomie in Belgisch en Nederlands recht', 2019 *TPR*, pp. 141-144, n°. 27.

31 Apers, 2021, p. 68, n°. 45.

> "An inherent component of a good is an essential element of this good that cannot be separated from it without detracting from the physical or functional substance of this good."[32]

Although the Explanatory Memorandum remains vague about the concrete interpretation of this concept,[33] in line with the aforementioned evolution of the incorporation criterium in case law (see *supra* 2.1),[34] two alternative standards for inherent components can be derived from this definition: (1) a physical and (2) a functional standard.[35] First, following the physical standard, a component is inherent if it cannot be separated from the main good without breaking or damaging the good or the inherent component itself.[36] The fact that there is only a temporary attachment does not prevent the property from being immovable by incorporation.[37] Secondly, according to the functional standard, a component is also inherent if it is necessary for the functioning of the good or to complete the main good, even though it can be removed without damage.[38] For example solar panels could meet this functional standard if they are necessary for the power supply of the building.[39] Moreover, a good also qualifies as a functional inherent component if it has been adjusted to the main good (for example building kitchen equipment).[40] The physical and functional criterion for component formation correspond respectively to the former traditional physical objective standard, on the one hand, and the more functional subjective criterion, on the other hand.

Although there might already be discussion in legal literature about the coherence of two elements in the definition of inherent components, namely 'essential elements' and

32 Before the property law reform, inherent components were described as "all physical and legal parts of a good which, according to their normal intended purpose, are not susceptible to an independent existence.". See Sagaert, 2014, p. 75, n°. 83.

33 Explanatory Memorandum, p. 26.

34 Explanatory Memorandum, pp. 117-118.

35 Belgian Court of Cassation 25 February 2019, 2019 *JLMB*, p. 1792; Sagaert, 2021, n°. 175; N. Bernard, 'Titre 1 : Dispositions générales (le droit commun)', *in* N. Bernard & V. Defraiteur (eds.), *Le droit des biens après la réforme de 2020*, Limal, Anthemis, 2020, n°. 49-50.

36 Article 3:4, 2nd paragraph Dutch CC paragraph prescribes a similar physical standard for inherent components. See Dutch Supreme Court 13 November 2020, *NJ* 2021/86 (*Glencore/Zalco II*); Bartels, Van Mierlo & Ploeger, 2021, n°. 67.

37 For example trees in a tree nursery, which are removed after a short time are nevertheless immovable. See Belgian Court of Cassation 19 April 1888, *Pas.* 1888, vol. I, pp. 198-199.

38 Following article 3:4, 1st paragraph Dutch CC a component becomes inherent if it is necessary to complete the main object in general or if it is specifically matched in structural terms for the main object. See also Dutch Supreme Court, 5 November 1991, *NJ* 1993, vol. 316 (*Dépex/Curatoren*); Bartels, Van Mierlo & Ploeger, 2021, n°. 67.

39 Explanatory Memorandum, p. 118. See also recently in case law: Luik 11 September 2014, 2016 *RGDC*, p. 220.

40 See in Dutch law: Dutch Supreme Court 1991 15 November 1991 (Dépex/curatoren).

'physical or functional substance',[41] we support Sagaert's view, that the physical or functional criterion should be read together with the necessity criterion. This way, the physical and functional criterion for inherent components is aligned with the aforementioned extended incorporation criterion (see *supra* 2.1). Since waterhouses meet the extended incorporation criterion (see *supra* 2.2), they can thus also be considered as functionally necessary inherent components: because of the special characteristics of the floating construction technique, they are specifically adjusted the underlying water volume and soil. Therefore, the addition of the notion 'inherent components' to article 3.47, 2nd paragraph, does not change the previously defended immovable status of floating homes.

3 IMMOVABLE ACCESSION: APPLICATION TO WATERHOUSES

The second property law issue for the legal design of floating real estate projects is whether article 3. 64 CC on immovable accession applies to waterhouses.[42] If this is the case, the owner of the underwater land plot would also become the owner of the incorporated waterhouse, which is a rather unwanted effect of the application of immovable accession. On the basis of the latter, the landowner acquires ownership of all goods that are directly or indirectly united with the ground, such as buildings.[43] The former owner of the acceded good loses his ownership right[44] and the ownership right of the land owner extends to the goods united with the ground.[45] Like the category of immovables by incorporation (see *supra* 2.3), the concept of accession is based on the unity principle of article 3.8, §2 CC.[46]

41 See also about this discussion: De Schepper, 2022 *TPR*, p. 327, n°. 38 with references to Baeck, 2021, p. 38, n°. 15 (who supports a separate necessity criterion); Sagaert, 2020 *TPR*, p. 435, n°. 54; Sagaert, 2020 *RW*, p. 865; Bernard & Defraiteur, 2020, p. 43, n°. 50 (who support an integrated necessity criterion).

42 See similar article 5 :20 Dutch CC.

43 Bouly, 2015, pp. 72-130; J. Hansenne, *L'accession* in *Répertoire notarial*, II, l. I, Brussel, Larcier, 1994; P. Lecocq, *Manuel de droit des biens*, Brussel, Larcier, 2012, I, pp. 272-297; Sagaert, 2014, p. 592, n°. 739.

44 Sagaert, 2021, pp. 1189-1190, n°. 1371; F. Werdefroy, 'Beschouwingen over de onroerende natrekking: het recht van erfpacht, het recht van opstal, en verlof tot bouwen', 1983 *TPR*, pp. 293-343.

45 Gent 9 mei 2006, *Fiscoloog* 2006, vol. 1052, p. 18; Gent 19 december 2006, 2007 *TFR*, p. 321, note D. Jacques; A. Apers, 'Afgrenzing van onroerende goederen uit hun aard', *TFR* 2011, vol. 405, n°. 12 (note under Gent 11 januari 2011); Bouly, 2015, pp. 50-52, n°. 36; Derine, Van Neste & Vandenberghe, 1975, p. 1049, n°. 712; P. Levie, *Traité théorique et pratique des Constructions érigées sur le Terrain d'Autrui*, Leuven, Publications Universitaires de Louvain, 1951, p. 155, n°. 58.

46 APERS, 2021, p. 68, n°. 45 *in fine*; Baeck, 2021, pp. 37-42; D. GRUYAERT, 'Eigendom', *in* J. Baeck *et al.* (eds.), *Het nieuwe goederenrecht*, Antwerpen, Intersentia, 2021, p. 266, n°. 30; Lecocq & Popa, 2020, p. 30, n°. 22; V. Sagaert, 'The background and general principles of the new Belgian property law', *EPLJ* 2021, vol. 10, pp. 19-20, n°. 19; Sagaert, 2020 *TPR*, p. 511, n°. 162; Verheye, 2019, p. 134, pp. 141-142, p. 150, n°. 22, 27 & 25.
As previously defended in Belgian legal doctrine: Sagaert, 2014, p. 743, n°. 970; Swinnen, 2014, p. 354, n°. 379.

Consequently, under the reformed property law, the same incorporation criterion exists for immovables by incorporation and immovable accession.[47] Based on the forgoing (see *supra* 2.2 and 2.3), waterhouses meet the modern extended incorporation criterion and are considered to be inherent components. Since there is a uniform incorporation criterion for immovable property by incorporation (article 3.47 CC) and immovable accession (article 3.50 *j.* 3.55 CC), immovable accession will also apply to floating houses. As a result of the application of immovable accession, the owner of the underlying land plot acquires the property of the floating home. This would be a problematic outcome, specifically in the case of floating projects, since the owner of the floating house in most cases does not own the underlying running water or ground (see 4).[48] Therefore, we will discuss below how a horizontal property split between the floating object and the underlying water and soil can be established through the creation of a building right (see *infra* 5).

In Dutch legal scholarship there is discussion about the relation between article 3:3, 3:4 and 5:20 Dutch Civil code. See for an overview: H.W. Heyman & S.E. Bartels, *Vastgoedtransacties: Koop*, Deventer, Kluwer, 2019, pp. 42-43 and p. 54 *et seq.*

47 Explanatory Memorandum, p. 118 & pp. 136-137: The legislator considered the simultaneous application of immovable accession and the qualification as immovable property essential. See also Apers, 2021, p. 69, n°. 46; Gruyaert, 2021, p. 266, n°. 30; Sagaert, 2020 *TPR*, p. 436, n°. 55, pp. 493-494, n°. 173 & p. 511 n°. 162. Most legal scholars were already in favour of a uniform incorporation criterium before the property law reform. See Apers, 2017, n°. 142 & n°. 167; De Page & Dekkers, 1975, pp. 601-602, n°. 633-637; Derine, Van Neste & Vandenberghe, 1975, p. 1049, n°. 712; Dekkers & Dirix, 2005, p. 13, n°. 27-28 & p. 154, n°. 384 *et seq.*; Hansenne, 1996, p. 635, n°. 684; Sagaert, 2014, n°. 978; Sagaert, 2020 *RW*, pp. 854-856. *Contra*: Some scholars, due to the systematic expansion of the incorporation criterion for immovable goods in case law (*supra* 2.1), were no longer in favour of a uniform incorporation criterion, but argued for a dualistic criterion, that should be interpreted stricter for immovable accession than for immovables by incorporation. See Bouly, 2015, n°. 94-99; S. Bouly, 'Does the expansion of the concept 'immovable' influence immovable accession?', in B. Akkermans & E. Marais (eds.), *Property Law Perspective*, Antwerpen, Intersentia, 2013, pp. 111-130. However since the property law reform confirmed the uniform incorporation criterion, this dualistic approach cannot longer be endorsed.
Dutch law also largely upholds a uniform incorporation criterium for immovables by incorporation (article 3:3 Dutch CC) and immovable accession (article 5:20 Dutch CC). See S.E. Bartels & A.A. Van Velten, *Mr. C. Assers Handleiding tot de beoefening van het Nederlands Burgerlijk Recht. 5. Zakenrecht, Eigendom en beperkte rechten*, Deventer, Kluwer, 2017, n°. 85a; V. Tweehuysen, 'Tiny houses. Does size matter?', *WPNR* 2017, vol. 7157, p. 513. *Contra:* Ploeger, *WPNR* 2002, vol. 6497, p. 520; G.E. Van Maanen, 'De boom van Bartels', *NTBR* 2012, vol. 1, p. 4, n°. 3.

48 On the question on the property status of the underlying water volume and subsoil, see *infra* 4. See likewise Ploeger & Van der Plank, but they conclude that immovable accession does not apply to floating projects (Ploeger & Van der Plank, 2021, p. 275).

4 UNDERLYING SOIL AS PUBLIC DOMAIN

4.1 *Subsoil and Water Volume as Public Domain Goods*

Article 3.45 CC stipulates the distinction between public and private goods in the reformed property law.[49] The original draft bill contained a definition of the term 'public domain' in article 3.59 as "Goods that are expressly or implicitly intended for the use of all or to a public service".[50] This broad definition followed the developments in case law and legal doctrine regarding the criterion for public domain goods. According to the Court of Cassation 'public domain property' means property which, by its nature or by a decision of a competent authority – express or implied[51] – is intended for the use of all or that is expressly included by law in the public domain.[52] In a judgment of 15 March 2018, the Court of Cassation added a new dimension to this criterion by concluding that not only "goods intended for the use of all", but also "goods intended for a public service" belong to the public domain.[53] The proposed article 3.59 mirrored this evolution by including both "intended for the use of all" and "intended for a public service" as a criterion.[54] Unfortunately this article did not make it through the property law reform.[55] Nevertheless, the definition remains relevant in recent case law.[56] Based on the classic criterion for public domain property, it can be assumed the underlying land and the water volume, will belong to the

---

49 Unlike Belgian law, there is in principle no longer a distinction between public and private goods in Dutch law. See M. Milo, 'Publiek domein in privaatrecht en administratief recht. Een negentiende-eeuwse discussie in gescheiden circuits', *in* F. Vanhemelryck (ed.), *Recht ende justicie. Handelingen van het XIIIe Belgisch-Nederlands Rechtshistorisch congres*, Brussel, KUB, 1997, p. 226 & pp. 240-248.

50 Draft bill Book 3 "Goods" for the new Civil Code, *Parl.St.* 2018-19, no. 54-3348/001, 531.

51 J. De Staercke, 'De finaliteit en totstandkoming van het openbaar domein', *in* R. Palmans, T. Leys & J. Toury (eds.), *Openbaar domein*, Antwerpen, Intersentia, 2019, pp. 47-48, n°. 44.

52 Belgian Court of Cassation 17 October 2014, 2015-2016 *RW*, pp. 1065-1071, note N. Van Damme; Belgian Court of Cassation 18 May 2007, 2007-2008 *RW*, p. 736, note V. Sagaert; Belgian Court of Cassation 20 April 1978, 1978 *Arr.Cass.*, p. 1191; Belgian Court of Cassation 3 May 1968, 1986 *Arr.Cass.*, p. 1100; Belgian Court of Cassation 9 March 1950, 1950 *Arr.Cass.*, p. 457; Belgian Court of Cassation 21 January 1926, *Pas.* 1926, vol. I, p. 187; Belgian Court of Cassation 11 November 1886, *Pas.* 1886, vol. I, p. 401.

53 Belgian Court of Cassation 15 March 2018, *T.Gem.* 2019, vol. 2, p. 87, note S. De Winter; S. De Winter, 'Openbare domeingoederen en erfpacht', *T.Gem.* 2019, vol. 2, pp. 88-89; A. Lemmerling, 'Openbaar domein', *in* J. Baeck *et al.* (eds.), *Het nieuwe goederenrecht*, Antwerpen, Intersentia, 2021, p. 108, n° 13.

54 Explanatory Memorandum, p. 111 *et seq.*; D. D'Hooghe & M. Van Den Langenbergh, 'Naar de opheffing van het leerstuk van het openbaar domein', *in* R. Palmans, T. Leys & J. Toury (eds.), *Openbaar domein*, Antwerpen, Intersentia, 2019, p. 272, n°. 63; Lemmerling, 2021, p. 119; Sagaert, 2021, pp. 238-240, n°. 247; V. Sagaert & P. Lecocq, *De hervorming van het goederenrecht*, Brugge, die Keure, 2019, p. 196.

55 The Belgian Council of State criticized the definition: *Parl.St.* Chamber 2019-20, no. 55-0173/004, pp. 23-26 & p. 78. Other actors, on the contrary, were explicitly in favour, see *Parl.St.* Chamber 2019-20, no. 55-0173/004, p. 68.

56 See for example Belgian Court of Cassation 25 November 2021, 2022 *RW*, p. 1592 (summary); Court of Antwerp 21 September 2021, *LRB* 2022, p. 45 (summary). See also Sagaert, 2021, p. 239, n° 247.

public domain. Both navigable and unnavigable rivers, streams and canals are part of the public domain, as they are in principle intended for the use of all.[57]

4.2 *Accession and Public Domain*

From the foregoing, it follows that immovable accession applies on floating houses (see *supra* 3) and the underlying water and soil are part of the Belgian public domain (see *supra* 4.1). However, in Belgian legal literature the question has risen whether essentially private structures, such as for example waterhouses, can be subject to accession if the acceding object belongs to the public domain. Traditionally, it has been assumed that accession does occur in favour of the public domain.[58] This would result in the public domain extending to incorporated structures, which do not necessarily meet the definition of public domain property. For this reason, several Belgian authors have criticised the traditional view.[59] The qualification as public domain could not extend to structures that are incorporated into the public domain, but that do not meet the criteria for public domain themselves.[60] The incorporated structures must also necessarily be "intended for the use of all" in order for them to be part of the public domain.[61] Nevertheless, the new

57 Decree 4 May 1994, *Belgian official Gazette* 16 July 1994; Article 16 Act of 28 December 1967 on the unnavigable streams, *Belgian Official Gazette* 15 February 1968 (https://codex.vlaanderen.be/Portals/Codex/documenten/1008791.html); Article 1 §2 Decision of the Flemish Government of 4 June 2004, *Belgian official Gazette* 14 July 2004; Rb. Brugge 12 December 1990, 1990-1991 *RW*, p. 994; Rb. Ieper 24 February 1960, 1959-1960 *RW*, p. 1856; Bouly, 2015, p. 293, n° 242; De Page & Dekkers, V, n°. 798; Derine, Van Neste & Vandenberghe, 1975, p. 177, n°. 92; Hansenne, 1996, n°. 121; M. Pâques, 'Présentation, champ d'application, nature et composition du domaine', *in* M. Pâques *et al.* (eds.), *Domaine public, domaine privé – biens des pouvoirs publics* in *Répertoire notarial*, Brussel, Larcier, 2008, p. 65, n°. 47; Sagaert, 2021, p. 239 & pp. 243-244, n°. 247 & n° 252. *Contra:* J. Goedertier, 1953-1954, p. 1659.
In Dutch law the water of streams, rivers, lakes or harbours cannot be an object of property but is a so-called 'res nullius'. See Bartels & Van Velten, 2017, n°. 97; H.D. Ploeger, 'Drijvend wonen', *De Notarisklerk* 2002, vol. 79, p. 114; Van Velten, 2018, p. 72; Snijders & Rank-Berenschot, 2022, n°. 173; W.H.M Reehuis *et al.*, *Goederenrecht* in *Het Nederlands burgerlijk recht, deel , Pitlo*, Deventer, Kluwer, 2019, p. 462, n°. 537.
However, the land below which public waterways are located is presumed to be owned be the property of the State. See article 5:24-5:28 Dutch CC; Dutch Supreme Court 5 June 1992, *NJ* 1992, vol. 539; Dutch Supreme Court 19 January 1962, *NJ* 1962, vol. 151; W.H.M. Reehuis *et al.*, 2019, p. 470, n°. 548; G. Snijders, *Overheidsprivaatrecht – bijzonder deel*, Deventer, Kluwer, 2016, p. 30; Van Velten, 2018, p. 46.

58 This theory refers to the so-called '*domanialité publique globale*'. See Belgian Court of Cassation 9 March 1950, 1950 *Arr.Cass.*, p. 457; Brussel 21 December 1966, *Pas.* 1967, vol. II, 184; Hansenne, 1996, p. 1246; J. Kokelenberg, T. Van Sinay & H. Vuye, 'Zakenrecht. Overzicht van rechtspraak (1995-2000)', 2001 *TPR*, p. 862, n°. 17; N. Verheyden-Jeanmart, P. Coppens & C. Mostin, 'Examen de jurisprudence (1989 à 1998). Les Biens', 2000 *RCJB*, p. 92, n°. 22.

59 L. Deridder & T. Vermeir, *Leidingen voor nutsvoorzieningen*, Brugge, die Keure, 2000, p. 19, n° 21; P. Flamme, 'Crise ou cure de jouvence de a domanialité publique: un obstacle au financement privé des équipements collectifs?', 1991 *JT*, p. 442; Pâques, 2008, p. 111, n°. 56; Sagaert, 2009, p. 76-77, n°. 66.

60 These authors refer to the so-called '*domanialité publique fragmentée*'. See Bouly, 2015, p. 420, n°. 336; Sagaert, 2019, pp. 259-260, n°. 411.

61 Bouly, 2015, p. 421, n°. 336; Flamme, 1991, p. 449, n°. 36.

Article 3.45, paragraph 2 CC implies that accession does apply.[62] In this contribution, we therefore take into account that floating homes can accede to the public domain, regardless of the question whether the acceding good does or does not become a part of the public domain good because of the accession rule. Consequently, we will explore how a horizontal property split between public and private domain can take place (see *infra* 5).

4.3 *The Creation of Rights in Rem on Public Domain*

For the realisation of the horizontal split between public and private property, we first have to check whether real rights can be established on public domain goods, in the case of floating real estate and the underlying soil. Article 3.45, 2nd paragraph CC confirms that under current property law, it is possible to establish personal rights and rights in rem on the public domain provided that these do not conflict with the public purpose of the property.[63] The possibility to create personal rights, such as a lease right, and certain rights in rem, such as a building right, was previously already applied in some legislation,[64] case law[65] and defended in legal doctrine.[66] Belgian law has evolved from a traditional absolute

62 Adversely, article 3.45 Belgian CC confirms that accession does not apply if the public domain property itself accedes to a private good. See Sagaert, 2020 *TPR*, p. 499, n°. 144. See earlier on this matter: Brussel 2 April 1980, 1981 *RNB*, p. 364; J. Kokelenberg, T. Van Sinay & H. Vuye, 'Zakenrecht. Overzicht van rechtspraak (1994-2000)', 2001 *TPR*, p. 862, n° 17.

63 Sagaert, 2021, pp. 264-265, n°. 279-280.
This is also possible under Dutch law, since there is in principle no distinction between public and private property. See Dutch Supreme Court 15 February 1918, 1918 *NJ* ; Dutch Supreme Court 19 January 1968, *NJ* 1968, vol. 166; W. Konijnenbelt, R.M. Van Malle & H.D. Van Wijk, *Hoofdstukken van bestuursrecht*, Den Haag, Elsevier, 2002, pp. 418-419, n°. 16; Snijders, 2016, p. 27, n°. 7; A.Q.C. Tak, *De overheid in het burgerlijk recht*, 's-Gravenhage, VUGA, 1997, p. 225 *et seq*. Additionally, next to the establishment of property right, for waterhouses, mooring licenses and rental agreements for moorings are possible. See Van Velten, 2018, p. 91, n°. 2.13.1.

64 Decree of 18 July 2003 on public-private cooperation, *Belgian Official Gazette* 19 September 2003, 46497; Article 185 Decree on Provinces of 9 December 2005, *Belgian Official Gazette* 29 December 2005, 56891; Article 191 Decree on Municipalities 15 July 2005, *Belgian Official Gazette* 31 August 2005, 38153; Article 6-7 Decree of 2 April 2004 on the public-law external independent agency 'De Vlaamse Waterweg NV', *Belgian Official Gazette* 26 May 2004; Article 13 Decree of 2 March 1999 on the policy and management of seaports, *Belgian Official Gazette* 8 April 1999. See also Sagaert, 2021, pp. 262-263, n° 277; Sagaert, 2019, p. 252.

65 Belgian Court of Cassation 18 May 2007, 2007-2008 *RW*, p. 736, note V. Sagaert. See on this decision also L. De Boel, 'Dan toch zakelijke rechten op het openbaar domein?' (note under Cass. 18 May 2007), 2008 *T.Gem.*, p. 75; V. Sagaert, 'Opstal en openbaar domein: een doorbraak' (note under Cass. 18 May 2007), 2007-2008 *RW*, pp. 737-740; D. Van Heuven, 'Zakelijke rechten op openbaar domein zijn mogelijk' (note under Cass. 18 May 2007), 2008 *TBO*, p. 11.

66 M.A. Flamme, *Droit Administratif*, Brussel, Bruylant, 1989, n°. 420bis ; C. Mostin, 'Superficie et emphytéose: aspects civils', in *Répertoire notarial*, Brussel, Larcier, 2004, n°. 110; Sagaert, 2014, pp. 134-135, n°. 156; V. Sagaert, 'Openbaar domein: van dijkbreuk tot doorbraak', *in* K. Deketelaere, D. D'Hooghe & A. Draye (eds.), *Liber amicorum Marc Boes*, Brugge, die Keure, 2011, p. 440-441, n°. 15; V. Sagaert & R. Jansen, 'Goederenrecht: de gestage groei naar een conventioneel vermogensrecht', 2011-2012 *RW*, p. 68-73; K.

non-disposability of the public domain[67] to an *in concreto* admissibility of property rights on the public domain.[68] New under the reformed property law, is the possibility to establish perpetual rights in rem when these rights are granted to erect structures belonging to the public domain.[69]

5 Horizontal Property Split and Multiple Land Use Through the Creation of a Perpetual Building Right

5.1 *Multiple Land Use*

As indicated earlier, the qualification of floating homes as immovable goods (see *supra* 2.2), subject to component formation (see *supra* 2.3) and immovable accession (see *supra* 3), on the one hand, is important for the legal design of the floating real estate project. On the other hand, we concluded (see *supra* 4) that that the underlying water and land, to which the waterhouse is connected by means of brackets and poles, is part of the public domain. All combined, the immovable waterhouse will accede to the underlying subsoil and thus could potentially become part of the public domain too. This would lead to the undesirable outcome that the waterhouse would be administered by the same public or private entity that manages the underlying river. Therefore, it will be necessary for the legal juritecture of floating real estate projects to create a horizontal property split between the floating object and the underlying ground.[70] In other words, it is crucial that the

---

Vanhove, 'Het private gebruik van overheidsgoederen', in *Themis. Goederenrecht*, Brugge, Die Keure, 2009, p. 12; H. Vuye & A. Vandenburie, 'Droits réels et personnels sur le domaine public: vers la fin des (in) certitudes …(?)', 2010 *TBBR*, pp. 114-129.

67 In traditional case law and legal doctrine, the creation of property rights on public domain goods was impossible. See Belgian Court of Cassation 25 September 2000, 2000 *Arr.Cass.*, p. 1428; Cass. 27 May 1983, *Pas.* 1983, vol. I, 1080; Dekkers & Dirix, 2005, n°. 392; J. De Staercke, 'Het Hof van Cassatie over het openbaar domein: vliegen op automatische piloot?', 2003 *TBO*, pp. 101-106; J. De Staercke, 'Onvervreemdbaarheid van het openbaar domein. Een rechtsvergelijkende studie', *TBP* 2003, vol. 2, p. 81, n°. 13; S. Van Garsse, *De concessie in het raam van de publiek-private samenwerking*, Brugge, Die Keure, 2007, p. 86, n°. 164; F. Van Neste, *Zakenrecht* in *Beginselen van Belgisch Privaatrecht*, Brussel, Story-Scientia ,1990, p. 181, n.° 98A.
Administrative use rights, such as a domain concession or license, on public domain property were already possible, but only if they were compatible with the destination of the public domain and the laws of public service. See Sagaert, 2021, pp. 250-256, n°. 258-268.

68 Sagaert & Lecocq, 2019, p. 196; D'Hooghe & Van Den Langenbergh, 2019, p. 272, n°. 63.

69 Article 3.169 paragraph 2 Belgian CC (emphyteusis right); Article 3.180 paragraph 2, 1° Belgian CC (building right); Sagaert, 2021, p. 915 & pp. 1015-1016, n°. 1013 & 1119; Sagaert & Lecocq, 2019, p. 355 & pp. 372-373.

70 See on the concept of a 'horizontal property split': Bouly, 2015, 600 p; Ploeger, 1997, p. 3, n°. 4; Sagaert, 2021, p. 975, n°. 1074; V. Sagaert, *De vergeten dimensie van het eigendomsrecht. Openingsrede op de Plechtige*

underlying land – and related to this, the water of the stream or river in which the waterhouse is placed – can be used by different actors, namely a private owner and a public body. In the case of so-called 'multiple land use', multiple parties may, on the basis of one or more limited rights in rem or via division into apartment rights use the available space above and below ground for different purposes.[71] In what follows, we examine how such horizontal property split and multiple land use for waterhouses can be legally formalised through the establishment of a building right.

5.2 *Building Rights: General Takings*

Immovable accession and, consequently, the ownership shift in favour of the landowner can be interrupted by the establishment of an – independent or accessory[72] – building right.[73] Article 3.177 CC defines the building right as: "A property use right, which grants ownership on volumes, whether or not built, which are situated, in their totality or partly, on, above or under the ground of someone else, in order to have constructions or plantations on it".[74] The building right must be established on a volume above, on or under the ground,[75] which, moreover, needs to be sufficiently independent. Consequently, no

Openingszitting van het 114e werkingsjaar van de Balie van Brussel, Antwerpen, Intersentia, 2008, p. 3, n°. 3; T.H.D. Struycken, *De numerus clausus in het goederenrecht*, Deventer, Kluwer, 2007, p. 447, n°. 6.9.2.2.

71 See Bouly, 2015, pp. 380-392 & pp. 481-496; Mes, Ploeger & Janssen, 2016, p. 167 *et seq.*; Ploeger, 1997, 375 p.; Sagaert, 2008, p. 3, n°. 3; Sagaert, 2009, pp. 21-103; Sagaert, 2019, p. 27, n°. 44 *et seq.*; N. Verheyden-Jeanmart & P.P. Renson, 'La propriété et les enjeux urbanistiques du troisième millénaire. La propriété des volumes', in A. Wijffels (ed.), *Le Code civil entre ius commune et droit privé européen*, Brussel, Bruylant, 2005, pp. 333-358.

72 An accessory building right arises from the establishment of another personal or property right, such as a lease right, usufruct right or emphyteusis right, on the basis whereof the holder of such right has a competence to erect a building. The holder then accessory acquires a building right, which is dependent of the main right in rem. See Article 3.182 Belgian CC; Bouly, 2015, pp. 312-356, n°. 262-294; I. Durant, *Droit des biens*, Brussel, Larcier, 2017, p. 421, n°. 556; D. Michiels, 'Het accessoir opstalrecht', 2007 *T.Not.*, pp. 213-227; M. Muylle & K. Swinnen, 'Het juridische regime van accessoire opstalrechten' (note under Cass. 12 juni 2014), 2016 *TBO*, pp. 303-307; V. Sagaert, 'Het opstalrecht in het nieuwe goederenrecht: een eigentijdse volume-eigendom', *T. Not.* 2022, vol. 6, pp. 531-559; N. Van Damme, 'Opstalrechten, verzakingen aan het recht van natrekking en wetsontduiking: stand van zaken en toekomstperspectieven', 2019 *T.Not.*, p. 87, n°. 12; T. Van Sinay, 'Bouwen op andermans grond', *in* J. Kokelenberg *et al.* (eds.), *Eigendom/Propriété*, Brugge, die Keure, 1996, p. 348, n°. 60.

73 G. Blockx, F. Lens & L. Wynant, *Erfpacht, opstal en erfdienstbaarheden*, Mechelen, Kluwer, 2006, p. 65; N. Carette, 'Opstalrecht', *in* J. Baeck, *Het nieuwe goederenrecht*, Antwerpen, Intersentia, 2021, p. 492, n°. 7-8; A. Heyvaert, 'Beschouwingen over de afstand van het recht van natrekking en de horizontaal gescheiden onroerende eigendom', 1964 *TPR*, p. 338, n°. 9; Lecocq, 2012, p. 277, n°. 110.
This is also the case in Dutch law: Book 5, Title 8 Dutch CC; Snijders & Rank-Berenschot, 2022, n°. 683; W.H.M. Reehuis *et al.*, 2019, p. 464, n°. 538.

74 See article 5:101 Dutch CC.

75 See on what is understood under the notion 'volume': Explanatory Memorandum, p. 332; N. Bernard, 'Droit d'emphytéose et de superficie' *in* N. Bernard (ed.), *Le droit des biens réformé*, Brussel, Larcier, 2021,

building right can exist on mere improvements and repairs, as they do not fit within the definition of 'autonomous volume'.[76] Although, as previously stated (see *supra* 2.3), they are inherent components, because they are at least functionally incorporated in the subsoil, waterhouses are still sufficiently independent constructions: they fulfill a different function than the underlying volume, namely housing (see also *infra* 5.2). The independent nature of floating houses seems at first sight largely contradictory with the qualification as inherent components and in conflict with the aforementioned unity principle (see also *supra* 2.3). However, it is in fact possible to create a building right on a sufficiently independent inherent component. The unity principle is thus to be interpreted on a spectrum.

5.3 *From Limited Duration to a Perpetual Building Right*

As stated in Article 3.180 paragraph 1 of the CC, a building right can be established for a maximum duration of 99 years.[77] Compared to the former property law, this is a significant extension of the time limit: before the property law reform, the maximum period for a building right was only 50 years.[78] Under the new property law, it is now even possible to create a perpetual building right for (1) purposes of public domain or (2) for a building right on complex and heterogeneous immovable property (see article 3.180, second paragraph CC). These two forms of perpetual building rights constitute a functional equivalent of the French so-called 'volume property'. The only difference is that the Belgian building right is still subject to negative prescription if it is not used for more than 30

pp. 266-270, n°. 51-56; Bouly, 2015, n°. 383; H. Perinet-Marquet, 'Actualités de la dissociation des droits sur le sol en droit privé', *RDI* 2009, vol. 1, p. 16; Sagaert, 2021, p. 999, n°. 1099.

76 Belgian Court of Cassation 23 December 1943, *Pas.* 1944, vol. I, p. 124; Brussel 27 February 2001, 2001 *RW*, p. 844; Rb. Kortrijk 14 November 1947, 1950 *T.Not.*, p. 17; Derine, Van Neste & Vandenberghe, 1974, n°. 1024; V. Sagaert, 'De zakenrechtelijke motoren van een circulaire vastgoedeconomie: een SWOT-analyse', 2021 *TPR*, p. 1547, n°. 7; A. Van Muylder & J. Verstappen, 'Actuele problemen inzake het recht van natrekking, de verzaking daaraan, en het recht van opstal', 1992 *T.Not.*, p. 293, n°. 22; Verheye, 2019, n°. 56. In Dutch law the same issue occurs. See Ploeger, 1997, p. 218; E.C.M Wolfert, 'Bestanddeel of zaak? Over het onderscheid en de samenhang tussen de artikelen 3:4 en 5:20 NBW (II, slot)', *WPNR* 2003, vol. 5625, p. 280; P.J. Van Der Plank, 'Is het mogelijk artikel 3:4 BW bestanddelen te verzelfstandigen door middel van het vestigen van een recht van opstal?', 2016 *WPNR*, pp. 399-403.

77 Sagaert, 2021, pp. 1009-1011, n°. 1111-114.
According to article 5:104 paragraph 2 *iuncto* 5:86 Dutch CC, parties are free to determine the duration of building rights and can thus in principle establish a perpetual building right. Nevertheless, the building right can be ended by virtue of article 5:87 and 5:79 *iuncto* 5:104 Dutch CC. See W.H.M. Reehuis *et al.* (eds.), 2019, p. 556, n°. 676-677.

78 Article 4 Building rights act of 10 January 1824. However, if the building right was accessory to a emphyteusis right, consequently a maximum duration of 99 years applied to the accessory building right (article 2 Emphyteusis right act of 10 January 1824).

years, while a right of ownership is not.[79] Volume ownership implies: "the division of the ownership right of a property into different independent volumes, which are located both above and below the ground surface which may be both vertically and horizontally limited and each independently accessible".[80]

The first exceptional perpetual building right can be applied if the building volume belongs to the public domain on the one hand and the land belongs to a private individual (Article 3.180 paragraph 2, 1° CC).[81] This way, the legislator wanted to create a way to avoid that a private land owner would acquire the ownership of a public domain property as a result of immovable accession (see *supra* 3).[82] However, it does not seem possible to apply this first perpetual building right to floating houses, since in that case, the opposite situation occurs: the underlying ground and water mass belong to the public domain, but the waterhouse is itself private property.

Secondly, it is possible to divide "a complex and heterogeneous immovable property comprising several volumes which can be used independently and diversly and which do not have any common parts" in different volumes with various owners.[83] This way, it is for the first time possible to implement a perpetual ownership split outside the hypothesis of apartment co-ownership.[84] Four conditions must be met: there should be a (1) complex and (2) heterogeneous immovable property including (3) volumes that are susceptible to independent use or management and (4) that do not have any common parts.[85]

79 Explanatory Memorandum, p. 337; A. Appelmans, 'Emphyteusis rights (long lease) and superficies rights (building rights) in the new Belgian Property Law', in *EPLJ* 2021, vol. 10, p. 107, n°. 27; S. Bouly, 'Een plaats voor volume-eigendom naar Belgisch recht?', *in* X., *Opening Doors. Verslagboek Notarieel congres 2017*, Brussel, Larcier, 2017, pp. 362-386; Sagaert, 2021, p. 1012, n°. 1115; Sagaert, 2019, p. 131, n°. 211; L. Tranchant, 'Du droit de superficie à la propriété modulaire', *in* J.-Y. Chérot & S. Cimamonti, *Le droit entre autonomie et ouverture*, Brussel, Bruylant, 2013, p. 765, n°. 3.
Also under Dutch law recently - and specifically in the context of floating real estate - the introduction of a form of volume ownership has been proposed through so-called "three-dimensional ownership". See Mes, Ploeger & Janssen, 2016, pp. 181-182; A.J. Mes, 'Driedimensionaal eigendom', *WPNR* 2014, vol. 7043, pp. 1189-1199.

80 Sagaert, 2009, p. 25, n°. 2. See also J.-P. Bertrel, 'Les ensembles immobiliers complexes', 1994 *Droit et Patrimoine*, p. 45; Bouly, 2017, p. 373.

81 This can be for example the case when a public parking garage is built under a privately owned apartment building or when a metro network is located under private homes. See Explanatory Memorandum, p. 341; Sagaert, 2021, pp. 1015-1017, n°.1119-1122; Sagaert, 2019, pp. 264-265, n°. 416-417. Before the reform see: Brussel 2 April 1980, 1981 *RNB*, p. 364; Luik 7 December 1923, 1924 *BJ*, p. 198; P.-Y. Erneux, 'La propriété en volumes. Flexibilité et évolution des programmes immobiliers et par voie de conséquence, de leur organisation juridique', 2014 *JT*, p. 91, n°. 12; Hansenne, 1996, n°. 1239; P. Lecocq *et al.*, *Manuel de droit des biens, 2: Droits réels principaux démembrés*, Brussel, Larcier, 2016, p. 367, n°. 6.

82 J. De Staercke, *Domeingoederenrecht*, Antwerpen, Intersentia, 2006, p. 85, n°. 87; Erneux, 2014, p. 91, n°. 12; Lecocq, 2012, p. 367, n°. 6; Kokelenberg, Van Sinay & Vuye, 2001, p. 862, n°. 17.

83 Sagaert, 2021, pp. 1017-1021, n°. 1124-1130.

84 Explanatory Memorandum, p. 330; Appelmans, 2021, p. 107, n°. 27.

85 See on these conditions: Carette, 2021, pp. 503-506, n°. 20; Sagaert, 2019, p. 130, n°. 209; R. Timmermans & N. Van Damme, 'De volume-eigendom afgetoetst aan de wet van 4 februari 2020 houdende het nieuwe

The first condition requires that a 'complex' immovable property, including several (at least two) volumes, is the object of the building right. It must be a building in which different volumes are stacked on top of each other.[86] According to some authors, it is required that one or more specific building rights exist on the same land plot.[87] This first condition already calls into question the application of the perpetual building right to floating homes. Only one building right is established on the waterhouse itself. However, one could argue that this building right is not a general building right because the building right is established on a specific volume, namely the floating property only. The underlying water volume is not the object of the building right. *A contrario* there would still be two volumes, namely the residential volume and a so-called 'water volume', which are stacked on top of each other.

The second condition means that the volumes must have different functions or destinations.[88] It is therefore uncertain whether Article 3.180, 2° CC can apply to floating houses, because these do not have a heterogeneous function. Usually, they are purely intended for residential purposes.[89] However, like we said earlier, we could argue that the underlying water could be considered as a separate volume, with a separate function to fulfil: the water volume is part of the public domain and has a public purpose (see *supra* 4).

Thirdly, the volumes should be legally and factually autonomous or independent volumes: they should be separately accessible, possibly via an easement.[90] This condition is closely related to the fourth condition that there should be no common parts between the different volumes. It is most likely that the aforementioned 'housing volume' and 'water volume' would not have common parts, so this condition should not be an impediment for the legal design of floating houses.

To summarise, if we want to apply the perpetual building right of Article 3.180, paragraph 2, 2° CC, the conditions, and more specifically the concepts 'complexity' and 'heterogeneity' of the immovable property, should be interpreted broadly. Another, more

---

goederenrecht', 2020 *T.App.*, p. 6-8, n°. 7-12. According to the Explanatory Memorandum a residential building, a public place or an above-ground shopping centre with an underground car park fall within the scope of this provision. See Explanatory Memorandum, p. 339.

86 Sagaert, 2021, p. 1018, n°. 1026.

87 See article 3.179 Belgian CC concerning the object of the building right: a specific building right is explicitly limited in its scope (height x width x depth). See also Carette, 2021, pp. 494-495, n°. 11; Timmermans & Van Damme, 2020, p. 7, n°. 10.

88 For example residential vs. commercial vs. parking (Explanatory Memorandum, p. 339). However, see critically with regard to the required functional heterogeneity: Bouly, 2015, pp. 489-490; Carette, 2021, pp. 503-504, n°. 20 (who argues for replacing this condition with a criterion of 'multinormativity').

89 However, in more complex floating structures, such as for example floating cities, where different functions (residential, commercial, industrial etc.) may co-exist, this condition would undoubtedly be fulfilled. However, these floating structures are beyond the scope of this contribution.

90 Explanatory Memorandum, p. 339-340; Carette, 2021, p. 504, n. 20.

far-reaching, solution for the creation of a perpetual building right on floating homes could be to include, via amendment, a separate exception category (3°) for floating structures. At the moment, this amendment seems premature, given the current level of development of floating construction in Belgium, but this could possibly be considerable in the future.

6 Conclusion: Living on Water – 'Fluctuat Nec Mergitur'?

At the end of this chapter, we try to provide a comprehensive answer to the questions whether and how to structure the legal design of floating real estate projects. The findings of previous research are systematically explained.

6.1 Immovable by Incorporation

First, the qualification of waterhouses as movable or immovable goods is crucial. In the first part of this chapter, we have argued that under current reformed Belgian law, these houses can be considered as immovable goods by incorporation on the basis of the extended and subjectivised incorporation criterion for immovable property. The ability of the houses to move up and down, depending on the water level, does not prevent this qualification. An amendment to Article 3.47 Belgian Civil Code thus seems initially unnecessary for the immovable qualification of floating structures.

6.2 Immovable Accession

Secondly, we conclude that, given the existence of a uniform incorporation criterion for both immovables by incorporation and immovable accession, floating homes under Belgian law accede to the underlying soil, to which the waterhouse is connected. The landowner automatically acquires ownership of the waterhouse. Functionally, the exclusion of the immovable accession for floating real estate seems attractive, since in that case no horizontal property split is necessary. Nevertheless, we argue for the application of immovable accession for floating homes. Concluding the opposite would, given the uniform incorporation criterion, result in confirming the movable qualification, which is not a desirable outcome.

6.3 *Inherent Components*

The notion 'inherent component' lies at the basis of the incorporation criterion and the related unity principle forms, consequently, the foundation for both immovables by incorporation and immovable accession. Under Belgian law, floating homes are therefore qualified as inherent components of the underlying land plot. Since waterhouses meet the extended incorporation criterion for immovables by incorporation, they can also be considered as functionally necessary inherent components, regardless of whether or not they are necessary to complete the underlying soil.

6.4 *Public Domain*

A fourth fundamental issue for the legal design of floating real estate projects is the fact that under Belgian law the water volume and the subsoil on which the waterhouse is placed, is part of the public domain. Property rights can only be established on public domain goods if the public destination of the good does not prevent this and if this encumbrance does not interfere with the public service.

6.5 *Building Rights*

The above conclusions are crucial for the legal design or 'juritecture' of waterhouses. Subsequently, we explored the possibilities for multiple land use and horizontal property split. We limited this research to the question whether a building right could be created on a floating volume. Since the waterhouse can be considered as a sufficiently independent volume, a building right can be established. However, both under the former and reformed property law, building rights remain primarily limited in time. Even if two forms of perpetual building rights have been introduced, for floating homes, the application conditions 'complexity' and 'heterogeneity' of article 3.180, 2nd paragraph, 2° CC seem to remain problematic. Nonetheless, we think that this problem can be solved and the creation of a perpetual building right on waterhouses is possible, if a flexible interpretation of these criteria is adopted. This way, some sort of floating volume-property can be introduced in Belgian property law.

6.6 *Fluctuat Nec Mergitur*

On the basis of the forgoing, we conclude that the legal design of floating homes should be possible under current Belgian property law. As long as a broad interpretation of the incorporation criterion and the notion 'inherent components' is upheld and the conditions for the perpetual building right of article 3.180 CC are not interpreted too strictly, Belgian property law is flexible enough to realise this new form of 'water architecture'. 'Fluctuat nec mergitur'[91] is an appropriate phrase in this case. However, there are still a lot of uncertainties and the legal design of floating homes will have to follow the current evolutions in property law. The developments in Belgian case law and legal doctrine will therefore determine the legal and practical feasibility of floating real estate projects in the future.

91 'It is thrown back and forth by the waves but does not sink'. See Paris city emblem (https://www.parisunlocked.com/history-of-paris/fluctuat-nec-mergitur-paris-motto-meaning/)

7 PROPERTY AND REMEDIES IN THE CASE OF INTERFERENCE WITH CRYPTOASSETS: A VIEW FROM ENGLAND AND WALES

Katie McCay[*]

1 INTRODUCTION

If someone interferes with tangible property, the available private law causes of action in England and Wales are relatively settled.[1] The same is not true with intangibles, with the law still developing its approach. Early cases attempted to find a remedy through causes of action that protected a claimant's possessory interest in the thing. These causes of action failed, because intangible assets, which are incapable of possession, cannot be protected by actions protecting possession. Instead, the cases on the interference with cryptoassets have taken a different approach, one which emphasises the proprietary aspects of the asset in question. Some cases have gone down the route of injunctive relief. These are interim or temporary remedies that are usually granted before a full trial. Most of the remedies granted will only operate where the asset in question is property. This has led to some discussion about whether cryptoassets are property. The proprietary status of cryptoassets is very significant; not just at the interim remedy state. Whether or not an asset is property determines 'the nature and scope of potential rights, remedies and defences.'[2]

This chapter firstly considers cryptoassets within the wider personal property landscape in England. It then sets out the remedies that were unsuccessfully attempted where other intangibles were misappropriated. It then outlines some of the remedies for interference with cryptoassets that have been discussed in the case law. The purpose of this is to demonstrate that the remedies that have been used focus on the claimant's *property* right in the asset, rather than a possessory interest in it. This is to be expected, as it sidesteps the issue that intangibles cannot be possessed. The problem with this approach is that the relevant case law has concluded, without much discussion, that cryptoassets are property,

* PhD Candidate, University of Bristol Law School.

1 Later references to England in a jurisdictional context should be taken to mean England and Wales unless otherwise stated.

2 S. Baker & J. Bihary, 'From Cryptic to (Some) Clarity: English Law and Policy Rising to the Challenge of Cryptoassets', Journal of International Banking Law and Regulation, Vol. 37, No. 2 2022, p. 311.

at least in the particular context to which the particular case relates, such as for the purpose of an interim remedy.[3] There are obvious incentives for declaring cryptocurrencies as property, but without clearly articulating why these assets are property, the case law creates a shaky foundation on which to develop the law. It is therefore necessary to consider whether these assets are justifiably categorised as property in the first place, and whether the analysis on property aspects can apply beyond its current application at the interim stage.

The question of whether cryptoassets are property has two distinct but related threads. The first is whether cryptoassets can be called property even where they do not fit neatly into the pre-existing categories of property. The second is whether cryptoassets have the characteristics of property in general. This chapter seeks to consider the first question by giving an overview of the personal property landscape in English law as it relates to intangibles. It then considers the proprietary aspects of cryptoassets.

2 What Is a Cryptoasset and Where Do They Fit Within English Personal Property Law?

A cryptoasset is a type of intangible asset.[4] It is created on a decentralised network, using blockchain technology. It is verified by consensus using cryptography and exists virtually.[5] Popular cryptoassets include cryptocurrencies, such as Bitcoin. Unlike standard currency, which has a central authority, cryptocurrencies are created in a decentralised manner, without any input from a central authority or trusted third party.[6] Some cryptoassets have

3 The reason context is mentioned in these circumstances is that cases heard at interim level require a lower standard of proof than cases at full trial. As such, the argument that a cryptoasset is property requires less evidence at interim level than it would at full trial.

4 This chapter uses the term 'intangible', rather than 'intangible property'. This is deliberate, in an area with rapidly developing technology there are new types of digital assets which emerge that the law has not (yet) declared to be property. As will be seen throughout this chapter, the proprietary status of cryptoassets is very significant; whether or not an asset is property determines "the nature and scope of potential rights, remedies and defences": Steven Baker & Julia Bihary, 'From Cryptic to (Some) Clarity: English Law and Policy Rising to the Challenge of Cryptoassets' (2022) 37 Journal of International Banking Law and Regulation 311, 311.

5 S. Green, 'Cryptocurrencies: The Underlying Technology', in Cryptocurrencies in Public and Private Law, Oxford, Oxford University Press, 2019, paras. 1.01-1.05. Consensus means that a majority of participants (called nodes) on the network agree on the data recorded on the distributed ledger.

6 J. Brown & M. Pawlowski, 'The Challenge of Identifying Private Property under English Law,' Conveyancer and Property Lawyer, Vol. 3 2022, p. 309; S. Nakamoto, 'Bitcoin: A Peer-to-Peer Electronic Cash System', pp. 1-9; K. F. Low & E. G. Teo, 'Bitcoins and Other Cryptocurrencies as Property?', Law, Innovation and Technology, Vol. 9 No. 2 2017, p. 236.

been declared to be property, at least in a context specific manner to which the case relates.[7] Thus it is helpful to set out the property law landscape in which these assets fit.

English property law is divided into real property and personal property. Real property refers to land and interests in land. This category consists of not just the actual piece of land, but also the things attached to it, as well as rights relating to the land such as rights of way, mortgages and charges over the land.[8] Real property is not the focus of this chapter. Instead, it considers personal property. Personal property in England is a residual but broad category, consisting of any type of property which is not real property.[9] Within personal property, there are two categories, things in possession and things in action.[10] A thing in possession is a piece of tangible moveable property. The rights in this type of property can be enforced by taking possession of it. A thing in action is intangible personal property that is characterised as a right enforceable by action.[11] As it has no physical presence, the rights in it can only be enforced by legal action against a specific person. Examples of things in action include shares,[12] and Intellectual property.[13] Things in action have no existence outside of the legal system. The legal system is necessary to recognise the right, without a legal system to recognise the right, the thing does not exist. By contrast, irrespective of whether there is a legal system to recognise rights in things in possession, the tangible thing still exists.

This categorisation has traditionally been taken to be exhaustive in English law. Anything that is personal property is either a thing in possession or a thing in action, never both, never neither.[14] Digitalisation and the rise of cryptoassets have created intangible assets which do not fit neatly into this categorisation. In *AA v. Persons Unknown*,[15] a case which among other things, considered whether cryptocurrencies were property, Bryan J noted that cryptocurrencies were not a thing in possession because they are virtual and so cannot be possessed. They were also not a thing in action because 'they

7 AA v. Persons Unknown & Ors, [2019] EWHC 3556 (Comm); Osbourne v. Persons Unknown and Ozone Networks Inc, [2022] EWHC 1021 (Comm); Ion Science Ltd v. Persons Unknown and others, (unreported), 21 December 2020 (Commercial Court); Wang v. Darby, [2021] EWHC 3054 (Comm).

8 E. McKendrick, Goode and McKendrick on Commercial Law, 6th edn, (2021), paras. 2.17-2.18.

9 E. McKendrick, Goode and McKendrick on Commercial Law, 6th edn, (2021), paras. 2.15-2.16.

10 Colonial Bank v. Whinney, [1885] 30 ChD 261, (Fry LJ).

11 Howard W Elphinstone, 'What Is a Chose in Action? Law Quarterly Review Vol. 9, 1893, p. 311; WS Holdsworth, 'The History of the Treatment of "Choses" in Action by the Common Law' Harvard Law Review, Vol. 33, 1920, p. 997.

12 Colonial Bank v. Whinney, [1885] 30 ChD 261.

13 Chaplin v. Leslie Frewin (Publishers) Ltd, [1966] Ch 71, (Danckwerts LJ). Patents, a type of intellectual property, are not things in action: Patents Act 1977, s. 30, but this is only because patents are subject to statutory classification.

14 Colonial Bank v. Whinney, [1885] 30 ChD 261, (Fry LJ). Fry LJ dissented, but his decision was affirmed on appeal.

15 AA v. Persons Unknown & Ors, [2019] EWHC 3556 (Comm).

[did] not embody any right capable of being enforced by action.'[16] Bryan J nevertheless concluded that cryptocurrencies could be property.[17]

Although strictly speaking, things in action are a species of property that are only enforceable by legal action,[18] the category is broader, and has at times been interpreted as including all forms of intangible property, irrespective of whether they are in actual fact a right enforceable by action.[19] For instance, *Colonial Bank v. Whinney*[20] sets out that personal property is either a thing in possession or a thing in action. In his judgment, Fry LJ approves a very expansive definition of a thing in action.[21] Citing the work of Joshua Williams,[22] Fry LJ notes that other forms of personal wealth, such as shares, patents and copyrights are: 'usually spoken of as [things] in action' when they are, strictly speaking, 'personal property of an incorporeal nature.'[23] Fry LJ's dissent was affirmed on appeal and the House of Lords echoes Fry LJ's sentiments that the realm of things in action is broader than the strict literal definition. Lord Blackburn, writing in the late 1800s, notes that: 'in modern times lawyers have accurately or inaccurately used the phrase '[things] in action' as including all personal chattels that are not in possession.'[24] This leads to the result that what constitutes a thing in action is broad, with few unifying features.[25] It may be that a more accurate description of what unites property termed a 'thing in action' is that it is incorporeal, rather than a right enforceable by action. If that is correct, then the need for another additional category is redundant.

The issue of categorisation of personal property is relevant to cryptoassets for a number of reasons. Firstly, categorising an asset as property means that proprietary remedies may

16 AA v. Persons Unknown & Ors, [2019] EWHC 3556 (Comm), Bryan J.

17 Within the context of an application for a proprietary injunction.

18 Torkington v. Magee, [1902] 2 KB 427.

19 Bridge & others, The Law of Personal Property, 3rd ed., London, Sweet & Maxwell, 2021, para. 4-004. Historically, it was doubted whether Intellectual Property could be a thing in action as strictly speaking, they are negative rights to complain of interference, rather than a positive right to enforce. However, unless where statute says otherwise, Intellectual Property is classified as a thing in action: Chaplin v. Leslie Frewin (Publishers) Ltd, [1966] Ch 71, p. 93. For an example in the case law, see Fetch.AI Ltd and Another v. Persons Unknown and others, [2021] EWHC 2254 (Comm), para. 9.

20 Colonial Bank v. Whinney, [1885] 30 ChD 261.

21 I.e., a right enforceable by action. Fry LJ's approval of this broad definition suggests an acceptance of the inevitable; where property must be categorised as either a thing in action or a thing in possession, then choses in action will be a residual category that covers property which can neither be possessed nor enforceable by legal action.

22 J. Williams, Principles of the Law of Personal Property, 12th ed, 7.

23 Colonial Bank v. Whinney, [1885] 30 ChD 261, at p. 276.

24 Colonial Bank v. Whinney, (1886) 11 App. Cas. 426, at p. 440.

25 Holdsworth, 1920, 998. Indeed, Halsbury's Laws of England, Vol.13, 2017, para. 1, n. 2 suggests that the expression has so many meanings attached to it and has been and still is employed to denote so many and such various classes of things, that it is impossible to give an accurate and complete definition of what it means and may include at the present day. The various kinds of property included under the term have little in common beyond the characteristic fact of their not being subjects of actual physical possession."

apply. Secondly, there is the question of whether something that strictly falls outside the categorisation of the thing in action and thing in possession can be classified as property. The case law in England has concluded that even where an asset is strictly neither a thing in action nor a thing in possession,[26] it can still be personal property. This suggests that something that consists of neither a right enforceable by legal action nor a right to possession of a thing to be property. However, the view that a third category of personal property is necessary is misguided; instead the categorisation of a thing in action has had the flexibility to encompass property that is more accurately described as intangible or incorporeal. It has not been limited to only those intangible assets that are enforceable by action, nor does it need to be limited to these assets when considering new types of property, such as cryptoassets.[27]

3 EARLY CASES INVOLVING WRONGFUL INTERFERENCE WITH INTANGIBLES: THE INAPPLICABILITY OF THE PROPERTY TORTS

The first cases in England concerning interference with intangibles predate cryptoassets. Nevertheless, these cases set the scene and closed off a potential remedy that may have otherwise been tried in the cryptoassets context. The leading case here is *OBG v. Allan*.[28] *OBG* concerned, among other things, whether the wrongful but good faith interference with contractual debts, a type of thing in action, could amount to the tort of conversion.

The tort of conversion is the primary way tangible personal property is protected in England.[29] It is a tort that protects a claimant's *possessory* interest in a piece of tangible property.[30] As such, there is no way of using tort to directly protect a person's *ownership* rights in a thing. For a claimant to establish that the defendant has converted her property, she must prove that the defendant's conduct was inconsistent with her possessory rights in the thing, and the conduct was so extensive an encroachment on the rights to exclude her from use and possession of the property.[31]

In *OBG*, two receivers were appointed over a company that was struggling financially. The problem was that the receivers' appointment was invalid, but they were unaware of

26 AA v. Persons Unknown & Ors, [2019] EWHC 3556 (Comm); Swift v. Dairywise Farms Ltd (No 1), [2000] 1 WLR 1177; Armstrong DLW GmbH v. Winnington Networks Ltd, [2013] Ch. 156.

27 It does not just relate to cryptoassets, and includes other types of intangible personal property that are not rights enforceable by action, such as waste management licences, import quotas or carbon emissions allowances.

28 OBG Ltd v. Allan, [2007] UKHL 27.

29 This is the closest English law gets to the vindicatio and the modern-day equivalents such as that found in Bürgerliches Gesetzbuch §985.

30 OBG Ltd v. Allan, [2007] UKHL 27, para. 222.

31 Kuwait Airways Corp v. Iraqi Airways Co & Anor, [2002] UKHL 19, paras. 77-78 (Lord Nicholls).

this fact. The receivers, acting in good faith, liquidated assets, sold land and property, and settled debts with customers for a lower price than to that which they were entitled. A conversion action for the tangible assets was successful, but the conversion action for the contractual debts, which made up most of the business' capital, failed. Lord Hoffmann, who delivered the most significant speech for the majority, wanted to keep the tort rooted in its historical origins, as a tort protecting possession.[32] Lords Brown and Walker agreed. The minority of Baroness Hale and Lord Nicholls recognised the historical origins, but felt there was no reason to remain bound by history.[33] As the tort protects a claimant's possession, rather than their ownership, it is unsurprising that a majority of the House of Lords held that contractual rights, as things in action, which cannot be possessed, cannot be the subject matter of the tort of conversion. Nevertheless, *OBG* was and continues to be an important case concerning remedies for the interference with intangibles.

Subsequent cases have applied *OBG*, deciding that remedies involving possession did not apply to intangibles. For instance, in *Your Response v. Datateam Business Media*, a lien, a type of possessory security, did not cover an electronic database.[34] Other cases have held that the same action could not apply to emails,[35] nor other types of electronically stored information.[36] This was to be expected, given that these things were intangible and could not be possessed.[37]

4 Interim Remedies

Interim remedies are orders granted by a Court, usually before the issue has reached full trial. They give a court the power to do things in relation to persons or assets. One example is the interim injunction,[38] which is 'a court order prohibiting a person from doing something or requiring a person to do something.'[39] Interim remedies may alternatively require a defendant to deliver up property,[40] or restrain the defendant from dealing with particular property, irrespective of whether it is within the jurisdiction.[41]

Much of the discussion on remedies for the interference with cryptoassets has been at the interim stage. This is an important limitation, as it means that the interim remedies

32 OBG Ltd v. Allan, [2007] UKHL 27, paras. 100 and 106.

33 OBG Ltd and Others v. United Kingdom, ECtHR App No 48407/07 (November 2011), paras 221, 224-225, 308-309.

34 Your Response v. Datateam Business Media, [2014] EWCA Civ 281.

35 Thunder Air Ltd v. Hilmarsson, [2008] EWHC 355 (Ch).

36 The Environment Agency v. Churngold Recycling Ltd, [2014] EWCA Civ 909.

37 In addition, these things were not property.

38 Civil Procedure Rules, 25.1.

39 Civil Procedure Rules, Glossary; S. Gee, Gee on Commercial Injunctions, 7th ed, (2021), paras. 1-006.

40 Civil Procedure Rules, 25.1(e).

41 Civil Procedure Rules, 25.1(f).

applied where cryptoassets are misappropriated are not directly comparable to the final remedies that were unsuccessful when other intangibles were misappropriated. Nevertheless, discussion of interim remedies in the context is still valuable, as the questions about property considered at the interim level will be relevant in other contexts, such as at the stage of the final remedy.

This section starts by setting out interim injunctions in brief terms, before considering the most popular interim remedies for the misappropriation of cryptoassets, which have been considered in the case law.[42]

4.1 *Interim Injunctive Relief*

As stated above, an injunction is 'a court order prohibiting a person from doing something or requiring a person to do something.'[43] As an injunction can be a remedy that is sought without notice to the defendant, and given that the requirements of complying with an injunction can be a significant limitation on a defendant's freedom to deal with their property, and given that an interim injunction can, and usually does, apply before judgment against a defendant,[44] interim injunctions are subject to the 'balance of convenience test.'[45] The requirements of this are set out in *American Cyanamid Co v. Ethicon Ltd.* In order to grant an interim injunction, the claimant must firstly demonstrate that there is a 'serious question to be tried.'[46] The threshold is low, this requirement ensures that the claimant is not bringing a case that is 'frivolous or vexatious.'[47] Then, the claimant must show that damages are not an adequate remedy or that the defendant would not be

42 Although not all of the following remedies or processes succeeded, a flavour of the claims are as follows: Ion Science Ltd v. Persons Unknown and others, (unreported), 21 December 2020 (Commercial Court), para. 1 (proprietary injunction, a worldwide freezing order and an ancillary disclosure order); Toma v. Murray, [2020] EWHC 2295, para. 1 (interim injunction); Wang v. Darby, [2021] EWHC 3054 (Comm), para. 3 (worldwide freezing order, proprietary injunction, trusts); D'Aloia v. Binance Holdings, [2022] EWHC 1723 (Ch D), para. 1 (interim injunctive relief, disclosure and ancillary orders, trusts); Osbourne v. Persons Unknown and Ozone Networks Inc, [2022] EWHC 1021 (Comm), paras. 3-4 (proprietary freezing order, Bankers Trust order); AA v. Persons Unknown & Ors, [2019] EWHC 3556 (Comm), para. 38 (interim proprietary injunction); Vorotyntseva v. Money-4 Ltd, [2018] EWHC 2596 (Ch), para. 1 (freezing order); Liam David Robertson v. Persons Unknown, (unreported 15th July 2019) (preservation order); L. Chambers, 'The Keepers of the Keys: Remedies and Legal Obligations Following Misappropriations of Cryptocurrency', Journal of Banking and International Finance Law, Vol.11 2016, p. 673; Armstrong DLW GmbH v. Winnington Networks Ltd, [2013] Ch. 156, para. 2 (restitution, proprietary restitution, knowing receipt).

43 Civil Procedure Rules, Glossary; Gee, Gee on Commercial Injunctions, para. 1-006.

44 Shown by reading the Civil Procedure Rules, Part 25.1(a) and 25.2(a) together.

45 American Cyanamid Co. v. Ethicon Ltd., [1975] A.C. 396.

46 American Cyanamid Co., p. 407 (Lord Diplock).

47 American Cyanamid Co., p. 407 (Lord Diplock).

in the 'financial position to pay them.'[48] If damages are not an adequate remedy, the focus then shifts to whether the claimant would be able to give an undertaking in damages in the event that the defendant is successful at trial. These damages are there to compensate the defendant for the restrictions placed on him or her between the application and the trial.[49] In a case where there is doubt over the adequacy of damages for either party, or both parties, then this is resolved by considering the balance of convenience between the parties. The factors to consider vary in type and weight depending on each case.[50] If, following the balance of convenience test, the factors are evenly balanced, then the court will take measures that 'are calculated to preserve the status quo.'[51]

Traditionally, injunctions are not granted where damages would be an adequate remedy,[52] such as where the thing in question is fungible and can easily be replaced on the market, or where the assets could be dissipated.[53] Within the crypto sphere, damages have been inadequate due to the risk of the asset being dissipated or where the defendant is of unknown means, making it unclear whether the defendant will have the financial means to pay.

4.2 Freezing Orders

According to the Civil Procedure Rules, a freezing order is a remedy which restrains a party from moving their assets out of the jurisdiction,[54] or restrains a party from dealing with their assets irrespective of whether these assets are in the jurisdiction.[55] Freezing orders[56] are interim remedies where a (potential) claimant can protect themselves against a defendant who may undermine the efficacy of a future judgment by disposing of certain assets.[57] Unlike that suggested by the terminology, this remedy acts *in personam*, not *in rem*, and so does not usually attach to a specific piece of property.[58] This limitation in the remedy is crucial in cases involving cryptoassets, with the effect that claimants opt for the

48 American Cyanamid Co., p. 408 (Lord Diplock).
49 American Cyanamid Co., p. 408 (Lord Diplock).
50 American Cyanamid Co., p. 408 (Lord Diplock).
51 American Cyanamid Co., p. 408 (Lord Diplock).
52 Co-Operative Insurance Society Ltd v. Argyll Stores (Holdings) Ltd, [1998] AC 1; American Cyanamid Co. v. Ethicon Ltd., [1975] A.C. 396.
53 Watson's Dairies Ltd v. AG Lambert and Partners, [2020] EWHC 2825 (Ch), para. 20 (Marcus Smith J). See generally Hugh Beale (ed), Chitty on Contracts 34th ed., London, Sweet & Maxwell, 2021, pp. 30-79.
54 Civil Procedure Rules, 25.1(1)(f)(i).
55 Civil Procedure Rules, 25.1(1)(f)(ii).
56 Originally called Mareva injunctions after Mareva Compania Naviera SA v. International Bulkcarriers SA, [1975] 2 Lloyd's Rep. 509, [1980] 1 All E.R. 213 CA.
57 I. Goldrein, R. Aird, and A. Grantham, eds., Commercial Litigation: Pre-Emptive Remedies, 3rd ed, (2019), paras. A10-001, A10-010; Les Ambassadeurs Club Ltd v. Songbo Yu, [2021] EWCA Civ 1310, para. 14.
58 Gee, Gee on Commercial Injunctions, para. 1-036.

property freezing order instead. This is a distinct remedy that seeks to preserve assets that belong to the claimant that are in the defendant's control. As above, the *American Cyanamid* principles apply to these claims.[59]

Against this backdrop, proprietary freezing orders have been granted over digital assets which are fungible, such as cryptocurrencies. For instance, in *Ion Science*,[60] Butcher J justifies such an order over fungible (readily interchangeable) property because in a judgment against persons unknown, there was no evidence that the defendants would be able to satisfy the significant monetary judgment.[61] *Danisz v. Persons Unknown*[62] reaches the same conclusion. In *Danisz*, Lane J's reason for favouring an injunction instead of damages was that the assets had already started to be dissipated, and the order was necessary to prevent this.[63] Similar considerations were at play in *AA*, where Bryan J was willing to grant a freezing order over cryptocurrencies. Damages were an inadequate alternative as there was a substantial risk of the assets being dissipated.[64]

5 Can We Call Cryptoassets Property?

This section considers some of the arguments in the case law for treating cryptoassets as property.[65] As will be seen, few cases in England have considered this question in much detail. Other common law jurisdictions have set out the legal principles in a more detailed manner, and so these cases will also be discussed. Additionally, this section will explore the academic arguments for treating cryptoassets as property. These arguments have been much more detailed and considered than the case law. The arguments advanced in this section are that:

- The case law in England and Wales has not considered the question of whether cryptoassets are property in much detail.
- The case law has been poor at identifying the subject of property rights.[66] In other words, the case law has not confidently identified the thing to which property rights attach when cryptoassets are declared to be property.

59 Polly Peck International Plc v. Nadir, [1992] 4 All E.R. 769; AA v. Persons Unknown & Ors, [2019] EWHC 3556 (Comm), para. 62.

60 Ion Science Ltd v. Persons Unknown and others, (unreported), 21 December 2020 (Commercial Court).

61 Ion Science Ltd., para. 17 (Butcher J).

62 [2022] EWHC 280 (QB).

63 Danisz v. Persons Unknown, [2022] EWHC 280 (QB), para. 15 (Lane J).

64 AA v. Persons Unknown & Ors, [2019] EWHC 3556 (Comm), para. 65 (Bryan J).

65 The case law does not set out any arguments *against* cryptoassets being property. This is most likely because the property aspect is uncontested, as it is advantageous for all players in the industry to regard the asset as property.

66 See generally S. Li and S. Wei, 'Cryptocurrencies, Money and Law', Journal of International Banking Law and Regulation, Vol. 38 No. 2, 2023, pp. 57-67.

- Academic contributions have been much stronger at identifying the subject of property. Identifying this is crucial, it is only then that it becomes possible to determine whether this 'thing', the subject of property, is rightfully called property.

5.1 *The Case Law in England and Wales*

This section considers some of the case law that has considered the proprietary status of cryptoassets. It begins with *AA v. Persons Unknown*,[67] the first case to consider the issue in England. It then discusses subsequent cases, arguing that while the case law has considered the proprietary aspects of cryptoassets, it has not done so in much detail.

In *AA*, a Canadian insurance company was hacked, and their computer system encrypted, with the hackers demanding payment of $1,200,000, paid in Bitcoin, for the decryption tool. This ransom was paid by the Canadian company's insurer.[68] After payment and decryption, the insurer who paid the ransom sought to track down the location of the Bitcoin, which was in a wallet in the British Virgin Islands controlled by an unknown person. In respect of this Bitcoin, a proprietary injunction was sought.[69] The reason behind pursuing this remedy was the perceived advantages of a proprietary remedy that attached to the thing, rather than a personal remedy against an unknown defendant.[70]

Unsurprisingly, given the remedy pursued, the question of whether Bitcoin, as a cryptoasset, was property, was central. Without this aspect, a proprietary injunction would fail.[71] The first consideration made by Bryan J was whether Bitcoin could be property for the purposes of a freezing order where it did not clearly fall within the traditionally exhaustive and mutually exclusive categories of things in action and things in possession. Although outside of the traditional categorisation, Bryan J did not see this as precluding the finding that Bitcoin could be property.[72] In short, Bitcoin specifically, and cryptocurrencies in general, could be property, even if they did not fit neatly into the pre-existing sub-categories of property in English Law.

---

67 AA v. Persons Unknown & Ors, [2019] EWHC 3556 (Comm) .

68 This was negotiated down to $950,000.

69 Other remedies, namely a Bankers Trust order and a Norwich Pharmacal order were initially sought, though due to the issues of serving these outside of the jurisdiction, they were withdrawn: AA v. Persons Unknown & Ors, [2019] EWHC 3556 (Comm) at paras 38 and 49. Since AA, there has been an amendment to the Civil Procedure Rules, adding a new Gateway 23 into Civil Procedure Rules Practice Direction 6B. This aims to simplify the procedure to serve out of jurisdiction. For more, see M. Pelling, 'Issues in Crypto Currency Fraud Claims, Speech from the Crypto Disputes Conference', 29 June 2022, available at https://www.judiciary.uk/wp-content/uploads/2022/07/CRYPTO-DISPUTES-CONFERENCE.pdf, n.9, (accessed 24 February 2023).

70 Personal remedies, such as restitution for unjust enrichment could well succeed on these facts. However, in practice they are less desirable or perhaps even worthless against an unknown defendant.

71 AA v. Persons Unknown & Ors, [2019] EWHC 3556 (Comm) para. 55.

72 AA v. Persons Unknown & Ors, [2019] EWHC 3556 (Comm) para. 58.

In reaching this conclusion, Bryan J relied heavily on a report on *Cryptoassets and Smart Contracts* authored by the United Kingdom Jurisdiction Taskforce (UKJT),[73] a group of judges, academics and practitioners with expertise in the field. As far as it relates to the UKJT Report, Bryan J in *AA* states that the 'analysis as to the proprietary status of crypto currencies is compelling and for the reasons identified therein should be adopted by this court.'[74] In his judgment, Bryan J uses paragraphs 71-84 inclusive of the UKJT Report to justify the conclusion that 'at least to the level required for [...] interim relief that [cryptocurrencies] constitute property.'[75] What is evident from these paragraphs of the UKJT Report is that there is more concern about whether cryptoassets can fall within the overall category of property where the asset does not fit neatly into either of the pre-existing categories of property, rather than concern about whether cryptocurrencies displayed the necessary characteristics of property. The main argument in the relevant paragraphs on the UKJT Report cited in *AA* was that just because something does not fall neatly within a sub-category of property, does not mean it is precluded from being property at all.[76] To this end, the UKJT extensively refers to *Colonial Bank v. Whinney*,[77] a case which asks whether shares, unequivocally a type of personal property, fell within the category of a thing in action for the purposes of the Bankruptcy Act 1883, s44(iii), something which was ultimately considered as a matter of statutory interpretation, rather than a matter of personal property law.[78] The value of *Whinney* was to show that the case does not limit the scope of things that can be property in law.[79] It is possible for something to be property, even though the law has not conceptualised such a thing as property before.

While *AA* set out the case for intangible assets that are not things in action to be recognised as a species of intangible property, it said comparatively little about why cryptoassets should be property. The discussion of this point in *AA* is limited to Lord Wilberforce's *dicta* in *National Provincial Bank v. Ainsworth*.[80] Although the facts are far removed from the present discussion,[81] the definition of property rights in *Ainsworth* has been applied to all types of property rights, in land or in things. In *Ainsworth*, Lord

73 UK Jurisdiction Taskforce Report, Legal Statement on Cryptoassets and Smart Contracts, 2019.

74 AA v. Persons Unknown & Ors, [2019] EWHC 3556 (Comm), para. 57 (Bryan J).

75 AA v. Persons Unknown & Ors, para. 63 (Bryan J).

76 This accords with the reference in AA, para. 59, that the UKJT Report was influential, although no more of the report was covered in AA.

77 Colonial Bank v. Whinney, (1886) 11 App. Cas. 426.

78 D. Fox and S. Green, eds., Cryptocurrencies in Public and Private Law, Oxford, Oxford University Press, 2019, para. 6.33; UK Jurisdiction Taskforce, Legal Statement on Cryptoassets and Smart Contracts, 2019, paras. 70 and 76.

79 UK Jurisdiction Taskforce, Legal Statement on Cryptoassets and Smart Contracts, 2019, para. 77; AA v. Persons Unknown & Ors, [2019] EWHC 3556 (Comm), para. 58.

80 National Provincial Bank v. Ainsworth, [1965] 1 AC 1175.

81 *Ainsworth* is a land law case, and considered whether the right of a deserted wife to remain in the matrimonial home was a property right or a personal right.

Wilberforce states that property rights, as opposed to personal rights are 'definable, identifiable by third parties, capable in its nature of assumption by third parties, and have some degree of permanence or stability.'[82] This definition is not without its problems. It is 'riddled with circularity,'[83] in that a thing is called property because it has proprietary characteristics, which would not exist without the thing being defined as property. It is this aspect of *Ainsworth* that is the problem when applied in *AA*.[84] In *AA*, Bryan J assumed, without much discussion, that cryptoassets met the four *Ainsworth* requirements.[85]

Notwithstanding the problem that *Ainsworth*'s application erroneously fails to distinguish between the questions of whether a thing is property and whether a right in a thing has proprietary characteristics, it does set out some of the characteristics of property.[86] In particular, it reiterates the important fact that property rights are rights which are effective against the whole world. This is in contrast to contractual rights which usually only have legal effects for those who are party to the contract. The trouble is that the characteristics of the rights in the thing necessarily flow from whether the asset is property. In this context, then, *AA*'s treatment of *Ainsworth* prioritises these two issues incorrectly, and does not adequately *justify* why cryptoassets should be property in the first place.

Although there have been several cases in England concerning proprietary aspects of cryptoassets in the context of their interference,[87] it is perhaps easy to overstate what the case law has said about their proprietary status. To date,[88] the case law in England has held that there is a 'realistically arguable case' that cryptoassets are property.[89] No case has held that these assets are property in the general sense,[90] although it is increasingly unlikely that any future case law will challenge this assertion.[91] The reason for this is that cases decided

82 National Provincial Bank v. Ainsworth, p.1248.

83 K. Gray and S. F. Gray, Land Law, 7th edn, Oxford, Oxford University Press, 2011, p. 45.

84 It is not the *only* problem in *AA*. *Ainsworth* concerns a possessory interest and there is no reason why it should be extended to apply to the non-possessory.

85 This aspect is considered in more detail in the Singaporean case of B2C2 Ltd v. Quoine Pte Ltd, [2019] SGHC(I) 3.

86 These are necessary, but not sufficient, requirements for a thing to be property.

87 AA v. Persons Unknown & Ors, [2019] EWHC 3556 (Comm); Ion Science Ltd v. Persons Unknown and others, (unreported), 21 December 2020 (Commercial Court); Liam David Robertson v. Persons Unknown, (unreported 15th July 2019); Osbourne v. Persons Unknown and Ozone Networks Inc, [2022] EWHC 1021 (Comm).

88 February 2023.

89 Osbourne v. Persons Unknown and Ozone Networks Inc, [2022] EWHC 1021 (Comm), para. 13; D. Wyatt, C. Whitehouse, and G. Fahey, 'Osbourne v. Persons Unknown - Injunction Granted over Stolen NFTs Held on Constructive Trust', Computer and Telecommunications Law Review, Vol. 28 No. 6 2022, p. 137.

90 The cases limit their discussion to property in the context to which the case relates.

91 For the view in a criminal law context, see DPP v. Briedis and Reskajs, [2021] EWHC 3155 (Admin), para. 10. Indeed, some later cases, such as D'Aloia v. Binance Holdings, [2022] EWHC 1723 (Ch D), para. 22, Mr Dollar Bill Ltd v. Persons Unknown [2021] EWHC 2718 (Ch), para. 10 and Fetch.AI Ltd and Another v. Persons Unknown and others, [2021] EWHC 2254 (Comm), para. 9, merely assume that

on an interim basis have a lower standard of proof than required when these questions can be considered at trial, with the benefit of both parties making submissions. Thus, for an interim injunction, it is sufficient to demonstrate that an asset is arguably property for the injunction to operate. Whether the asset is property may then be considered at trial, depending on whether the final remedy sought is proprietary or personal.

The issue with the current approach in England is not, strictly speaking, that cases seeking interim remedies have not considered the finer points on the proprietary aspects of cryptoassets. The issue is that there is a danger that later cases read too much into earlier cases, concluding that cryptoassets are property, without giving the thought which such an important aspect deserves.[92] This issue is not fanciful. Using the authority of *AA v. Persons Unknown* and *Ion Science v. Persons Unknown*, two cases involving interim proprietary injunctions, the case of *Wang v. Derby*, a case on whether a cryptocurrency could be property that was the subject matter of a trust, decided that 'it is common ground that fungible and non-identifiable digital assets [...] constitute property that is capable of being bought and sold as well as held on trust as a matter of English law.'[93]

This statement goes beyond what *AA* and *Ion Science* decided, with *Ion Science* noting that there was at least *a serious issue to be tried* that cryptoassets were property,[94] while in *AA*, Bryan J was 'satisfied at least to the level required for the purposes of this application for interim relief that Bitcoins constitute property.'[95] In any case, the substantive reasoning in *AA* is very brief, concluding that cryptoassets fall within the *Ainsworth* criteria. *AA* also uses the reasoning in the Singaporean case of *B2C2 v. Quoine*,[96] even though the question of whether a cryptocurrency constituted property was a point conceded by one of the parties.[97]

---

cryptoassets are property, without even paying lip service to previous case law. See also L. Gullifer, H. Chong and H. Liu, 'Client-Intermediary Relations in the Crypto-Asset World' University of Cambridge Faculty of Law Research Paper No 18/2021, at n. 2.

92 What is property for the purposes of an interim remedy may not be property more widely: Templeton Insurance Ltd v. Motorcare Warranties Ltd, [2012] EWHC 795 (Comm) (goodwill as asset in the context of a freezing injunction). It is therefore important to consider the reasoning behind why a particular asset is property and in what contexts it is considered to be property.

93 Wang v. Darby, [2021] EWHC 3054 (Comm), para. 55.

94 Ion Science Ltd v. Persons Unknown and others, (unreported), 21 December 2020 (Commercial Court), para. 11 (emphasis added).

95 AA v. Persons Unknown & Ors, [2019] EWHC 3556 (Comm), para. 63.

96 B2C2 Ltd v. Quoine Pte Ltd, [2019] SGHC(I) 3, para. 142.

97 B2C2 Ltd v. Quoine Pte Ltd, [2019] SGHC(I) 3, para. 142. In addition, Simon Thorley IJ uses a very wide definition of 'intangible property' of the case, namely 'an identifiable thing of value' (para. 142). This approach is not unique to Singapore, with some English cases defining property in equally broad terms: Hanger Holdings v. Perlake Corporation SA & Anor [2021] EWHC 81 (Ch), paras. 68-69, 74. AA also cites Vorotyntseva v. Money-4 Ltd, [2018] EWHC 2596 (Ch) to support the view that cryptoassets can be property. The case itself merely notes that the respondents did not suggest that cryptoassets could not be property (para. 13).

The common ground in *Wang v. Derby* was that the parties agreed that cryptoassets could be property.[98] The problem with *Wang v. Derby* is twofold. Firstly, the property point was already an aspect of common ground between the parties, meaning the substantive arguments were not discussed. Secondly, *Wang v. Derby* applies the reasoning in *Ion Science* and *AA*, seemingly overlooking the contexts of those cases.

Other cases which consider this issue are more cautious, and mindful of the context in which the case sits. For instance, in *Tulip Trading*,[99] a case primarily considering whether those that controlled the Bitcoin network owed fiduciary duties to users,[100] Falk J is much more cautious in her analysis of the proprietary aspects of cryptocurrencies when compared to *Wang v. Derby*.[101] In *Tulip Trading*, Falk J goes not further than stating that the claimant, in suggesting that cryptoassets were property had "the better of the arguments" in terms of previous authority, albeit in the context of interim relief.[102]

In sum then, some early cases such as *AA* were limited and cautious, careful not to overstate the proprietary characteristics of cryptoassets in first instance decisions. Some other cases have been less cautious, assuming that cryptoassets are property. While this is hardly surprising, based on the precedent of earlier cases, it is important to be mindful that the reasons for categorising cryptoassets as property have not been extensively set out in English case law. In the wider common law world, the reasoning has been more detailed, and it is that which we now consider.

5.2 *The Case Law in the Common Law World*

Some case law in other common law jurisdictions has, in contrast to the English cases, been more willing to set out the reasons to treat cryptoassets as property. This section focuses on the decision of *Ruscoe v. Cryptopia* in the High Court of New Zealand, which set out the property aspects of cryptoassets in some detail.[103] Although New Zealand's approach to intangible assets has diverged from that of England in some respects,[104] the

98 This is referred to earlier in the case, see Wang v. Darby, [2021] EWHC 3054 (Comm), para. 8.

99 Tulip Trading Limited v. Bitcoin Association for BSV and others, [2022] EWHC 667 (Ch).

100 A fiduciary duty is a status-based duty owed from one party to another. It is characterised by undivided loyalty from the fiduciary to the principal: Bristol & West Building Society v. Mothew, [1998] Ch 1, p. 18. See also in the cryptoasset context: Gullifer et al., 2021, p. 10.

101 In both cases the proprietary nature of cryptocurrencies was not contested.

102 Tulip Trading Limited v. Bitcoin Association for BSV and others, [2022] EWHC 667 (Ch), para. 141.

103 This was necessary on the facts as one party in the proceedings contented that such assets were not property: Ruscoe v. Cryptopia Limited (in liquidation), [2020] NZHC 728 (2020), para. 67.

104 For instance, in Dixon v. R, [2015] NZSC 147 digital files were treated as property in the context of theft. Furthermore, Henderson v. Walker, [2019] NZHC 2184 extends the tort of conversion to intangibles, expressly diverging from the English approach in OBG Ltd v. Allan and Your Response v. Datateam Business Media.

case is still useful to the discussion in England, reflected by the fact that *Ruscoe* has been approved in England at first instance.[105]

Other common law jurisdictions have discussed this matter, but they are not discussed in this chapter, as *Ruscoe* considers the issue in the most detail. For instance, in Singapore, in *Quoine v. B2C2* Sundaresh Menon CJ states that there 'have been some other cases in the Commonwealth that have implicitly accepted that cryptocurrency may be regarded as property,'[106] although no court in the common law world has 'attempted to identify the precise nature of the property right, if any.'[107] In *Copytrack v. Wall*,[108] the Supreme Court of British Colombia ordered tracing of the cryptocurrency Ethereum, suggesting that it was a type of property. There are hints of this in the judgment,[109] but the issue is not discussed in detail.

Ruscoe arose following the liquidation of Cryptopia, a cryptocurrency exchange platform. The liquidators firstly asked for clarification about whether cryptocurrencies were property,[110] under s2 of the Companies Act 1993, which defines property as:

> property of every kind whether tangible or intangible, real or personal, corporeal or incorporeal, and includes rights, interests, and claims of every kind in relation to property however they arise.[111]

The second question was, if the assets were property, were they held on trust for the account holders?[112] This section only considers the first of these questions. On the property question, Glendall J sets the scene by explaining why the classification of cryptoassets as property matters,[113] before considering whether such an asset is property. Some of the discussion draws similarities between cryptoassets and money, reasoning that if the latter was broad enough to fall within the 1993 Act, then so can the former. The value in Glendall J's *dicta* for the purposes of this chapter comes from his treatment of *Ainsworth*. Although the criticisms of *Ainsworth* are noted above, the case nevertheless prompts useful

105 Wang v. Darby, [2021] EWHC 3054 (Comm), para. 56.
106 Quoine Pte Ltd v. B2C2 Ltd, [2020] SGCA(I) 2, para. 139.
107 Quoine Pte Ltd v. B2C2 Ltd, [2020] SGCA(I) 2, para. 139.
108 Copytrack Pte Ltd v. Wall, 2018 BCSC 1709.
109 Copytrack Pte Ltd v. Wall, 2018 BCSC 1709, para 35 (Skolrood J).
110 Ruscoe v. Cryptopia Limited (in liquidation), [2020] NZHC 728 (2020), para. 53.
111 Companies Act 1993, s. 2 as reproduced in Ruscoe, paras. 70-71.
112 Ruscoe v. Cryptopia Limited (in liquidation), [2020] NZHC 728 (2020), para. 134.
113 This is not a novel point. The proprietary status of assets matters for reasons such as remedies, insolvency, succession and commercial in general: Ruscoe para. 66. See generally D. Harvey, Collisions in the Digital Paradigm: Law and Rule-Making in the Internet Age, Oxford, Hart Publishing 2017, Ch. 5 for an overview of the issues.

discussion of whether an asset is property, even though *Ainsworth* itself was considering whether a right was proprietary, not whether a thing was property.

The first aspect of *Ainsworth* is the identifiable subject matter, which Glendall J identifies as 'computer-readable strings of characters recorded on networks of computers established for the purpose of recording those strings[...]'[114] The problem with this analysis is that it identifies the subject matter, as characters on computers. The problem is that this is data, which is non-rivalrous,[115] and thus unfit to be the subject of property rights.[116] This is something later expressly acknowledged in the judgment,[117] so it is evidently not the subject of property by itself. Taken as a whole, the subject of property that Glendall J appears to be suggesting is a public key, combined with a private key, facilitates transactions which are recognised on the particular network.[118] As such, the subject of property is the 'transactional power'.[119] More will said about this in the next section, but at this point it is worth noting whether this transactional power can be considered property where such transactional power is not strictly a right enforceable by action.[120] The problem with Glendall J's analysis is that in the first stage of *Ainsworth*, the identifiable subject matter, the subject matter that could be the subject of property, is not something that has proprietary characteristics. It is up to later in the judgment for the potentially proprietary characteristics of the thing to be revealed. This is a recurring issue in many of the judgments involving intangibles or cryptoassets, which are reticent to pin down the precise nature of the thing they are declaring to be property.[121]

Related to the first requirement is the second requirement of the thing being identifiable by third parties, which Glendall J frames in the language of excludability.[122] What is

114 Ruscoe v. Cryptopia Limited (in liquidation), [2020] NZHC 728 (2020), para. 105.

115 According to the Law Commission, Digital Assets: Consultation Paper, Law Com No 256, 28 July 2022, p. 22, n.87, a thing is rivalrous where 'A thing is rivalrous if use or consumption of the thing by one person, or a specific group of persons, inhibits use or consumption of the thing by one or more other persons.'

116 Non-rivalrous data usually does not exhibit the characteristics of property, such as exclusive use of the thing: Law Commission, Digital Assets: Consultation Paper, Law Com No 256, 28 July 2022, para. 2.62.

117 Ruscoe v. Cryptopia Limited (in liquidation), [2020] NZHC 728, para. 111.

118 Ruscoe v. Cryptopia Limited (in liquidation), [2020] NZHC 728, para. 112.

119 D. Fox, 'Digital Assets as Transactional Power,' Journal of International Banking and Financial Law, Vol.1 2022, p. 3.

120 If not a right enforceable by action it would not fall within the traditional categorisation of property. Transactional power is something seen with bank money, which is a right enforceable by action: D. Fox, Property Rights in Money, Oxford, Oxford University Press, 2008, para. 1.38-1.42, citing Lipkin Gorman v. Karpnale Ltd, [1991] 2 AC 548 and Foley v. Hill, (1848) 2 HL Cas. 28; 9 ER 1002 .

121 Tulip Trading Limited v. Bitcoin Association for BSV and others, [2022] EWHC 667 (Ch), para. 140 (Falk J); Fetch.AI Ltd and Another v. Persons Unknown and others, [2021] EWHC 2254 (Comm), para 10.

122 Ruscoe v. Cryptopia Limited (in liquidation), [2020] NZHC 728 (2020), para. 111. The role of exclusion as the fundamental feature of property rights is well-known in the literature. See for example L. M. Katz, 'Exclusion and Exclusivity in Property Law', The University of Toronto Law Journal, Vol. 58 No. 3, 2008, pp. 275-315; T. Merrill, 'Property and the Right to Exclude', Nebraska Law Review, Vol. 77 1998, p. 730; J.

interesting here is that Glendall J uses the analogy of personal identification numbers to demonstrate how the private key used to effect transfer of cryptoassets is something which can be used to exclude the ability to transfer the cryptocurrency from third parties. Although there are similarities, the problem remains that there is no compelling reason that a private key or its effects should be propertised when a PIN number is not property.[123] The final two requirements, respectively the asset being capable of assumption by third parties,[124] and some degree of permanence or stability are less controversial, perhaps because they are more readily evident in the cryptoasset landscape where these assets are routinely traded.

The underlying problems of the approach in *Ruscoe* stem from the imprecision at the heart of identifying the precise subject of property rights, and from the fact that *Ainsworth* is an unsuitable instrument for determining if something should be property. More will be said on the first point in the next section. As for the second issue, there is a difference between a thing being property and a right exhibiting proprietary characteristics. The discussion on cryptocurrencies concerns the former, *Ainsworth* concerned the latter.

5.3 *Academic Arguments*

The last section identified some difficulties that arise when conceptualising cryptoassets as property. The conceptualisations either fail to identify the precise subject of property, or alternatively there has not been close enough attention paid to the justification for such an asset as property. This is not to say that cryptoassets cannot be considered property. These assets can be property, but it is necessary to clearly assert what it is that is the precise subject of property and why that is the case.

This section considers some of the academic views on cryptoassets as property. It focuses on two main points, firstly, the attempt to define cryptoassets as something other than pure information, to ensure they are not excluded from the remit of property for this reason,[125] and secondly, identifying the precise thing or right in cryptoassets that can attract property rights.

One of the main objections to describing cryptoassets as property is that some categorise the distributed ledger that records blockchain transactions as information.

Penner, The Idea of Property in Law, Oxford, Oxford University Press, 2000; K. Gray, 'Property in Thin Air', Cambridge Law Journal, Vol. 50 No. 2 1991, pp. 268-270.

123 It is the right that is property in the bank account example. It is unclear whether such an equivalent exists in the cryptoasset context. It is worth noting that the analogy itself need not necessarily undermine the case for cryptoassets to be property.

124 The assets are capable of assumption by third parties as they can be transferred between parties.

125 UK Jurisdiction Taskforce, Legal Statement on Cryptoassets and Smart Contracts, 2019, para. 65.

Subject to exceptions,[126] there is hostility in English law to treating information as property.[127] This is because information is non-rivalrous, and the same piece of information can be used by multiple parties concurrently without inhibiting any other party's use of the information.[128] To propertise information would risk hampering the free flow of information.[129] As such, fundamental to the arguments for cryptoassets being property is the argument that the thing that should constitute property is not just information.[130]

One of the ways this is done is to highlight the rivalrous nature of cryptoassets,[131] to characterise cryptoassets as not just a string of characters making up a public and private key, but to instead consider what the data enables the holder to do.[132] David Fox terms this 'transactional power.'[133] For Fox, these assets are 'ideational constructs,'[134] that is, something without a tangible existence but that is still treated as a thing that 'represents some specific locus of tradeable value in a market.'[135] There is an ideationally constructed 'thing' to which property rights could attach. This is transactional functionality, the fact that the asset is recognised on a particular network as being able to effect transactions. Even though Fox identifies a composite thing to which property rights could attach,[136] the question is whether this is possible as the law currently stands. Fox is clear that the complexity of this approach is greater because the thing in question is intangible, and that ideational creation at play (in our case a cryptoasset) has the ideational quality because of its *technical* functionality, rather than the legal attribution of the thing.[137] Both of these problems are discussed in turn.

126 One example of an exception is Intellectual Property. For instance, patents and patent applications are property under Patents Act 1977, s30; Copyright, Designs and Patents Act 1988, s. 1(1) categories Copyright as a property right.

127 Oxford v. Moss, (1979) 68 Cr App Rep 183; Boardman v. Phipps, [1967] 2 A.C. 46.

128 Law Commission Digital Assets: Consultation Paper, Law Com No 256, 28 July 2022, at n.87 states that 'A thing is rivalrous if use or consumption of the thing by one person, or a specific group of persons, inhibits use or consumption of the thing by one or more other persons.'

129 See the discussion in J. D. Michels & C. Millard, 'The New Things: Property Rights in Digital Files?', Cambridge Law Journal, Vol.81 No.1 2022, p. 3.

130 Ruscoe v. Cryptopia Limited (in liquidation), [2020] NZHC 728 (2020), para. 127; Michels & Millard, 2022, p. 14. It is in these arguments that we get more of a sense of what exactly should be the subject of property if we call cryptoassets property.

131 For a brief discussion of rivalrousness in this context, see T. Cutts, LSE Law Policy Briefing Series 36, Crypto-Property? Response to Public Consultation by the UK Jurisdiction Taskforce of the LawTech Delivery Panel, LSE Law Policy Briefing Series 36, 2019, pp. 2-3.

132 The UK Jurisdiction Taskforce, Legal Statement on Cryptoassets and Smart Contracts, 2019, para. 60 states that is that the data is not the cryptoasset, but is instead a record of it. The commercial value of a cryptoasset 'is not in the recorded data itself but in the fact that the person possessing that data is able to effect and authenticate dealings in the cryptoasset in accordance with the rules of the system.'

133 Fox, 2022.

134 Fox, 2022, p. 3.

135 Fox, 2022, p. 3. Cryptoassets fit that description.

136 The importance of the thing is clear from the outset: Fox, 2022, p. 3.

137 Fox, 2022, p. 3; See also Low and Teo, 2017, p. 245.

The tangibility aspect is not insurmountable. The transactional power in a cryptoasset is not dissimilar to the transactional power in money in the form of coins and banknotes. In essence, a blockchain register, in recording transactions, is similar to the historical origins of banknotes, which initially recorded coin deposits or loans, but these later became transferable themselves.[138] Tangibility prevents double-spending the asset, and gives the note rivalrous qualities. Although intangible, the same can be said of the blockchain ledger and spending cryptoassets. The requirement for a unique key with each transaction,[139] and the technical features of blockchain technology preventing double spending, mean that in this aspect, cryptocurrencies are functionally similar to money. The problem in the analysis comes with the second aspect, that of technical functionality rather than legal attribution. In this aspect, it is helpful to compare cryptoassets to bank money.[140] The argument, in sum, is that although the problems of tangibility and rivalrousness can be circumvented, it is less clear whether the character of the right (if it can even be called that) is one in which property rights can exist. Money in a bank account is a thing in action,[141] that is, a legal right, enforceable by action, to be paid.[142] In contrast, there does not appear to be a legal right to enforce cryptoassets.[143] It is plausible that English law could declare such a right to be enforceable by action, and thus allow cryptoassets to be property. This would demand some clarity about what this type of right is and what it does.

6 CONCLUSION

This chapter began by setting out the early remedies that were argued when intangibles were misappropriated. Fatal to these claims succeeding was the fact that intangibles, even if property, were and still are incapable of possession and thus cannot fall within the property torts which protect a claimant's possessory interest in a thing. Later cases involving different types of intangibles have skipped the possessory conundrum, and have instead focused on the proprietary aspects of the asset in order to ground an interim remedy. Although the final remedies found in the property torts cannot be compared with the interim remedies in every respect, the value of outlining the earlier attempted remedies was to demonstrate the development of the law. The focus on proprietary elements at the

138 D. Fox, 'Bona Fide Purchase and the Currency of Money' Cambridge Law Journal Vol.55, 1996, p. 555, cited in Fox, 2008, para. 1.36, n. 26.

139 Low and Teo, 2017.

140 Fox, 2008, para. 1.38.

141 Low and Teo, 2017, p. 242.

142 A thing in action, although consisting of a purely personal right, is a type of property.

143 Admittedly, Bryan J in AA v. Persons Unknown & Ors, [2019] EWHC 3556 (Comm), para. 59, makes it clear that intangibles things that do not give rights enforceable by action are property.

interim stage is in contrast to the range of proprietary and personal remedies that are presented as final remedies.

In the backdrop of legal consultation and a range of first instance decisions that are either reticent to declare cryptoassets as property in all circumstances, or work on the assumption that the property status of cryptoassets is all a foregone conclusion, it is useful to reflect upon what makes a thing property, what it is to which property rights attach and what the nature of the legal rights are where something is property.

8 Property Law and Space Resources: The Last Frontier of Property Law

Sirio Zolea[*]

1 Introduction

This chapter aims to analyse the problematic issues of property law in the space context. According to the Outer Space Treaty of 1967, the Moon and other celestial bodies are excluded from any form of national appropriation by claim of sovereignty, by use or occupation, or by any other means. The commercial exploitation of space resources, which did not seriously seem, at that time, a topical issue, is not clearly allowed nor clearly prohibited. In addition, the new role of private actors and their activities in space gives rise to regulatory ambiguities. The Moon Agreement of 1979, unfortunately ratified just by a few states, tried to set out a detailed regime of common heritage of mankind of space resources and to govern their exploitation in the interest of all the countries, and of present and future generations. Recently, states such as the United States of America, Luxembourg, the United Arab Emirates and Japan have unilaterally adopted internal legislation about the exploitation of space resources and their appropriation by national entities, once extracted. However, the compatibility of such laws with the international framework is criticised by several scholars and by some states. Furthermore, the Artemis Accords, regulating the cooperation of the USA and their allies within the space program aiming to send human beings back to the Moon, and this time to stably remain there, contain several references to the presence of private commercial partners and to the extraction and use of space resources. This chapter analyses the relationships between all these levels of regulation, highlighting the importance of the efforts to peacefully interpret the existing space treaties and to conceive new multilateral treaties, in respect of the various national interests and of the common interest of mankind.

2 The International Law Level

This chapter analyses the problematic issues of property law in the outer space context, with particular reference to space resources: in the general framework of the multilateral

* Senior researcher in Private Comparative Law, Roma Tre University, Law Department.

international treaties, in some other international agreements and in national legislation. The first layer of space law is the international level. Therefore, in the field of property rights in space, the essential rules are to be found in the United Nations treaties on outer space,[1] especially the Treaty on Principles Governing the Activities of States in the Exploration and Use of Outer Space, including the Moon and Other Celestial Bodies, of 1967, and the Agreement Governing the Activities of States on the Moon and Other Celestial Bodies, of 1979.

2.1 The Outer Space Treaty

The Treaty on Principles Governing the Activities of States in the Exploration and Use of Outer Space, Including the Moon and Other Celestial Bodies, is the main treaty governing the whole of outer space, ratified by many countries, including the main space powers. It is inspired by humanistic ideas of coexistence and cooperation between the nations, and it affirms, on a base of equality between the states, principles such as free access, free use, free exploration and scientific investigation in outer space. Its exploration and use must be carried out only for peaceful purposes, for the benefit and in the interest of all countries, and must be the province of all mankind (art. 1). It is specifically stated that the Moon and other celestial bodies are excluded from any form of national appropriation by claim of sovereignty, by means of use or occupation, or by any other means (art. 2).

The commercial exploitation of space resources, which did not seriously seem, at that time, a topical issue, is not clearly allowed nor clearly prohibited. Obviously, the question of private space activities did not concretely arise. The Treaty did not explicitly deal with these activities, even though such operations are undoubtedly concerned by the rule according to which the states bear international responsibility and liability for national activities in outer space, without distinction if they are carried out by public or private entities.

Today, the increasing role of the private sector in the use and exploration of space, a role which now concerns to varying degrees all the space powers, urgently raises the issues of new international agreements aiming for better regulation of such use and exploration through consensus of the international community. But it is a good thing that the foundations of space law have been laid by that Treaty, negotiated in a historical phase of expansion throughout the world of progressive and humanistic emancipation values, during the decolonisation era. Considering both the economic and the geopolitical importance of space, it is clear that a multilateralist approach is the only general defence

1 *See, amplius*, S. Zolea, 'Space Law and Inequalities: an Uncertain Future', in M. García Goldar, J. Núñez Cerviño (Eds.), *El derecho ante la tecnología: innovaciòn y adaptaciòn*, A Coruña, Editorial Colex, 2022, pp. 376-379.

against the danger that the space ambitions of the nations and geopolitical blocks may escalate into an open military conflict.[2]

2.2 *The Moon Treaty*

It is important to refer that the more progressive and cooperative elements of the abovementioned Treaty have been even more developed in the forward-looking Agreement Governing the Activities of States on the Moon and Other Celestial Bodies, of 1979. This is the last of the space treaties sponsored by the United Nations and regrettably, to the present day, the less successful, as it has never been signed by most of the states with space capabilities. It is somehow the culmination, but also, with its failings, the evidence of the crisis, of the period of the space treaties of the 60s and the 70s. It significantly accommodates the claims of the emerging countries. First of all, the Agreement points out and develops principles coming from the previous treaties. Moreover, while recognising the potential benefits arising from the exploitation of natural space resources, this treaty highlights the orientation of the exploration and use of the space, as a province of all mankind, toward the common good and the interests of all the countries, irrespective of their degree of economic or scientific development. The interests of present and future generations are mentioned, as well as the need to promote higher standards of living and conditions of economic and social progress and development. The more remarkable rules of this treaty can be found in its article 11, which considers the Moon and its natural resources as a common heritage of mankind, with the consequence that the states parties to the Agreement undertake to establish an international regime to govern the exploitation of the natural resources of the Moon as such exploitation is about to become feasible. The Agreement provides an international regime aiming to the orderly and safe development of the natural resources of the Moon; their rational management; the expansion of opportunities in their use; an equitable sharing by all states parties in the benefits derived from them, whereby the interests and needs of the developing countries, as well as the efforts of those countries which have contributed either directly or indirectly to the exploration of the Moon, should be given special consideration. Article 11 of the Moon Agreement also reaffirms and specifies that the Moon cannot be subject to national appropriation and that neither the surface, nor the subsurface, nor any part thereof or natural resources "in place" might become property of any state, international (intergovernmental or non-governmental) organisation, national or non-governmental

2 *See* R.S. Jakhu, S. Freeland (Eds.), *McGill Manual on International Law Applicable to Military Uses of Outer Space*, vol. I, *Rules*, Montreal, Centre for Research in Air and Space Law, McGill University, 2022.

entity, or of any natural person. In this way, the private sector is finally, to some extent, taken in account.

The non-ratification of the Agreement by the main space powers shows that it was, perhaps, too far advanced to obtain the necessary general consensus. The complex and uncertain current legal regime of the moon and other celestial bodies arises from this situation. Thus, the principle of common heritage of mankind may only be referred to the states having ratified the Moon Agreement, while for the other states the principle should apply of the surface and the subsoil of the celestial bodies as *res communes omnium*, namely 'first come first served'.[3] In fact, the silence of the Outer Space Treaty about the exploitation of resources of celestial bodies gives way to discordant interpretations regarding its legitimacy, but, according to most of the opinions, the principle of the freedom of use and exploration, which is affirmed there, should allow the exploitation, or at least some forms of exploitation.[4]

2.3 *The Uncertainties of the International Law Framework*

To better understand the complex system of properties in space, it is necessary to accurately distinguish between the artificial space objects, the soil and subsoil, and the natural resources. As for the manufacts, brought or even fabricated in space or on a celestial body, the jurisdiction and control of the states remain undisputed, without prejudice to the property rights attributed accordingly to the legal order of origin, thus allowing, insofar as the national legislation permits it, the ownership by private entities.[5] This is why the property regime of an artificial space object will depend on the international agreements of space cooperation in which the state of origin is involved, on national space legislation, and, for the rest, on the general internal property regime (statute law and/or case law). One can observe that, in space, the legal principle *superficies solo cedit* never applies, in contrast to the general rule of many legal traditions on Earth (both the common law and

3 *See* G. Catalano Sgrosso, *Diritto internazionale dello spazio*, Florence, LoGisma, 2011, pp. 48-49, 62-63.

4 *See* F. Tronchetti, 'The Non-Appropriation Principle as a Structural Norm of International Law: a New Way of Interpreting Article II of the Outer Space Treaty', *Air & Space Law*, vol. 33, n. 3, 2008, p. 301: "The Outer Space Treaty does not contain any reference to the use of space resources for non-scientific purposes. As a consequence, legal authors have highly debated the feasibility of such a hypothesis. Some of them strongly refute this option. Others, by using an analogy with the rules regulating the freedom of high seas, argue that such use merely forms part of the freedom of exploration and use of outer space. I partially agree with this theory. Outer space is a *res communis omnium*. States are entitled to use its resources so long as their activities do not involve any claim over outer space areas and until such activities do not prevent others to do the same (Article IX of the Outer Space Treaty). Moreover, States have to comply with the principle that the exploration and use of outer space must be carried out for the benefit and in the interests of all countries".

5 *See* H.R. Hertzfeld, F.G. Von der Dunk, 'Bringing Space Law into the Commercial World: Property Rights without Sovereignty', *Chicago Journal of International Law*, vol. 6, n. 1, 2005, pp. 81 ff.

civil law, in particular): the legal regime of the soil and subsoil does not affect the legal regime of the spacecraft or base and the (public or private) owner of a landed spacecraft or even lunar base does not become the owner of the underlying soil and subsoil, having no right to them.

As for the soil and subsoil of the Moon and other celestial bodies, the applicable international legal regime is very different between the states which are only parties of the Outer Space Treaty and the states parties of the Moon Agreement. In fact, the Treaty of 1967 establishes for them a regime of *res communes omnium*,[6] while the Agreement of 1979 of common heritage of mankind. These two regimes have in common the principle of free exploration and use for non-exploitative activities, but when it comes to the exploitation of the resources, they imply important differences. Of course – despite of the (symbolic) real estate sale contracts on celestial bodies that some private entities feel free to propose to purchasers[7] – the ban on national appropriation also includes private entities, as, according to article 6 of the Outer Space Treaty, the states bear international responsibility for national activities in outer space, carried out by both governmental or non-governmental subjects, and this is why their national legislation could not allow anyone to sell portions of land on celestial bodies without violating the Treaty.[8] The legal principle of the non-appropriation of the celestial bodies, according to many authors, meets both the requirements of the constant and uniform repetition of the practice and of its acceptance by states as law, implying its qualification as a customary rule of international law, binding for all the states, even the ones which are not parties of the Treaty of 1967.[9] Furthermore, claims of sovereignty and appropriation from the latter states could be scarcely effective, as all the space powers of the world have signed that Treaty.

---

6 About the stars as *res communes omnium, see* already J. Domat, 'Les lois civiles dans leur ordre naturel', in *Œuvres complètes*, new ed., t. I, Paris, Didot, 1828, p. 114.

7 *See* G. Gál, 'By Any Other Means - Some Remarks to Interpretation of Article II Space Treaty', in *Proceedings of the Forty-Ninth Colloquium on the Law of Outer Space (2-6 October 2006, Valencia, Spain)*, Washington, American Institute of Aeronautics and Astronautics, 2007, pp. 172 ff.; F.G. Von der Dunk *et alii*, 'Surreal estate: addressing the issue of "Immovable Property Rights on the Moon"', in F.G. Von der Dunk (Ed.), *International Space Law*, Cheltenam, Northampton, Edward Elgar, 2018, pp. 639 ss.

8 Catalano Sgrosso, 2011, p. 62; *cf. Statement by the Board of Directors of the International Institute of Space Law. On Claims to Property Rights Regarding The Moon and Other Celestial Bodies*, IISL, 2004, available at: https://iislweb.space/wp-content/uploads/2020/01/IISL_Outer_Space_Treaty_Statement.pdf (last accessed 17 January 2023); S. Hobe, 'Adequacy of the Current Legal and Regulatory Framework Relating to the Extraction and Appropriation of Natural Resources in Outer Space', *Annals of Air and Space Law*, vol. XXXII, 2007, pp. 115 ff.; V. Pop, *Who Owns the Moon? Extraterrestrial Aspects of Land and Mineral Resources Ownership*, Dordrecht, Springer, 2009, p. 72; P.J. Delage, *Vers l'appropriation privée des ressources naturelles célestes: quelques remarques et critiques*, Paris, Dalloz, 2016, p. 551; S. Marchisio, 'Lo sfruttamento delle risorse minerarie dei corpi celesti nel diritto internazionale', in E. Triggiani *et alii* (Eds.), *Dialoghi con Ugo Villani*, t. II, Bari, Cacucci, 2017, p. 886.

9 Tronchetti, 2008, pp. 277 ff.

The most controversial issue remains, in any case, the regime of the space resources, susceptible to be extracted and exploited. The silence, on this regard, of the Treaty of 1967, allows several possible interpretations on the legitimacy of their exploitation, even though the principle there affirmed of freedom of use and exploration supports the arguments in favour.[10] Otherwise, the Agreement of 1979, ratified only by a few states, has a consistently different approach, as it not only states the non-appropriability "in place"[11] also of the resources of the Moon and other celestial bodies, as a common heritage of mankind, and prohibits their appropriation by private entities too, but it also sets up the institution of a specific international regime for their exploitation. It has been observed that "the 'classical' concept of terra communis went with the presumption of complete freedom of activities, whereas those advocating the common heritage of mankind on the contrary presumed that any substantial - especially commercial - exploitive activities required the consent of the community of States. Consequently, they proposed to establish an international body to preserve such rights of the world community and act as a caretaker. Individual States (or their private entities) should only be allowed to undertake commercial activities as long as this caretaker would see to it that all States, especially the developing countries, would actually and materially benefit from those activities".[12] Sketched out only in its key features, the innovative solution contained in the Moon Agreement would imply to set aside a quota for the developing states with little or no space capacities space capacities. This point especially did not attract the space powers, having invested, over time, huge financial resources and, nowadays, finally being economically and technically close[13] to be able to start the exploitation of the space resources, with relevant chances of profit for their national private actors. These countries undermined the success of the Agreement, while

10 *See* Tronchetti, 2008, p. 301; *cf.* G. Gál, 'Acquisition of Property in the Legal Regime of Celestial Bodies', in *Proceedings of the Thirty-Ninth Colloquium on the Law of Outer Space (October 7-11, 1996, Beijing, China)*, Reston, American Institute of Aeronautics and Astronautics, 1997, pp. 45 ff.; Hertzfeld, Von der Dunk, 2005, pp. 81 ff.; Hobe, 2007, pp. 115 ff.; T. Masson-Zwaan, 'Lunar Exploration and Exploitation as a Special Case of Planetary Exploration: Legal Issues', in A.Y. Kapustin, G.P. Zhukov (Eds.), *The Contemporary Problems of International Space Law*, Moscow, People's Friendship University, 2008, pp. 159 ff.; J. Su, 'Legality of Unilateral Exploitation of Space Resources under International Law', *International and Comparative Law Quarterly*, vol. 66, issue 4, 2017, pp. 991 ff.

11 This subtle specification is important, as the Moon Agreement implicitly distinguishes between the natural resources "in place", before their extraction and removal, and after such activities, once they are made movable goods, at that point susceptible of appropriation, in accordance with the modalities provided in that same treaty for the common good of mankind, under an international regime; *see* Hobe, 2007, p. 124; F. Tronchetti, *The Exploitation of Natural Resources of the Moon and Other Celestial Bodies: a proposal for a legal regime*, Leiden, Boston, Nijhoff, 2009, pp. 218 ff.

12 F.G. Von der Dunk, 'The Moon Agreement and the Prospect of Commercial Exploitation of Lunar Resources', *Annals of Air and Space Law*, vol. XXXII, 2007, p. 98.

13 *See* R.J. Lee, *Law and Regulation of Commercial Mining of Minerals in Outer Space*, Dordrecht, New York, Springer, 2012, pp. 21 ff.

supporting the rule 'first come first served' instead, namely freedom of the activities of exploitation as long as they respect the previous Treaty of 1967.[14]

This is how the uncoordinated dualism of the principles of the two treaties remains, and the more innovative principles of the Moon Agreement do not meet the requirements to be considered as customary rules of international law,[15] as they currently bind just a few states with limited space capabilities. Both legal scholars and international actors argue about whether or not to keep the Moon Agreement,[16] perhaps amended (as the revision mechanism of art. 18 of the Agreement allows) in order to make it openly compatible with certain kinds of commercial utilisation of space resources,[17] or if the best choice would be writing a new treaty susceptible to get more international acceptance.[18] In any case, the notion of 'common heritage of mankind'[19] – implying solidarity between developed and developing countries, and between present and future generations – with its interpretative doubts and controversies,[20] seems to be a very general clause, susceptible to be filled with

14 Catalano Sgrosso, 2011, pp. 62-63.

15 G.M. Danilenko, 'The Concept of the Common Heritage of Mankind in International Law', *Annals of Air and Space Law*, vol. XIII, 1988, p. 263.

16 *See* Committee on the Peaceful Uses of Outer Space Legal Subcommittee, Forty-seventh session, *Joint statement on the benefits of adherence to the Agreement Governing the Activities of States on the Moon and Other Celestial Bodies by States parties to the Agreement*, United Nations Digital Library, 3 April 2008, digitallibrary.un.org/record/633417; S. Hobe, 'Moon Agreement - Let's Use the Chance', *ZLW*, 2010, pp. 372 ff.; R.S. Jakhu, Y.O. Mankata Nyampong, 'Some Legal Aspects of Space Natural Resources', *European Journal of Law Reform*, vol. 18, n. 1, 2016, pp. 86-104.

17 *See* the detailed amendment proposition of the New Delhi conference of 2002 of the International Law Association, Space Law Committee, *Final Report on the Review of Space Law Treaties in View of Commercial Space Activities - Concrete Proposals*, by Prof. M. Williams, general rapporteur, in *Black Holes*, available at: www.black-holes.eu/resources/ILA.pdf (last accessed 17 January 2023); *see* also Von der Dunk, 2007, pp. 109 ff.; S. Hobe *et alii*, 'The 1979 Agreement Governing the Activities of States on the Moon and Other Celestial Bodies', in S. Hobe *et alii* (Eds.), *Cologne Commentary on Space Law*, vol. II, Cologne, Heymanns, 2013, pp. 423-426; V. Aloia, 'Regulation of Commercial Mining of Space Resources at National and International Level. An Analysis of the Moon Agreement and the National Law Approach', *Proceedings of the International Institute of Space Law*, issue 5, 2019.

18 The *Statement of the Board of Directors of the International Institute of Space Law* of 22 March 2009, available at: https://iislweb.space/wp-content/uploads/2020/01/Statement-BoD.pdf (last accessed 17 January 2023), just wishes to keep the idea of a specific legal regime for the exploitation of the space resources, elaborated through the United Nations; *contra*, openly against the 1979 Agreement, and favorable to unilateral national approaches, *see* H.R. Hertzfeld, B. Weeden, C.D. Johnson, 'How Simple Terms Mislead Us. The Pitfalls of Thinking about Outer Space as a Commons', *Proceedings of the International Institute of Space Law*, issue 5, 2015, pp. 533 ff.

19 *See* also, trying to soften the more radical aspects of this principle, which discourage the participation of many states to the Agreement, *Declaration on International Cooperation in the Exploration and Use of Outer Space for the Benefit and in the Interest of All States, Taking into Particular Account the Needs of Developing Countries*, Adopted by the UN General Assembly, 51st session, 13 December 1996.

20 *See* Tronchetti, 2009, pp. 85 ff.; *cf.* R. Wolfrum, 'The Principle of the Common Heritage of Mankind', *ZaöRV*, 1983, pp. 312 ff.; Danilenko, 1988, pp. 247 ff.; C.Q. Christol, 'The Moon Treaty and the Allocation of Resources', *Annals of Air and Space Law*, vol. XXII(II), 1997, pp. 31 ff.; Hertzfeld, Weeden, Johnson, 2015, pp. 533 ff.

different contents, according to historical contingencies and, at the dawn of a period when the exploitation of the space resources is going to be effective, according to the (often conflicting) interests of the parties involved. This is why different interpretations of the concept of the common heritage of mankind are possible, and can be made more or less open to the possibility of including economic and commercial utilisations.[21]

3 Some National Experiences of Legislation

Although the period of the great multilateral space treaties ended in 1979, space law is now again in turmoil, pushed by the evolution of new, increasingly ambitious, space programs, firstly aiming at the Moon. Some states have recently tried to regulate the exploitation of space resources in their internal law: this is the case with the United States of America, with Luxembourg and, more recently, with the United Arab Emirates and Japan.

3.1 *The USA*

In the USA, the Commercial Space Launch Competitiveness Act, of 2015, attributes to the national exploiter of space resources a sort of proprietary position over them. In fact, paragraph 51303 (to be read together with the definitory paragraph 51301, according with the detailed style of the common law legislators), concerning "asteroid resource and space resource right" stipulates that a US citizen engaged in commercial recovery of an asteroid resource (in the sense of a space resource found on or within a single asteroid) or of a space resource (in the sense of an abiotic resource in situ in outer space, including water and minerals) shall be entitled to any asteroid resource or space resource obtained, including to possess, own, transport, use, and sell the asteroid resource or space resource obtained in accordance with applicable law, including the international obligations of the United States. The intent is clear: to attribute to the US exploiter of the resources *de facto* property rights over them, wide enough to protect him against the possibility of having his rights successively called into question by the national authorities.[22] It is a choice, aiming

21 *Cf.* B. Cheng, 'The Moon Treaty: Agreement Governing the Activities of States on the Moon and Other Celestial Bodies Within the Solar System Other than the Earth, December 18, 1979', *Current Legal Problems*, vol. 33, 1980, p. 233: "just as the conclusion of the Moon treaty was a matter of political will, so will be its implementation. Whether the new concept of the heritage of mankind introduced by the treaty develops into a striking reality or degenerates into a myth will depend on whether in the years to come the States Parties display the necessary will to comply with not only the letter of the treaty, but also its spirit".

22 *See* F. Tronchetti, 'Title IV – Space Resource Exploration and Utilization of the US Commercial Space Launch Competitiveness Act: A Legal and Political Assessment', *Air & Space Law*, vol. 41, n. 2, 2016, p. 148: "Essentially, even if the expression "property rights" is never utilised, the Space Act recognises, under US

to foster private commercial development of the space sector, that responds to the requests made by the American enterprises interested in this potential business. Even though the law ensures that, by the enactment of this act, the USA does not assert sovereignty or the ownership of any celestial body, several scholars and countries[23] express concerns over the dangers implied by American unilateralism, with the risk of a race to control of space resources. It is important to remember how the archetype of the Homestead Acts of the second half of the 19th Century is really deep-rooted in the American legal culture. This kind of unilateralism, confirmed and strengthened by several Presidential documents and executive orders,[24] seems radically hostile to the spirit and to the contents of the Moon Agreement.

3.2 *Luxembourg*

The legislation of Luxembourg, of 2017 (law of 20 July 2017 on exploration and utilisation of space resources), was passed due to the ambition of this country to become a relevant centre in the European space industry and to attract entrepreneurs interested in operating in this sector. It is the first country in Europe to try to guarantee legal certainty for private entities about the appropriability of the space resources extracted, if they fulfil the conditions required for the authorisation of the mission, which are precisely indicated in

---

law, de facto property rights of its citizens over asteroids and space resources that they have obtained. Importantly, however, such an obtainment shall be in accordance with applicable law, including the international obligations of the US".

23 *See Reviewing Opportunities for Achieving the Vienna Consensus on Space Security Encompassing Several Regulatory Domains*, working paper submitted by the Russian Federation, UNOOSA, 17 February 2016, pp. 5-7, available at: www.unoosa.org/oosa/oosadoc/data/documents/2016/aac.105c.12016crp/aac.105c.12016crp.15_0.html (last accessed 17 January 2023); *cf.* Tronchetti, 2016, pp. 152-153.

24 *See*, in particular, *Executive Order on Encouraging International Support for the Recovery and Use of Space Resources*, The White House, 6 April 2020, available at: https://trumpwhitehouse.archives.gov/presidential-actions/executive-order-encouraging-international-support-recovery-use-space-resources/ (last accessed 17 January 2023), Sec. 1: "Outer space is a legally and physically unique domain of human activity, and the United States does not view it as a global commons. Accordingly, it shall be the policy of the United States to encourage international support for the public and private recovery and use of resources in outer space, consistent with applicable law"; Sec. 2: "The United States is not a party to the Moon Agreement. Further, the United States does not consider the Moon Agreement to be an effective or necessary instrument to guide nation states regarding the promotion of commercial participation in the long-term exploration, scientific discovery, and use of the Moon, Mars, or other celestial bodies. Accordingly, the Secretary of State shall object to any attempt by any other state or international organization to treat the Moon Agreement as reflecting or otherwise expressing customary international law"; *A New Era for Deep Space Exploration*, The White House and National Space Council, 23 July 2020, available at: https://csps.aerospace.org/sites/default/files/2021-08/NSpC%20New%20Era%20for%20Space%2023Jul20.pdf (last accessed 17 January 2023); *Memorandum on The National Space Policy*, The White House, 9 December 2020, available at: https://trumpwhitehouse.archives.gov/presidential-actions/memorandum-national-space-policy/ (last accessed 17 January 2023).

the text of the law.[25] In contrast to the US choice, the Luxembourgian nationality of the enterprise is not required. The text of the law clarifies already in its article 1 that space resources are susceptible to appropriation. Asteroids are not specifically mentioned, although the attention of the Luxembourgian policymakers was originally focused on their resources. The law states that no one can explore or use space resources without a written mission authorisation from the competent ministers. The operator is required to comply with the licensing conditions and with the international obligations of Luxembourg (which, in particular, has ratified the 1967 Treaty). Analysing the parliamentary proceedings, one can notice the attention of the lawmakers to present the bill as compliant with international law, on the basis of the distinction between non-appropriability of the celestial bodies in themselves and appropriability of the resources. The explanatory comments also refer to a prestigious classic Belgian legal doctrine,[26] mentioning the legal regime of the sea,[27] where fish and shells are appropriable, but not the sea in itself. In addition, these comments refer to the fact that the authors of the bill, paradoxically, might even have omitted to explicitly state article 1, in the sense that its content is just a mere consequence of the notion of property of the Civil Code (art. 544), closely inspired by the original French Napoleonian Civil Code.[28]

3.3 *The United Arab Emirates and Japan*

In the United Arab Emirates, the Federal Law n. 12 of 2019 on the regulation of the space sector, issued on 19 December 2019,[29] considers a space resource any non-living resource present in outer space, including minerals and water. This law specifically regulates space resources exploration or extraction activities, envisaging scientific, commercial and other purposes. Article 18 states that – subject to the general provisions concerning permits for space activities – the conditions and controls relating to permits for the exploration, exploitation and use of space resources, including their acquisition, purchase, sale, trade,

25 *See* M. Hofmann, 'Entered into Force: the 2020 Space Law of Luxembourg', *Air & Space Law*, vol. 46, n. 4/5, 2021, pp. 587-602.

26 F. Laurent, *Principes de droit civil français*, t. VI, III ed., Bruxelles, Paris, Bruylant, Marescq, 1878, pp. 6 and 10.

27 Criticizing this analogy, *see* J. Steele, 'Luxembourg and the Exploitation of Outer Space', *Nottingham Law Journal*, vol. 29, n. 1, 2021, pp. 36-38.

28 'Exposé des motifs', in *Projet de loi sur l'exportation et l'utilisation des ressources de l'espace*, n. 7093, Chambre des députés, Session ordinaire 2016-2017, pp. 6-8; *see* also (at p. 8): "La notion d'appropriation inclut tous les attributs classiques du droit de la propriété et notamment celui de posséder, transporter, utiliser et vendre les ressources visées en conformité avec les dispositions du présent projet de loi et des textes internationaux applicables en la matière".

29 Text of the law available online in English translation, at: http://www.moj.gov.ae/assets/2020/Federal%20Law%20No%2012%20of%202019%20on%20THE%20REGULATION%20OF%20THE%20SPACE%20SECTOR.pdf.aspx (last accessed 17 January 2023).

transportation, storage and any space activities aimed at providing logistical services in this regard shall be determined by a decision issued by the Council of Ministers or by whomever the Council of Ministers delegates power. The legislator of this country, first in the Arab and Islamic world to regulate such issues, avoids too technical discussions about the nature of the right of the exploiter and specifies its practical utilities, following the model of the US law and developing it in an even more pragmatic way, in order to offer the maximum legal certainty to national companies and attract investors and global companies.[30]

Finally, in Japan, the Act on the Promotion of Business Activities Related to the Exploration and Development of Space Resources, Act n. 83 of 15 June 2021, allows business activities for the exploration and development of space resources and permits to acquire the ownership of them. Japanese private entities can explore, extract and use water, minerals and other natural resources existing in outer space, acquiring ownership of the resources mined or extracted in accordance with their business activity plan (which must preemptively be submitted for approval to the government, including in the application the purpose, the term, the place, the methods and the content of the activity, in addition to obtaining the 'simple' permission for launching an artificial satellite).[31]

4 THE ARTEMIS ACCORDS

It is finally important to mention the Artemis Accords, which can be considered as politically and legally foundational for the new ascent into space of the US and of its allies. These agreements, of 13 October 2020, take their name from the current US-led program aiming to send humans back to the Moon, this time with the idea of building permanent settlements. They contain principles for the cooperation in the exploration and utilisation for civil purposes of the Moon, Mars, comets, and asteroids, including their surfaces, subsurfaces and orbits. They refer to the more general and shared framework of the UN treaties that have been ratified by most of the countries (not the Moon Agreement), particularly the 1967 Treaty. They develop the provisions of these treaties, of course only

30 *See National Space Policy of the United Arab Emirates*, September 2016, available at: https://space.gov.ae/Documents/PublicationPDFFiles/UAE_National_Space_Policy_English.pdf (last accessed 17 January 2023), par. 2.3, par. 5.1.6.

31 H. Yotsumoto, D. Ishikawa, T. Odan, 'Japan', *The Space Law Review* (3rd ed.), 9 December 2021, available at: https://thelawreviews.co.uk/title/the-space-law-review/japan (last accessed 17 January 2023); this article also specifies that "the government may not grant permission unless:
a. the business activity plan conforms to the basic principles of the Basic Space Law and is not likely to have an adverse effect on the accurate and smooth implementation of the conventions concerning the development and use of outer space and the maintenance of public safety; and
b. the applicant has sufficient ability to carry out the business activity plan".

with effects among the parties to the Artemis Accords, in view of the next steps of space exploration.

There are several references to the presence of private commercial partners and to the extraction and use of space resources, according to standards of safety and sustainability of the activities, specifying that such operations (and the contracts and other legal instruments relating to space resources) should be executed in a manner that complies with the Outer Space Treaty and that they do not constitute national appropriation, as prohibited by this Treaty (section 10). Nevertheless, some problems may arise from the section 11 of the Accords, even though it is named after the purpose to encourage "deconfliction" of space activities. This section establishes the creation of temporary "safety zones",[32] which the other states parties are required to respect, through a mechanism of notification of the activities and of commitment to coordination with any relevant actor to avoid harmful interferences. Safety zones should be areas where nominal operations of a relevant activity or an anomalous event could reasonably cause harmful interference, the size and scope of which, as well as the notice and coordination, should be determined in a reasonable manner and reflect the nature and the environment of the operations being conducted. The signatory state establishing, maintaining, or ending a safety zone should do so in a manner that protects public and private personnel, equipment, and operations from harmful interference and should, as appropriate, make relevant information regarding such safety zones, including the extent and general nature of operations. The states commit to use safety zones, which will be expected to change over time, evolve, or end based on the status of the specific activity, in a manner that encourages scientific discovery and technology demonstration, as well as the safe and efficient extraction and utilisation of space resources in support of sustainable space exploration and other operations.

Despite the references to the principle of free access to all areas of celestial bodies and to the other provisions of the 1967 Treaty, it still remains necessary to define in detail how the states parties will actually enact and enforce the institution and the protection of safety zones, and how the rest of the international community will be willing to accept such

32 About the ambiguous concept of 'safety zone', *see* J.W. Nelson, 'Safety Zones: A Near-Term Legal Issue on the Moon', *Journal of Space Law*, vol. 44, n. 2, 2020, pp. 604-624; M. de Zwart, 'To the Moon and Beyond. The Artemis Accords and the Evolution of Space Law', in M. de Zwart, S. Henderson, *Commercial and Military Uses of Outer Space*, Singapore, Springer, 2021, pp. 65-80.

modalities,[33] particularly in relation to the ban on national appropriation of the space.[34] In the Accords, there is no express reference to the legal status of the resources, in place or once extracted, so that this matter is left to national legislation and further agreements. Nevertheless, the presence in the Artemis Accords of the states (USA, Luxembourg, UAE, Japan) having adopted – right before or right after the Accords – national laws allowing forms of property over the space resources confirms the idea that such Agreements also aim to create a favourable international framework, in coordination between allied states, for the adoption of regulations promoting the commercial appropriation of the resources, mostly from private bodies. This could tend to generalise, among a larger geopolitical block, the US-led approach[35] towards the space resources, in an effort to strengthen and legitimise such approach[36] in the face of other, rival or adverse, geopolitical actors (Russia, China, etc.). This choice seems a try to bypass the path of general multilateral hard law or soft law (such as the documents adopted by the UN General Assembly) instruments, or maybe also to determine in advance the content of the future multilateral agreements by putting the other space powers in front of the *fait accompli*.[37]

---

33 J.W. Nelson, 'The Artemis Accords and the Future of International Space Law', *ASIL Insights*, vol. 24, issue 31, 10 December 2020; highlighting the risk of a new Moon Race, *see* G. Wang, 'NASA's Artemis Accords: the path to a united space law or a divided one?', *The Space Review*, 24 August 2020, available at: www.thespacereview.com/article/4009/1 (last accessed 17 January 2023); about the concerns of the scientific community towards the consequences of the Artemis Accords, *see* A. Boley, M. Byers, 'U.S. Policy Puts the Safe Development of Space at Risk', *Science*, vol. 370, n. 6513, 2020, pp. 174-175.

34 *See* Y. Takaya-Umehara, 'The Exploitation of Natural Resources on Celestial Bodies', in P. Achilleas, S. Hobe (Eds.), *Fifty Years of Space Law – Cinquante ans de droit de l'espace*, Leiden, Boston, Brill/Nijhoff, 2020, pp. 543 ff.; for the debate of legal scholars about the compatibility of the Accords with the Outer Space Treaty, *see*, *ex ceteris*, R. Deplano, 'The Artemis Accords: Evolution or Revolution in International Space Law?', *International and Comparative Law Quarterly*, vol. 70, n. 3, 2021, p. 819; S. Mosteshar, 'Artemis: the Discordant Accords', *Journal of Space Law*, vol. 44, n. 2, 2020, pp. 591-603.

35 *See* C.D. Johnson, 'Renewed Ambitions in Space-Exploration Lawmaking', *The Air & Space Lawyer*, vol. 33, n. 3, 2020, p. 21: "These two initiatives, the White House Executive Order and the Artemis Accords, demonstrate an energetic and proactive stance taken by the United States [...] to address current and emerging space activities head on by regulating carefully but robustly what needs to be regulated and creating an enabling environment for anticipated governmental, public-private, and wholly private space activities"; Mosteshar, 2020, p. 602: "Rather than engage in modification or clarification of the Outer Space Treaty appropriation provisions through a friendly understanding with other parties, it appears that through the Artemis Accords the United States is inviting likeminded States to join in freeing themselves of the appropriation prohibitions of the Outer Space Treaty, declaring that 'space resource extraction and utilization can and will be conducted...'".

36 *See* W.A. Smith, 'Using the Artemis Accords to Build Customary International Law: A Vision for a U.S.-Centric Good Governance Regime in Outer Space', *Journal of Air Law and Commerce*, vol. 86, n. 4, 2021, p. 699: "By casting the Accords as an outgrowth of the Outer Space Treaty and incorporating provisions from the other U.N. treaties on outer space, the U.S. seeks to use the Accords to build customary international law through state practice and *opinio juris* in essential areas like disclosure of scientific data, resource extraction, and deconfliction of activities".

37 *See* E.A. Taichman, 'The Artemis Accords: Employing Space Diplomacy to De-Escalate a National Security Threat and promote Space Commercialization', *National Security Law Brief*, vol. 11, n. 2, 2021, pp. 145-146.

5 Concluding Remarks

We live in a historical time when, finally, it seems that we are very close to the beginning of an economic exploitation of the space resources, to which public and private entities of several countries aim now in an effective way and with tangible plans. This is why, in constitutional democracies, the internal regulation – and the national contribution to the drafting of the international regulation – of this strategic field should not be handed to the technicians or to the alleged self-regulatory skills of the market, but it should be conceived and managed under the sign of the values of peace, harmony and equality between the peoples, and of internal solidarity and redistribution of wealth, that characterise contemporary constitutionalism.[38]

In conclusion, property issues are not completely resolved by the space treaties. In fact, these treaties are partially obsolete, fragmentary and insufficient,[39] and they have several grey areas. Moreover, the various international and national sources are at risk of overlapping and contradiction.[40] Some principles, such as the prohibition of appropriation of the celestial bodies, which can now be seen as a customary rule of international law, still remain fundamental for a peaceful development of human space exploration. The ambiguous situation of property law in space under the treaties has given rise to the unilateral initiative of some national lawmakers. This initiative might encourage the development of an area of international law which remains seriously incomplete, but it also increases unilateral approaches and international tensions in space, implying a new, conflictual space race. Actually, it will only be possible to generally sort out these problems when there is an effective collaborative will within the international community.[41] A more detailed multilateral agreement, involving all the space powers and the greatest number of countries with current or future space capabilities, is indispensable to ensure the peaceful development of the human adventure in space, hopefully at least in part inspired by the cooperation and solidarity principles of the neglected Moon Treaty. When drafting a new agreement, it would be important to take in account the variety of models and cultures of property among the space powers (at least common law, civil law, Asian market socialism), drawing inspiration from all of them in order to create an original paradigm of property

38 Zolea, 2022, p. 380.

39 *See* J. Tjandra, 'The Fragmentation of Property Rights in the Law of Outer Space', *Air and Space Law*, vol. 46, n. 3, 2021, pp. 373-394.

40 *See* S. Hobe, R. Popova, 'Space mining: the Delineation between National and International Jurisdiction', *Proceedings of the International Institute of Space Law*, issue 5, 2019.

41 *Cf.* P.B. Larsen, 'Is There Legal Path to Commercial Mining on the Moon?', *University of Pittsburgh Law Review*, vol. 83, n. 1, 2021, pp. 1-50.

of space resources, more stable and consensual, accepted and applied by all the actors involved.[42]

42 *See, amplius*, S. Zolea, 'Esplorazione spaziale e nuove forme di appartenenza: spunti comparativi', *The Cardozo Electronic Law Bulletin*, Vol. 26, No. 1, 2020, pp. 1-41.

Maastricht Law Series

The Maastricht Law Series is created in 2018 by Boom juridisch and Eleven International Publishing in association with the Maastricht University Faculty of Law. The Maastricht Law Series publishes books on comparative, European and International law. The series builds upon the tradition of excellence in research at the Maastricht Faculty of Law, its research centers and the Ius Commune Research School. The Maastricht Law Series is a peer reviewed book series that allows researchers an excellent opportunity to showcase their work.

Published in this series:

Volume 1: Reinhard Zimmermann, Does the Law of Succession Reflect Cultural Differences?, ISBN 978-94-6236-856-9

Volume 2: Anna Berlee, Access to personal data in public land registers, ISBN 978-94-6236-841-5

Volume 3: Marcus Meyer, The Position of Dutch Works Councils in Multinational Corporations, ISBN 978-94-6236-848-4

Volume 4: Jaap Hage, Foundations and Building Blocks of Law, ISBN 978-94-6236-860-6

Volume 5: Bastiaan van Zelst, The End of Justice(s)?, ISBN 978-94-6236-881-1

Volume 6: Agustín Parise & Lars van Vliet (eds.), Re- De- Co-dification? New Insights on the Codification of Private Law, ISBN 978-94-6236-900-9

Volume 7: Caroline Rupp, Rafael Ibarra Garza & Bram Akkermans, Property Law Perspectives VI, ISBN 978-94-6236-904-7

Volume 8: Aalt Willem Heringa, Europees Nederlands Staatsrecht, ISBN 978-94-6290-604-4

Volume 9: Symeon C. Symeonides, The "Private" in Private International Law, ISBN 978-94-6236-949-8

Volume 10: Jaap Hage, European Integration: A Theme, ISBN 978-94-6236-981-8

Volume 11: Jan M. Smits, Five Uneasy Pieces. Essays on Law and Evolution, ISBN 978-94-6236-982-5

Volume 12: Hannah Brodersen, Vincent Glerum, & André Klip, The European Arrest Warrant and In Absentia Judgements, ISBN 978-94-6236-985-6

Volume 13: Bram Akkermans & Gijs van Dijck, Sustainability and Private Law, ISBN 978-94-6236-986-3

Volume 14: Antonia Waltermann, David Roef, Jaap Hage & Marko Jelicic, Law, Science, Rationality, ISBN 978-94-6236-989-4

Volume 15: Frans L. Leeuw, Van Legal Realism naar Legal Big Data, ISBN 978-94-6290-781-2

Volume 16: Josua Sitompul, Cross-border Access to Electronic Evidence, ISBN 978-94-6236-133-1

Volume 17: Bram Akkermans & Jill Robbie, Property Law Perspectives VII, ISBN 978-946236-181-2

Volume 18: Bram Akkermans & Anna Berlee, 'Sjef-Sache', ISBN 978-94-6236-197-3

Volume 19: Froukje van den Borne, Luca Cox, Youri Cremers, Daan Groenewoud, Sven Schaghen & Tom Stijns, Het stopzetten van KEI-civiel nader bezien, ISBN 978-94-6290-955-7

Volume 20: Nicholas Mouttotos, The Impact of Europeanization in Cyprus Contract Law and the Spill-Over to Matters of Civil Procedure, ISBN 978-94-6236-206-2

Volume 21: Katja Zimmermann, Facilitating Cross-Border Real Estate Transactions in Europe, ISBN 978-94-6236-220-8

Volume 22: Alexis E. Antoniades, Remedies for human rights violations by the European Union, ISBN 978-94-6236-275-8

Volume 23: André Klip, European Arrest Warrant, ISBN 978-94-6236-284-0

Volume 24: Bram Akkermans, Sustainable Property Law, ISBN 978-94-6236-289-5

Volume 25: Sarah Schoenmaekers & Pauline Melin, The Art of Moving Borders, ISBN 978-94-6236-296-3

Volume 26: Agustín Parise & Olivier Moréteau, Comparative Perspectives on Law and Language, ISBN 978-94-6236-328-1

Volume 27: Renata Barbosa, Vincent Glerum, Hans Kijlstra, André Klip & Christina Peristeridou, Improving the European Arrest Warrant, ISBN 978-94-6236-327-4

Volume 28: Cedric Vanleenhove & Lotte Meurkens, The Recognition and Enforcement of Punitive Damages Judgments Across the Globe, ISBN 978-90-4730-162-2

Volume 29: Jill Robbie, Flore Vavourakis, Víðir Smári, Ivan Allegranti & Aleksa Radonjić, Property Law Perspectives VIII, ISBN 978-90-4730-171-4

www.ingramcontent.com/pod-product-compliance
Lightning Source LLC
LaVergne TN
LVHW080809011026
849160LV00015B/1585